(Continued on next card)

77–153440

71 (4)

GREAT LIVES OBSERVED

Gerald Emanuel Stearn, *General Editor*

EACH VOLUME IN THE SERIES VIEWS THE CHARACTER AND ACHIEVEMENT OF A GREAT WORLD FIGURE IN THREE PERSPECTIVES—THROUGH HIS OWN WORDS, THROUGH THE OPINIONS OF HIS CONTEMPORARIES, AND THROUGH RETROSPECTIVE JUDGMENTS—THUS COMBINING THE INTIMACY OF AUTOBIOGRAPHY, THE IMMEDIACY OF EYEWITNESS OBSERVATION, AND THE OBJECTIVITY OF MODERN SCHOLARSHIP.

ERIC FONER, *editor of this volume in the* Great Lives Observed *series, is Associate Professor of History, Columbia University. He is the author of* Free Soil, Free Labor, Free Men: The Ideology of the Republican Party Before the Civil War *and* America's Black Past: A Reader in Afro-American History.

GREAT LIVES OBSERVED

Nat Turner

Edited by ERIC FONER

It is astonishing that such a parcel of wretches have dared the murderous deeds which they have committed. Their ultimate object, as well as the means they took to perpetrate so many murders, whence they came, and whither any of them is going, are circumstances not yet explained. . . . Who is this Nat Turner?

—*Richmond Compiler*, AUGUST 17, 1831

Deep down inside, even when we didn't know his name, Nat Turner was always alive. Nat, by whatever name we called him, or dreamed of him, or told stories about him, Nat was our secret weapon, our ace in the hole, our private consciousness of manhood kept strictly between us.

—OSSIE DAVIS, 1968

A SPECTRUM BOOK

PRENTICE-HALL, INC., ENGLEWOOD CLIFFS, N. J.

To J. P. S.

The title-page quotation by Ossie Davis is taken from "Nat Turner: Hero Reclaimed," *Freedomways* 8, no. 3 (Summer 1968): 231. Reprinted by permission of *Freedomways* Magazine, 799 Broadway, New York City.

A SPECTRUM BOOK

10 9 8 7 6 5 4 3 2 1

ISBN: C-0-13-933143-3

P-0-13-933135-2

Library of Congress Catalog Card Number: 77-153440

Printed in the United States of America

PRENTICE-HALL INTERNATIONAL, INC. (*London*)
PRENTICE-HALL OF AUSTRALIA, PTY. LTD. (*Sydney*)
PRENTICE-HALL OF CANADA, LTD. (*Toronto*)
PRENTICE-HALL OF INDIA PRIVATE LIMITED (*New Delhi*)
PRENTICE-HALL OF JAPAN (*Tokyo*)

P85590

Contents

v

Acknowledgments

I would like to thank Martin E. Dann, Herbert Aptheker, and my father, Professor Jack D. Foner, for suggesting materials on Nat Turner for use in this collection. I am also extremely grateful to Mr. Henry I. Tragle, who generously shared with me the results of his lengthy investigation into the Southampton Insurrection, and who made available a number of tape-recorded interviews with residents of Southampton County. Professors James P. Shenton and Eric McKitrick of Columbia University read and criticized the introduction. Thanks are also due to the staffs of a number of libraries, who willingly assisted me in locating and reproducing materials, especially the librarians of Columbia University, the Boston Public Library, the New York Historical Society, New York Public Library, Library of Congress, the Library of the Department of State, Virginia State Library, and North Carolina Department of Archives and History. Research for this project was assisted by a grant from the Council for Research in the Social Sciences, Columbia University. Finally, I would like to thank the editor of this series, Gerald E. Stearn, for his advice and encouragement.

Introduction

Despite the fact that he organized and led the most important slave rebellion in this nation's history, most of the life of Nat Turner is shrouded in mystery. We know a great deal—although by no means enough—about the days in August, 1831, when he and his followers cut a bloody path through Southampton County, Virginia, and indelibly inscribed the name "Nat Turner" in the psyches of both white and black Americans. But the only important information about his life prior to 1831 comes from the *Confessions* he dictated to the white lawyer Thomas Gray, while awaiting trial and execution. Other contemporary sources add only a few tantalizing hints. One newspaper account of September, 1831, records that Turner had once been whipped for predicting that slaves would gain their freedom, and mentions in passing Turner's wife, who had been forced "under the lash" to give up her husband's papers. But what Thomas Wentworth Higginson wrote over a hundred years ago is still true today: of the "private experiences and special privileges or wrongs" of any slave, including Nat Turner, we know virtually nothing.

Nat Turner was born on October 2, 1800, on the farm of Benjamin Turner in Southampton County. Five days later, another great Virginia slave rebel, Gabriel Prosser, was executed in Richmond. Turner may have inherited some of his rebelliousness from his parents, for according to local tradition, his African-born mother had to be restrained from killing her infant son rather than see him a slave, and his father escaped when Nat was a boy. Turner seems to have been a precocious child. He early learned to read and write, and apparently acquired from books and experimentation the ability to make paper and gunpowder. From an early age, his parents imbued in him the idea that he was "intended for some great purpose," and he intentionally held himself aloof from the rest of the slaves. "Having soon discovered [myself] to be great," he told Gray, "I must appear so, and therefore studiously avoided mixing in society, and wrapped myself in mystery, devoting my time to fasting and praying."

Religion increasingly formed the focus of Turner's life. His grandmother, "to whom I was much attached," had been very religious, and Turner spent many hours poring over the Bible, praying, and developing a religious commitment that bordered on fanaticism. Although not officially ordained or a member of any church, he was accepted as a Baptist preacher by the slaves, and once even baptized a local white man. His status as a preacher allowed him far greater freedom of

1

movement than other slaves, and he appears to have made himself familiar with all the paths and byways of Southampton County. One newspaper in 1831 suggested that he had traveled as far as Richmond.

By the 1820s, Turner had acquired an immense reputation and influence among the county's slaves. It was said that he had the ability to recall events that had taken place before his birth and to heal diseases by the touch of his hands. Historians like C. L. R. James, Vincent Harding, Sterling Stuckey, and Eugene Genovese have recently begun investigating the alternative culture and community which slaves strove to create, beyond the direct control of their masters. Although we still know far too little about the culture and values of the slaves, it is certain that Turner's position as a preacher made him a leader of the slave community and of one of that community's focal points, the slave church. Turner's role as the organizer of a slave rebellion cannot be understood unless his position of leadership among the slaves of Southampton is remembered; it was a leadership voluntarily accorded him by the slaves themselves.

When Turner first experienced his miraculous religious visions is not clear from the *Confessions*; but one day, while praying, a Spirit approached him saying, "Seek ye the kingdom of Heaven and all things shall be added unto you." A few years later, he ran off to the woods, apparently because of a disagreement with an overseer; but thirty days later, after another vision, he returned, to the amazement of the other slaves. Turner's visions now became increasingly graphic and bloody. Once, against a darkened sun and thunderous sky, he witnessed a battle between black and white spirits in which streams of blood flowed in the air; another time, the Spirit revealed to him "the knowledge of the elements, the revolution of the planets, the operation of the tides, and changes of the seasons." Finally, in May, 1828, the Spirit informed him that, like Christ, he was to take up the "fight against the Serpent," and that a sign would soon be given for the war to commence.

As Nat Turner reached adulthood and began his mystical encounters with the Spirit, the state of Virginia entered a prolonged period of economic decline. Because tobacco had exhausted much of her soil and white families were increasingly moving to the South and West, the agricultural depression of the 1820s hit Virginia especially hard. In eastern Virginia, where the slave population was concentrated, the decaying town and farm became all-too-familiar sights. As the value of slaves and land hit rock-bottom in the late 1820s, many large plantations were broken up into smaller farms, and as whites emigrated, the proportion of slaves and free blacks in the population steadily increased. Southampton County, located in southeastern Virginia along the North Carolina border, shared in these developments. In 1830 it ranked forty-sixth in the state in the assessed value of its land; thirty years earlier it had ranked fifth. Blacks comprised almost 60 percent of the county's population in 1830. The slaves, however, were not concentrated on large plantations. One resident of the county did own eighty blacks, but three or four to a family was the rule. Few slaveholders employed overseers in Southampton, and most worked beside their slaves in the field, growing tobacco, cotton, potatoes, and corn, or harvesting apples for the county's renowned apple brandy. Virginians prided themselves on the claim that slavery there was much less harsh than on the large plantations of the deep South. Even Nat Turner, who had been purchased by Thomas Moore upon the death of Benjamin Turner, and was now owned by Moore's infant son Putnam, but worked for Moore's widow and her new husband, Joseph Travis, said he "had no cause to complain" of Travis's treatment. It is easy to understand why Virginians would find a slave rebellion completely inexplicable.

The sign for which Turner had been waiting appeared in February, 1831—an eclipse of the sun. Turner now "communicated the great work laid out for me to do" to the four slaves in whom he had the greatest confidence, and they agreed on July 4 as the day of their uprising. But Turner fell ill on the appointed day. Then on August 13, the sun rose with a strange greenish tint; later, it turned to blue, and in the afternoon a dark spot was visible on its surface. The Richmond *Whig* reported that this occurrence "stimulated" the slaves' "religious devotion," but to Turner it was a new sign, and according to one contemporary account he told his followers, "as the black spot passed over the sun, so shall the blacks pass over the earth." One week later, he decided to meet with a few trusted men, "and then to concert a plan, as we had not yet determined on any," as Turner later told Gray. On Sunday, August 21, Hark Travis (called "General Moore" by his fellow slaves) brought a pig, and Henry Edwards some brandy, to the meeting spot on a stream near Joseph Travis's home. Four other slaves joined them and in midafternoon, Nat Turner arrived. When one of the plotters expressed apprehensions because of the small size of the group, Turner said he had intentionally avoided involving too many slaves in his planning. Other plots, he said, had "always leaked out," and he intended "that their march of destruction and murder should be the first news of the insurrection." After dining and drinking into the night these seven slaves, under the leadership of Turner, set out on their mission.

We will probably never know with certainty the precise extent of the plot or the aims of the rebels. Turner's *Confessions* is silent as to what plan was agreed upon at the Sunday meeting or what the ultimate objectives of the rebellion were, and the trials of the conspirators uncovered only a few hints. One slave, a teen-age girl, testified that she had heard the conspiracy discussed among the slaves for at least eighteen months, but this is the only mention of any planning so far in advance. There is evidence, however, that the plot was discussed on at least two farms in the week before it occurred, and that the rebels expected many slaves to join them once the first whites were killed. As for the aims of the conspirators, contemporary Virginians seemed mystified. At first they believed the rebellion was merely an attempt at plunder; some suggested later that Turner's aim was to seize the town of Jerusalem and march to the Great Dismal Swamp, the hiding place for many fugitive slaves. Others believed the rebels intended to march to Norfolk, seize ships, and sail to Africa. According to one report, a map was later found, "drawn by Nat Turner, *with pokeberry juice,* which was descriptive of the county of Southampton." Another paper reported: "Brodnax's servants stated their object to be to reach the free states, where they expected to make proselytes, and return to assist their brethren." The evidence is obviously inconclusive, but perhaps the simplest interpretation is also the most accurate. It is suggested by a slave who testified that on the day before the rebellion one plotter told him "that Gen. Nat was going to rise and murder all the whites."

Joseph Travis and his family attended church services on Sunday, August 22, and arrived home near midnight. Soon afterwards, Turner entered the house through a second-story window, unbarred the door to let in the other rebels, and Travis and his family were murdered. Salanthiel Francis, the owner of the rebels Sam and Will, was the next victim, killed in his farmhouse six hundred yards away. As the rebels moved from farm to farm, they gathered muskets, swords, and other weapons, and their numbers slowly increased—from seven to fifteen, to forty, to sixty. One slave joined the rebels wearing his dead master's shoes and socks. No white along the route was spared, with the exception of one family so poor that, Turner observed, they "thought no better of themselves than they did of the negroes." For several hours, the rebels met no resistance, but by morning the alarm was spreading in the neighborhood, and the whites were hastily organizing. Raising the militia proved difficult, for many whites were attending a camp meeting in North Carolina. But a small militia unit did confront the rebels on Monday afternoon at Parker's field, three miles from the town of Jerusalem. Turner had sent a band of slaves to gather recruits at the farm of James Parker, but the slaves, discovering Parker's cellar of apple brandy, did not return quickly. As Turner went to rally them, a group of eighteen whites approached and fired on the rebels, but Turner organized his men and drove them off. Almost immediately, however, a militia unit from Jerusalem arrived on the scene and the reinforced whites, better armed and organized, proved too much for the slaves, who quickly dispersed. The defeat at Parker's field prevented the rebels from marching on Jerusalem where, according to one report, some three or four hundred women and children had fled for safety. The rebellion was now for all practical purposes over, but Turner did not abandon hope. That night he tried to rally his forces and gather new recruits and the next day the rebels appeared at the home of Dr. Simon Blunt, where the final skirmish was fought. It appears that Blunt armed his slaves and that they helped resist the rebels, although a few reports state that Blunt and his sons did the work themselves. But the rebellion was now over. Somewhere around sixty whites—more than half of them women and children—had been killed, although as one Virginian noted with evident surprise, "not one female was violated." Of the victims only one, Margaret Whitehead, was killed by Turner himself. Between sixty and eighty slaves had joined the rebels along with at least four free blacks, one of whom, Bill Artis, in order to avoid execution or sale into slavery, walked into the woods, placed his hat on a stake, and shot himself.

Now, on Tuesday and Wednesday, as militia units from the surrounding countries hurried to Jerusalem and United States troops embarked from Fortress Monroe, a massacre of the blacks of Southampton began. Most of the torture and killing was done by vigilante groups, such as the party of horsemen that set out from Richmond, "with the intention of killing every black person they saw in Southampton County." The militia, however, also took part. One unit from North Carolina beheaded a group of prisoners and placed their heads on poles, where they remained for weeks. How many blacks were killed is unknown, but the number certainly ranges into the hundreds. That the massacre subsided was largely due to the efforts of the militia commander, General Eppes, who quickly disbanded and sent home the militia and the artillery and infantry units, and strongly condemned the "inhuman butchery." The editor of the Richmond *Whig,* who came to Southampton to investigate the rebellion at first hand, commented, "some of the scenes are hardly inferior in barbarity to the atrocities of the insurgents."

On Wednesday, August 31, the court of Southampton County convened to try the rebels. By this time, almost all had been captured except Turner. Despite a large-scale manhunt and a continuing stream of newspaper accounts of his escape or capture, he was able to hide in the woods of Southampton, not far from where the rebellion had begun, until October 31, when Benjamin Phipps captured him. The next day, Thomas Gray began questioning Turner and composing the *Confessions,* and on November 5, Turner was convicted of insurrection and sentenced to hang. He went to his execution six days later with dignity and composure, refusing an invitation to make a final statement to the large crowd that had gathered to watch him hang. He was the last of seventeen slaves executed for the rebellion; another twelve were transported out of the state. The heirs of Turner's owner were awarded

$375 in compensation by the court; Turner's body was given to surgeons for dissection; and, according to tradition, souvenir purses were made of his skin.

"This will be a very noted day in Virginia," Governor John Floyd wrote in his diary on hearing of the insurrection. Few Virginians reacted so calmly. The haunting fear of slave revolt was deeply imbedded in the white southern mind; it never faded as long as slavery existed. Throughout Virginia, and in areas of the South as far away as Louisiana and Alabama, slaveholders wondered, as one resident of Richmond put it, "if the slaves in that county would murder the whites, whether they are not as ready to do it in any *other county* in the State." "A Nat Turner might be in any family," another Virginian later observed; and throughout the state, rumors of insurrection spread, slaves were arrested and executed, and vigilante groups tightened patrols and made plans to scour the Great Dismal Swamp for fugitive slaves. Requests for arms and reports that slaves were either in rebellion or unusually unruly poured in upon Governor Floyd. Floyd himself seemed unruffled. "I am disgusted with the cowardly fears of [Norfolk]," he wrote in his diary. "They have exhibited more fear, cowardice and alarm than the whole state besides. . . ." Governor Montfort Stokes of North Carolina received similar reports and requests for military aid. In September, Raleigh was thrown into a panic over reports that two thousand rebellious slaves had burned the town of Wilmington and were marching on the state capital. Free blacks were dragged before vigilante committees, and many slaves were jailed and executed. "Fear was seen in every face," read one report from North Carolina, "women pale and terror-stricken, children crying out for protection, men fearful and full of foreboding. . . ." Like Floyd, Governor Stokes kept his head, although he did send military assistance, largely to quiet the fears of the whites. He later confessed that many innocent slaves had been executed during the hysteria, and pardoned one slave who had been told by his master to confess to involvement in a plot to avoid being tortured.

The Nat Turner rebellion occurred at a time of rising antislavery militancy in the northern states, and many southerners, seeking a scapegoat for the insurrection, seized upon the abolitionists. Two years earlier, the Boston free black David Walker had published his *Appeal,* an eloquent and bitter condemnation of racism and slavery that called upon the nation to repent of its sins or face the wrath of God in the form of servile insurrection. Copies of the *Appeal* had been discovered in a number of southern states in 1830, and several legislatures had enacted laws prohibiting the circulation of "incendiary publications." Some southerners now suggested that Turner had read and been influenced by the pamphlet. Walker, however, had died in 1830; most of the South's indignation in 1831 was directed at William Lloyd Garrison, whose *Liberator,* demanding the complete and immediate end of slavery, had begun publication in Boston the previous January. Governor Floyd believed Garrison's "express intention" was "inciting the slaves and free negroes in this and the other States to rebellion and to murder the men, women and children of those states," and he insisted its publication be stopped. Newspapers throughout the South denounced Garrison, legislatures tightened their laws, and Georgia even offered a $500 reward for the capture of Garrison and his transportation to the state—an open invitation to kidnapping. Other southerners wrote Mayor Otis of Boston, inquiring whether anything could be done to suppress the publication at its source, and Otis, who had never even heard of Garrison, was forced to wander through the back streets of Boston's black district to locate the newspaper.

Despite the suggestion by several historians that Turner may have seen Walker's pamphlet, there is no evidence that he was influenced by either Walker or Garrison. Nor was it true that Garrison advocated slave rebellion. On the contrary, he had condemned Walker's *Appeal* precisely because it advocated violence. Garrison was a nonresistant who believed that moral suasion would convince slaveholders of their sins, and who condemned the use of force by any group—whether government, slaveholders, or slaves. He did write, soon after the Turner rebellion, that the slaves had more right to rebel than any other men, but his point was to demonstrate the hypocrisy of those who revered the rebels of the American Revolution, yet condemned Turner and his followers. He also used the occasion to warn the South that if slavery were not abolished peacefully, more insurrections were inevitable. Ironically, despite his pacifism, it was the Turner rebellion which made Garrison a national figure. Southern attacks gave him instant notoriety and enabled him to win new allies by linking his antislavery crusade with the preservation of freedom of the press.

Every slave rebellion in southern history culminated in the execution of the rebels, the murder of innocent slaves, and a tightening of slave codes. In one respect, Turner's insurrection was exceptional. For a brief moment, Virginians openly questioned not only the loyalty of their slaves, the efficiency of police controls, and the influence of outside agitators, but the very nature, necessity, and possible abolition of the slave system itself.

It has been an enduring myth in historical literature that in 1831 Virginia was on the verge of abolishing slavery and that Turner's rebellion prevented such action. As recently as 1970, Frank Vandiver wrote in his history of the Confederacy that Turner "killed the debate for manumission." Yet the very opposite is true: far from killing the debate, Nat Turner opened it. In the closing months of 1831, petitions poured into the Virginia legislature from throughout the state. Some called for the removal of all free blacks from the state, blaming them for fomenting unrest among the slaves; some demanded new restrictions on the black population; but many, arguing mainly from the fear and insecurity the Turner revolt had created and pointing to the continuing increase of black population, called for the gradual emancipation of the slaves and their colonization outside the country. Governor Floyd, who believed that outside agitators and black preachers were to blame for the rebellion, was convinced by the continuing alarm that something had to be done to remove slavery gradually from the state. Although he did not mention abolition in his message to the legislature in December, Floyd pledged in his diary, "I will not rest until slavery is abolished in Virginia."

The famous debate on slavery that occupied the Virginia House of Delegates in January, 1832, was precipitated when a committee to which the legislative petitions had been referred recommended that no action be taken "for the abolition of slavery." At the same time, Thomas Jefferson Randolph, the grandson of the third president, proposed a plan whereby all slaves would become the property of the state at the age of twenty-one and be hired out to pay for their transportation to Africa. For several weeks the legislature engaged in a heated debate, in which virtually every argument against slavery which would be used by northerners in the next thirty years was aired. It was a remarkable, unprecedented spectacle. The Richmond *Enquirer* commented, "The seals are broken which have been put for fifty years upon the most delicate and difficult subject of state concernment"; and the *Whig* added, "Nat Turner, and the blood of his innocent victims have conquered the silence of fifty years."

Most of the antislavery speeches in this crucial debate came not from the eastern, slaveholding delegates, but from representatives of western Virginia, who had long resented the political dominance of the east and who had fought unsuccessfully in the Constitutional Convention of 1829–30 for a revision of legislative apportionment to end the representation of slave property. Moreover, while a few delegates did condemn slavery as a violation of natural rights and a moral evil, most were concerned with the institution's effects on whites. Slavery was condemned primarily because it was held responsible for the economic decline of the state, the emigration of white farmers and laborers, and the encouragement of idleness, luxury, and arbitrary power. Some westerners also warned that future slave revolts and racial warfare were inevitable unless steps toward emancipation were taken. Every emancipation scheme, however, was coupled with colonization; the antislavery sentiments of many westerners were based on fear of the spread of slavery—and blacks—into their area.

In reply, a few eastern delegates defended slavery as a rational and just system, but many, admitting it to be an evil, were content simply to attack the program of the westerners. No plan of emancipation was possible, they argued, because the cost of compensation would be prohibitive, and any plan not based on voluntary cooperation by the slaveholders would undermine the rights of property. The defenders of slavery also tended to downgrade the size and importance of the Turner revolt and to argue that most slaves were loyal and contented. In the end, a resolution urging legislative action against slavery was defeated by a vote of 73 to 58.

The Virginia slavery debate ended not with steps toward abolition, but with further legal repression of the slaves and free blacks. The Virginia Senate did reject a bill that passed the House in February providing for the deportation of free blacks. But measures barring slaves or free blacks from holding religious meetings, strengthening the patrol system and militia, and prohibiting free blacks from owning firearms were enacted. Added to the measures barring the instruction of free blacks and slaves in reading and writing, which the legislature had passed in April, 1831 in reaction to the Walker pamphlet, the new laws marked a significant deterioration of the position of blacks in Virginia society. A large number of informal black schools were eliminated, and the activities of black preachers were all but suppressed. And other states followed suit. North Carolina barred free blacks and slaves from preaching; Maryland and Tennessee prohibited the entrance of free blacks into the state; and Alabama made the circulation of incendiary pamphlets a capital offense. Three states of the deep South—Alabama, Mississippi, and Louisiana—even moved to outlaw the interstate slave trade, fearing Virginians would sell off their most troublesome and rebellious slaves. Such laws were never effectively enforced, but they reveal the lengths southern legislatures were prepared to go to strengthen the slave system in the aftermath of Nat Turner's rebellion.

The years 1831 and 1832 mark a significant turning point in the history of slavery. With the emergence of Garrison, Nat Turner's rebellion, and the Virginia debate on slavery, the peculiar institution seemed under assault both at home and from the outside. Yet the ultimate result of the debate of 1832, which seemed at the time so auspicious to the friends of emancipation, was a hardening of Virginia sentiment along proslavery lines. In January, 1832, an antislavery delegate could inform the legislature he was gratified that none of the proslavery spokesmen had risen to defend the institution as a positive good; and throughout the South, even at this late date, the defense of slavery was generally tentative and qualified. But as a reaction to the Virginia debate, Professor Thomas Dew composed his famous *Review of the Debates,* in which the program of the emancipationists was systematically demolished, and, far more important, an elaborate theoretical defense for the institution of slavery was erected, drawing on religion, history, and political economy, and ultimately resting on racial superiority. At the same time, Virginians and other southerners recoiled from open discussion of emancipation, fearing that further debate would incite the slaves to further outbreaks and encourage northern abolitionists. And, as the value of land and slaves skyrocketed in the 1830s and the renewed interstate slave trade dampened fears of too great an increase in the black population, the economic impetus behind antislavery sentiment waned. Antislavery Virginians withdrew from politics, changed their views, or fell silent, and a curtain of censorship and repression fell upon the southern mind. By 1840 the ranks of southern society had closed in defense of slavery.

Chronology of Nat Turner and the Southampton Insurrection

1800, October 2	Nat Turned born on farm of Benjamin Turner in Southampton County, Virginia.
1822	Denmark Vesey conspiracy suppressed in Charleston, South Carolina.
1825	"Spirit" reveals to Turner "the knowledge of the elements" and "the revolution of the planets."
1828, May 12	"Spirit" tells Turner to take up the yoke of Christ and "fight against the Serpent."
1829	Publication of David Walker's *Appeal*.
1831, January 1	First issue of William Lloyd Garrison's *The Liberator*.
February 12	Eclipse of sun, taken by Turner as sign for rebellion.
April	Virginia legislature bars teaching free blacks and slaves to read and write.
July 4	Date planned for rebellion; Turner ill.
August 13	Sun takes on greenish color, taken by Turner as new sign for rebellion.
August 21	Turner and six followers meet to plan rebellion.
August 22 early morning	Rebellion begins with murder of Joseph Travis and family.
August 22, afternoon	"Battle" at Parker's field; dispersal of rebels.
August 23	Attack on Dr. Blunt's farm; final suppression of revolt.
August 23–26	Massacre of unknown number of Southampton blacks.
August 31	Trial of rebels begins.
September 4	Execution of rebels begins.
October 30	Turner captured by Benjamin Phipps.
November 1–3	Thomas Gray transcribes Turner's *Confessions*.
November 5	Trial of Nat Turner.
November 11	Execution of Turner in Jerusalem, Virginia.
November	Publication of *The Confessions of Nat Turner*. . . .

1832,
January Debate on slavery in Virginia House of Delegates.
March Virginia legislature outlaws black preachers and tightens slave code.

PART ONE

NAT TURNER AND THE SOUTHAMPTON INSURRECTION

1

Contemporary Accounts

W. G. PARKER TO GOVERNOR JOHN FLOYD [1]

This is the most complete physical description of Nat Turner. It was addressed to Governor John Floyd by W. G. Parker of Jerusalem and was used, with only a few minor changes, in Floyd's proclamation offering a $500 reward for Turner's capture. The proclamation was printed in many newspapers, among them the Washington, D.C. United States Telegraph, September 19, 1831.

September 14, 1831
Sir,

Understanding you are anxious to have a description of Nat the contriver and leader of the late insurrection in this county, I have been at some pains to procure an accurate one. It has been supervised and collected by persons aquainted with him from his infancy.

"He is between 30 and 35 years old, 5 feet six or 8 inches high—weighs between 150 and 160, rather bright complexion but not a mulatto—broad shouldered—large flat nose—large eyes broad flat feet —rather knock-kneed—walk brisk and active—hair on the top of the head very thin—no beard except on the upper lip and the tip of the chin, a scar on one of his temples produced by the kick of a mule also one on the back of his neck by a bite—a large knot on one of the bones of his right arm near the wrist produced by a blow."

May I again take the liberty of requesting your immediate attention to the volunteer corps, proposed to be raised in this county.

Respectfully,
yr obd sevt
W. G. Parker

[1] From *Executive Papers,* Governor John Floyd, Archives Branch, Virginia State Library.

Before the invention of the telegraph and high-speed presses,
newspapers had to rely on messengers and mails for news, and
freely copied articles from newspapers closest to the scene of
major events. Thus, throughout the North and South, most
papers picked up accounts of the rebellion from the three lead-
ing newspapers of Richmond—the Whig, Enquirer, *and* Compiler—*and, less frequently, from Norfolk newspapers. The same*
stories appeared over and over again in newspapers throughout
the country. Especially in Virginia and North Carolina, rumors
and alarms spread much faster than the newspapers, and many
editors prefaced their stories with reassurances that the rebellion
had been suppressed and that the rumors flying through the
South were thoroughly unjustified. Note the variety of sug-
gestions in the newspaper accounts about Turner's motives and
aims.

RICHMOND *WHIG,* AUGUST 29, 1831

John Hampden Pleasants, the editor of the Whig, *went to*
Southampton County for a firsthand look at the situation. This
is his first dispatch, dated Jerusalem, Southampton County,
August 25.

The Richmond Troop arrived here this morning a little after 9
o'clock, after a rapid, hot and most fatiguing march from Richmond.
On the road we met a thousand different reports, no two agreeing,
and leaving it impossible to make a plausible guess at the truth. On
the route from Petersburg, we found the whole country thoroughly
alarmed; every man armed, the dwellings all deserted by the white
inhabitants, and the farms most generally left in possession of the
blacks. On our arrival at this village, we found Com. Elliott and Col.
Worth, with 250 U. State troops, from the neighborhood of Old Point,
and a considerable militia force. A Troop of Horse from Norfolk and
one from Prince George, have since arrived. Jerusalem was never so
crowded from its foundation; for besides the considerable military
force assembled here, the ladies from the adjacent country, to the
number of 3 or 400, have sought refuge from the appalling dangers
by which they were surrounded.

Here for the first time, we learnt the extent of the insurrection,
and the mischief perpetrated. Rumor had infinitely exaggerated the
first, swelling the numbers of the negroes to a thousand or 1200 men,
and representing its ramifications as embracing several of the adjacent
counties, particularly Isle of Wight and Greensville; but it was hardly

in the power of rumor itself, to exaggerate the atrocities which have been perpetrated by the insurgents: whole families, father, mother, daughters, sons, sucking babes, and school children, butchered, thrown into heaps, and left to be devoured by hogs and dogs, or to putrify on the spot. At Mr. Levi Waller's, his wife and ten children, were murdered and piled in one bleeding heap on his floor.—Waller himself was absent at the moment, but approaching while the dreadful scene was acting, was pursued, and escaped into a swamp, with much difficulty. One small child in the house at the time, escaped by concealing herself in the fire place, witnessing from the place of her concealment, the slaughter of the family, and her elder sisters among them. Another child was cruelly wounded and left for dead, and probably will not survive. All these children were not Mr. Waller's. A school was kept near his house, at which, and between which and his house, the ruthless villains murdered several of the helpless children. Many other horrors have been perpetrated. The killed, as far as ascertained, amount to sixty-two; I send a list believed to be correct, as far as it goes. There are probably others not yet known hereafter to be added. A large proportion of these were women and children. It is not believed that any outrages were offered to the females.

How, or with whom, the insurrection originated, is not certainly known. The prevalent belief is that on Sunday week last, at Barnes' Church in the neighborhood of the Cross Keye, the negroes who were observed to be disorderly, took offense at something; (it is not known what) that the plan of insurrection was then and there conceived, matured in the course of the week following, and carried into execution on Sunday night the 21st August. The atrocities commenced at Mr. Travis'. A negro, called captain Moore, and who it is added is a preacher is the reputed leader. On Monday, most of the murders were perpetrated. It is said that none have been committed since that day. The numbers engaged are not supposed to have exceeded 60—one account says a hundred—another not so many as 40. Twelve armed and resolute men, were certainly competent to have quelled them at any time. But, taken by surprise—with such horrors before their eyes, and trembling for their wives and children, the men, most naturally, only thought in the first place, of providing a refuge for those dependent upon them. Since this has been effected, the citizens have acted with vigor. Various parties have scoured the country, and a number of the insurgents, (differently reported) have been killed or taken. There are thirteen prisoners now at this place, one or more of them severely wounded; the principal of them, a man aged about 21, called Marmaduke, who might have been a hero, judging from the magnanimity with which he bears his sufferings. He is said to be an atrocious offender, and the murderer of Miss Vaughan, celebrated for her beauty. The Preacher-Captain has not been taken. At the

Cross Keys, summary justice in the form of decapitation has been executed on one or more prisoners. The people are naturally enough, wound up to a high pitch of rage, and precaution is even necessary, to protect the lives of the captives—scouring parties are out, and the insurrection may be considered as already suppressed.

Jerusalem, Saturday 27

Since writing the accompanying letter, which was expected to have been sent off immediately, other prisoners have been taken, and in one or two instances, put to death forthwith by the enraged inhabitants. Some of these scenes are hardly inferior in barbarity to the atrocities of the insurgents; and it is to be feared that a spirit of vindictive ferocity has been excited, which may be productive of farther outrage, and prove discreditable to the country. Since Monday, the insurgent negroes have committed no aggression, but have been dodging about in the swamps in parties of three and four. They are hunted by the local militia with great implacability, and must all eventually be slain or made captive. All the mischief was done between Sunday morning and Monday noon. In this time, the rebels traversed a country of near 20 miles extent, murdering every white indiscriminately, and wrecking the furniture. They set fire to no houses, and as far as is known, committed no outrage on any white female. What the ulterior object was is unknown. The more intelligent opinion is that they had none; though some of them say it was to get to Norfolk, seize a ship and go to Africa. My own impression is that they acted under the influence of their leader Nat, a preacher and a prophet among them; that even he had no ulterior purpose, but was stimulated exclusively by fanatical revenge, and perhaps misled by some hallucination of his imagined spirit of prophecy.—Committing the first murder, finding themselves already beyond the reach of pardon, drunk and desperate, they proceeded in blind fury, to murder and destroy all before them. It will be long before the people of this country can get over the horrors of the late scenes, or feel safe in their homes.— Many will probably migrate. It is an aggravation of the crimes perpetrated, that the owners of slaves in this country are distinguished for lenity and humanity. Cotton and corn are the staples here, and the labor of attending to these is trifling compared with what is necessary in other parts of the State.

RICHMOND *WHIG*, SEPTEMBER 3, 1831

This is Pleasants' complete report, written after his return to Richmond.

Southampton Affair

We have been astonished since our return from Southampton, (whither we went in Capt. Harrison's Troop of Horse,) in looking over the mass of exchange papers accumulated in our absence, to see the number of false, absurd and idle rumors, circulated by the Press, touching the insurrection in that county. Editors seem to have applied themselves to the task of alarming the public mind as much as possible, and of persuading the slaves to entertain a high opinion of their strength and consequence. While truth is always the best policy, and the best remedy, the exaggerations to which we have alluded, are calculated to give the slaves false conceptions of their numbers and capacity, by exhibiting the terror and confusion of the whites, and to induce them to think that practicable, which they see is so much feared by their superiors.

We have little to say of the Southampton Tragedy, beyond what is already known. The origin of the conspiracy, its prime agents, its extent, and ulterior direction, is matter of conjecture. The universal opinion in that part of the country is that Nat, a slave, a preacher, and a pretended Prophet, was the first contriver, the actual leader, and the most remorseless of the executioners. According to the evidence of a negro boy whom they carried along to hold their horses, Nat commenced the scene of murder at the first house (Travis') with his own hand. Having called upon two others to make good their valiant boastings so often repeated, of what they would do, and these shrinking from the requisition, Nat proceeded to despatch one of the family with his own hand. Animated by the example and exhortations of their leader, having a taste of blood, and convinced that they had now gone too far to recede, his followers dismissed their qualms and became as ferocious as their leader wished them.—To follow the bloody dogs from the capture of Travis' home, before day, to their dispersion at Parker's cornfield early in the afternoon, where they had traversed near twenty miles, murdered 63 whites, and approached within 3 or 4 miles of the village of Jerusalem, the immediate object of their movement—to describe the scenes at each house, the circumstances of the murders, the hair breadth escapes of the few who were lucky enough to escape—would prove as interesting as heart rending. Many of the details have reached us, but not in so authentic a shape as to justify their publication, nor have we the time or space. Let a few suffice. Of the events at Dr. Blount's we had a narrative from the gallant old gentleman himself, and his son, a lad about 15, distinguished for his gallantry and modesty, and whom we take leave to recommend to Gen. Jackson, for a warrant in the Navy or at West Point. The Doctor had received information of the insurrection, and that his house would be attacked, a short time before the attack was made. Crippled with the gout, and indisposed to fly, he resolved to defend his house. His force was his son, overseer, and three other white men. Luckily, there were six guns, and plenty of powder and shot in the house. These were barely loaded, his force posted, and the instructions given, when the negroes from 15 to 30 strong, rode up about day break. The Doctor's orders were that each man should be particular in his aim, and should fire one at a time; he himself reserved one gun, resolved if the house was forced, to sell his life as dearly as he could. The remaining five fired in succession upon the assailants, at the distance of fifteen or twenty steps. The blacks upon the fifth fire, retreated, leaving one killed (we believe) and one wounded, (a fellow called Hark,) and were pursued by the Doctor's negroes with shouts and execrations. Had the shot been larger, more execution would doubtless have been done.

Mrs. Vaughan's was among the last houses attacked. A venerable negro woman, described the scene which she had witnessed with great emphasis. It was near noon, and her mistress had been making some preparation in the porch for dinner, when happening to look towards the road, she descried a dust and wondered what it could mean. In a second, the negroes mounted and armed, rushed into view, and making an exclamation indicative of her horror and agony, Mrs. Vaughan ran into the house. The negroes dismounted and ran around the house, pointing their guns at the doors and windows. Mrs. Vaughan appeared at a window, and begged for her life, inviting them to take every thing she had. The prayer was answered by one of them firing at her, which was instantly followed by another, and a fatal shot. In the mean time, Miss Vaughan, who was up stairs, and unapprised of the terrible advent until she heard the noise of the attack, rushed down and begging for life, was shot as she ran a few steps from the door. A son of Mrs. Vaughan, about 15, was at the still house, when hearing a gun and conjecturing, it is supposed, that his brother had come from Jerusalem, approached the house, and was shot as he got over the fence. It is difficult for the imagination to conceive a situation so truly and horribly awful, as that in which these unfortunate ladies were placed. Alone, unprotected, and unconscious of danger, to find themselves without a moment's notice for escape or defence, in the power of a band of ruffians, from whom instant death was the least they could expect! In a most lively and picturesque manner, did the old negress describe the horrors of the scene; the blacks riding up with imprecations, the looks of her mistress, white as a sheet, her prayers for her life, and the action of the scoundrels environing the house and pointing their guns at the doors and windows, ready to fire as occasion offered. When the work was done, they called for drink, and food, and becoming nice, damned the brandy as vile stuff.

The scene at Vaughan's may suffice to give an idea of what was done at the other houses. A bloodier and more accursed tragedy was never acted, even by the agency of the tomahawk and scalping knife. Interesting details will no doubt be evolved in the progress of the trials and made known to the public.

It is with pain we speak of another feature of the Southampton Rebellion; for we have been most unwilling to have our sympathies for the sufferers, diminished or affected by their misconduct. We allude to the slaughter of many blacks, without trial, and under circumstances of great barbarity. How many have thus been put to death (generally by decapitation or shooting) reports vary; probably however some five and twenty and from that to 40; possibly a yet larger number. To the great honor of General Eppes, he used every precaution in his power, and we hope and believe with success, to put a stop to the disgraceful procedure. We met with an individual of intelligence, who stated that he himself had killed between 10 and 15. He justified himself on the ground of the barbarities committed on the whites; & that he thought himself right, is certain from the fact of his having narrowly escaped losing his own life in an attempt to save a negro woman whom he thought innocent, but who was shot by the multitude in despite of his exertions. We (the Richmond Troop) witnessed with surprize, the sanguinary temper of the population, who evinced a strong disposition to inflict immediate death, upon every prisoner. Not having witnessed the horrors committed by the blacks, or seen the unburied and disfigured remains of their wives and children, we were unprepared to understand their feelings, and could not at first admit of that extenuation, which a closer observation of the atrocities of the insurgents suggested. Now, however, we individually, feel compelled to offer an apology for the people of Southampton, while we deeply deplore that human nature urged them to such extremities. Let the fact not be doubted by those whom it most concerns, that another such insurrection will be the signal for the extirpation of the whole black population in the quarter of the State where it occurs.

The numbers engaged in the insurrection are variously reported. They probably did not exceed 40 or 50, and were fluctuating from desertions and new recruits. About fifty are in Southampton Jail, some of them upon suspicion only. We trust and believe that the intelligent magistracy of that county, will have the firmness to oppose the popular passion, should it be disposed to involve the innocent with the guilty, and to take suspicion for proof.

The presence of the troops from Norfolk and Richmond, alone prevented retaliation from being carried much farther.

At the date of Capt. Harrison's departure from Jerusalem, Gen. Nat had not been taken. On that morning however, Dred, another insurgent chief, was brought prisoner to Jerusalem, having surrendered himself to his master, in the apprehension no doubt of starving in the swamps, or being shot by the numerous parties of local militia, who were in pursuit. Nat had not been certainly heard of since the skirmish in Parker's cornfield, which was in fact, the termination of the insurrection, the negroes after that dispersing themselves, and making no farther attempt. He is represented as a shrewd fellow, reads, writes, and preaches; and by various artifices had acquired great influence over the minds of the wretched beings whom he has led into destruction. It is supposed that he induced them to believe there were only 80,000 whites in the country, who being exterminated, the blacks might take possession. Various of his tricks to acquire and preserve influence have been mentioned, but they are not worth repeating. If there was any ulterior purpose, he probably alone knows it. For our own part, we still believe there was none; and if he be the intelligent man represented, we are incapable of conceiving the arguments by which he persuaded his own mind of the feasibility of his attempt, or how it could possibly end but in certain destruction. We therefore incline to the belief that he acted upon no higher principle than the impulse of revenge against the whites, as the enslavers of himself and his race; that being a fanatic, he possibly persuaded himself that Heaven would interfere; and that he may have convinced himself, as he certainly did his deluded followers to some extent, that the appearance of the sun some weeks ago, prognosticated something favorable to their cause. We are inclined to think that the solar phenomenon exercised considerable influence in promoting the insurrection; calculated as it was to impress the imaginations of the ignorant.

A more important enquiry remains—whether the conspiracy was circumscribed to the neighborhood in which it broke out, or had its ramifications through other counties. We, at first, adopted the first opinion; but there are several circumstances which favor the latter. We understand that the confessions of all the prisoners, go to show that the insurrection broke out too soon, as it is supposed, in consequence of the last day of July being a Sunday, and not as the negroes in Southampton believed the Saturday before. The report is that the rising was fixed for the fourth Sunday in August, and that supposing Sunday, the 31st July, to be the first Sunday in August, they were betrayed into the error of considering the 3d Sunday as the 4th. This is the popular impression founded upon confessions, upon the indications of an intention of the negroes in Nansemond and other places to unite, and upon the allegation that Gen. Nat extended his preach-

ing excursions to Petersburg and this city; allegations which we however, disbelieve. It is more than probable nevertheless, that the mischief was concerted and concocted under the cloak of religion. The
trials which are now proceeding or impending in Southampton,
Nansemond, Sussex and elsewhere will develop all the truth. We sus-
pect this truth will turn out to be that the conspiracy was confined
to Southampton, and that the idea of its extensiveness originated in
the panic which seized upon the South East of Virginia.

Such we believe to be a summary outline of the Southampton insurrection! That insurrection made some salutary lessons; to the
whites, the propriety of incessant vigilance; to the blacks, the madness
of all attempts such as that in Southampton. A few lives they may indeed sacrifice, but possession of the country even for a week, is the
most chimerical of all notions. We assert confidently that 20 armed
whites would put to the rout the whole negro population of Southampton, and we repeat our persuasion, that another insurrection will
be followed by putting the whole race to the sword.

To Gov. Floyd, South East Virginia, owes a large debt of gratitude,
for the prompt and silent energy with which he threw arms and men
into all the supposed disaffected districts; and to Brig. Gen. Eppes,
we tender the respects of those lately under his command, for the
vigilance and fortitude with which he surmounted difficulties, arising
not from the strength of the enemy, but the novelty of his situation,
and the alarm and agitation of the inhabitants. To the Ladies of
Southampton, we want words to express the warmth of gratitude inspired in the breasts of the Richmond Troop, by their unremitting
kindness and attentions. All that that troop regrets, is, that some occasion had not offered, in which they could have manifested by deeds,
their zeal for the public safety, and their devotion to their hospitable
and amiable country women of Southampton.

We regret to be under the necessity of adverting to any disagreeable
circumstance connected with the expedition of the Richmond Troop
of Cavalry to Southampton; but the conduct of one individual, deserves and shall receive at our hands, the exposure and the chastise-
ment, which in the opinion of all who have heard it, it most richly
deserves. On Thursday morning the 25th, we arrived at Jerusalem,
and took up our quarters at the tavern of Mr. Henry B. Vaughan.
This individual was the brother-in-law of Mrs. Vaughan, whose melancholy fate and that of her family is noticed above. He had no
family, and is wealthy. Under these circumstances, good feeling would
have suggested the propriety of his charging no more than would in-
demnify him; a base and sordid love of self, could alone have prompted
the idea of speculating upon men in our situation. We tended our own
horses, with little aid from his servants; did not sleep in his house;
were furnished with the coarsest, and sometimes, stinking fare; many

neither ate nor drank at his table, but were entertained by the hospitality of the inhabitants; detachments were absent on several occasions; and the troop left on Wednesday, making the time less than five days. It will excite astonishment to learn that for this time, with this accommodation, and under all the circumstances of the case, the Landlord produced a bill exceeding $800! To state the fact, is to inflict on him the severest punishment, the indignation of the public.

RICHMOND *WHIG*, SEPTEMBER 8, 1831

Extract of a letter from Southampton, to a gentleman in this City, dated Cedardale, Sept. 4, 1831

We expected you would be a little uneasy about us, from the many rumors that were abroad in the land.

It came upon us as unexpectedly as any thing possibly could, and produced a pretty general panic, especially among our females. In fact it was a desperate affair. I have been engaged three or four days, trying those scoundrels: fourteen have been tried—thirteen of whom have been condemned and one acquitted—these are some of the principal offenders. There are a number still in jail; about 40 is supposed to have been shot in the woods, and other places. One of the leaders, a free fellow, was found shot, two days ago; supposed by his own hand, as his hat was hung on a stake near him, and his pistol lying by him—so that all have been taken and destroyed, except their principal leader, Capt. Nat. This fellow is very improperly represented to be a Baptist Preacher. I wish you to see the Editors of your papers on this subject, and say to them, that that account from the best information I can obtain, is an entire mistake. He never was a member of the Baptist or any other Church; he assumed that character of his own accord, and has been for several years one of those fanatical scoundrels, that pretended to be divinely inspired; of bad character, and never countenanced, except by a very few of his deluded black associates. To give this explanation, is an act of justice, to which I am sure they will readily accord.

It gives us pleasure to make the correction which this letter furnishes, in regard to Capt. Nat. That he should have been a Baptist Preacher, argues however, no discredit to that respectable and patriotic denomination. It is not the fault of the creed, that scoundrels now and then profess it, for nefarious purposes.

It is a little remarkable how little is known of Captain Nat. We could find no person who had ever seen him.

NEW YORK *MORNING COURIER AND ENQUIRER*, SEPTEMBER 17, 1831

Extract of a letter from a friend, dated Petersburg, Sept. 10, 1831.

Our town, in common with the greater portions of southern Virginia, has recently been thrown into a great state of excitement in consequence of an insurrection among the slaves of Southampton county. The newspapers have given many and contradictory accounts of this bloody affair.—And among others, I have seen in the Mercantile Advertiser, a letter dated at Petersburg, stating the insurgents to have been runaways from the Swamps, and their sole object, *plunder.* "The truth is" that there was not an absconding Negro among the murderous band, and plunder was scarcely a secondary object. For many weeks previous we were annoyed by night and day, with Negro Meetings, Preachings, and Baptizings. Hundreds of pretended converts in Petersburg, Richmond, and the surrounding country—nay thousands is no exaggeration, went down into the water and came thence *so pure,* that for all future *time they could do no wrong.* This is their doctrine, whether taught them by the respectable white breathren who have occasionally ministered in their churches, I am not prepared to say. At Cooke's mill in Prince George on the Sunday preceding the insurrection there was a negro baptizing, at which not less than 3,000 of these lambs of mercy were present, and then it is believed the final arrangements were made for the massacre by the leaders of the church. The majority of the lay-members of the brotherhood were only so far initiated in the mysteries of the hellish plot, as to be informed that Monday was to be the day of judgment—that a *black sun* was to rise in the east—(some said in the west) that there was to be oceans of bloodshed, etc. With the morning commenced the butchery—a "black sun" arose in the east with a vengeance!—a day of judgment came upon the heads of 64 innocent men, women, and children. The sentence of the judge and the blow of the executioner fell at once on the helpless victims of fanatic fury! Masters noted for their lenity —mistresses famed for their kindness—virgins renowned for their beauty and little helpless lisping infants in the cradle, were shot, hewed down with axes, butchered with knives, and had their brains dashed out against the house sides and fences, by these fiends in human form, these remorseless dealers in blood and carnage. Not once did they willingly spare—they went for extermination—determined that the news of their deeds and the deeds themselves should go together—intentionally they left none to tell the tale of horror. Some, however, did escape, gave the alarm and the course of the murderers was arrested.—Some twenty or thirty were shot by the whites, and about the same number have been or will be hung. The ringleader,

Nat Turner, (Gen. Cargill, as he called himself) is not yet taken, and my impression is, will never be, at the moment he became convinced that his enterprise must fail, he no doubt left the country, and ere this is secure in some one of the non-slave holding states.

Circumstances are every day coming to light, which go clearly to prove that this insurrection was to have been general; at least in the counties between the James and Roanoke rivers, and perhaps in some others. Lt. Harrison Cocke of the U. S. N., who went down as a volunteer with the Prince George cavalry, informed me that Hark (Hercules) one of the ringleaders, confessed to him that their principal force lay in Brunswick. He also saw the maps and papers of their General, Nat, from which however, little could be gathered, as they were filled with hieroglyphics of which the favourite figure was the crucifixion. Their banner was a red-cross in a white field. Some of the wretches wore red caps, and others had their hats ornamented with red bands of various materials. At no time could an attempt of this kind have been made with a greater chance of success. The militia were unarmed—the inhabitants perfectly unconscious of approaching danger from that course never dreamed that they were fostering adders in their bosoms who ere long would inflict the sting of death. Thanks to an energetic governor we are now prepared to meet danger at any moment. The recent attempt of these deluded fanatics has opened the eyes of the people and placed every man on his guard—another such an enterprize will end in total extermination of their race in the southern country—bloody as the remedy may be, it will be better thus to rid ourselves of, than longer endure the evil. . . .

RICHMOND *WHIG*, SEPTEMBER 26, 1831

This is one of the most important contemporary sources. It contains the only known reference to Turner's wife, and seems to be based on the interrogation of black prisoners and the testimony at the rebels' trials. It may well be that the author was Thomas R. Gray, the Jerusalem lawyer to whom Turner later dictated his Confessions.

We publish to-day, a detailed account of the late insurrection in Southampton, kindly furnished us by a gentleman well conversant with the scenes he describes, and fully competent from the sources of information he possesses, to arrive at a correct conclusion, as to the causes which prompted the ringleader, and the end he had in view. The writer's speculations are therefore, deserving serious considerations, and we are very much inclined to concur with him in the opinion that it was a sudden and unprepared outbreak of fanaticism and subtle craft, wholly unconnected with any concert in neighbouring counties. We expressed our belief of the contrary, when we heard the other day of the reported atrocious murders in North Carolina, but upon more mature reflection, we are now convinced, that we founded our opinions then, too hastily, upon the exaggerated account before us, and which we did not suppose could receive so general a belief, and so apparently an authentic shape, without a foundation in truth.

We owe the writer an apology, for the liberty we have taken, in abridging his remarks. Necessity compelled us to do so, or want of room, would have entirely excluded him. We have, however, taken care to omit no facts, related by him, and of these, the reader will find many new, and throwing much light on the shocking occurrence.

Southampton Insurrection

Jerusalem, Sept. 17, 1831

Messrs Editors: Being firmly convinced, that the public would be gratified by a detailed account, of the late unfortunate occurrence in our county; and likewise conscious, that justice to the innocent requires that the causes, the extent, and number of persons involved in the late insurrection, should be correctly understood, I have resolved to enter upon the task.—Professional duties prevent me, from bestowing as much attention to the drawing up of this narrative as I would wish.— And I must therefore, submit it to the public crude and undigested; sketched amid scenes, but ill calculated, to support me in my opinions. —Another inducement, exclusive of any sanctioned by humanity, is that there are so many rumors afloat, and so many misstatements in the public prints, that a sacred duty to my country, demands a correct view of this tragedy.

It is only since the affair appears to be settled, that I have thought seriously upon the subject.—In almost every section of our county, conversation instead of being as it was a month since, light and cheerful, is now cloathed in dismal forebodings.—Some of our citizens will leave us—and all agree, that they never again can feel safe, never again be happy. But let us examine into their apprehensions and see if we can administer no comfort.

I have heard many express their fears of a general insurrection, they are ignorant who believe in the possibility of such a thing.—What the relative proportion of black to white is, in the slaveholding states I know not—having no means of obtaining correct information at this time; but suppose the preponderance to be in favour of the blacks to any extent; and you cannot create causes for alarm. Is it possible for men, debased, degraded as they are, ever to concert effective measures?

Would the slaves alone in St. Domingo ever have attempted insurrection? I humbly apprehend not. It was the march of intellect among the free blacks, that first gave impulse to the tide, which poured its torrents throughout the Island.—Can any person entertain serious apprehensions from this portion of our population; situated as they are—without arms, without concert, what can be effected? Why nothing—and a serious attempt, will never be made while they are thus situated.

But if any desire there was to increase this spirit among our slaves, I would advise our citizens to permit coloured preachers to go on, as they have for several years past haranging vast crowds, when and where they pleased, the character of their sermons known only to their congregations.—Nor do I think some of our white brethren, exempt from censure, when they fill their discourses with a ranting cant about equality.—If our insurrection was known, beyond the neighborhood of its commencement—its cause must be attributed to the misguided zeal of good men, preaching up equality; and to ignorant blacks, who again retail the same doctrine, with such comments, as their heated imaginations may supply, to their respective circles of acquaintance. For my own part, I think when a minister goes into a pulpit, flies into a passion, beats his fist, and in fine plays the blockhead, that he gives a warrant to any negro who hears him, to do whatever he pleases provided his imagination, can make God sanction it.—If the insurrection was general, it is fortunate, that it happened at this time.—For if it had been delayed longer the minds of the blacks would have been better prepared, the plot more extensive and consequently the carnage much greater. But believing it highly improbable, that a serious attempt will ever be made while they remain in their present state of ignorance; satisfied that no general concert can ever be effected, unless by the means of education; and conscious from the advantage of the white over the blacks in moral firmness, that an attempt under any circumstances, would be futile and frivolous I feel perfectly easy.

But I would caution all missionaries, who are bettering the condition of the world, and all philanthropists, who have our interest so much at stake, not to plague themselves about our slaves but leave them exclusively to our own management. The only possible crisis, in which our slaves can ever become formidable, is in the event of civil wars.

Our insurrection, general, or not, was the work of fanaticism— General Nat was no preacher, but in his immediate neighbourhood, he had acquired the character of a prophet; like a Roman Sybil, he traced his divination in characters of blood, on leaves alone in the woods; he would arrange them in some conspicuous place, have a dream telling him of the circumstance; and then send some ignorant black to bring them to him, to whom he would interpret their meaning. Thus, by means of this nature, he acquired an immense influence, over such persons as he took into his confidence.—He, likewise, pretended to have

the court of Nansemond, has sentenced him to be hanged. Report says, Norfolk jail is full, upon similar evidence. What the courts will do in that quarter, with the oaths of 498, when weighed with two—I know not.

On the consequences of this rebellion, petty as it is, my opinions are almost exclusively my own; and therefore, it is impolite to mention them—but of the manner of treating it, together with other subjects, closely connected, I will presently speak.

I must here pay a passing tribute to our slaves, but one which they richly deserve—it is, that there was not an instance of disaffection, in any section of our country; save on the plantations which Capt. Nat visited, and to their credit, the recruits were few, and from the chief settlement among them, not a man was obtained.—Many from the course pursued by the negroes, were heard to remark, that if they had to choose a master, it would never be a black one. Had I time, I could detail many an act of true fidelity; but I believe, though the butcheries were inhuman, there was not a single instance of wanton torture.

This view of the subject, leads me to enquire, into Capt. Nat's design. His object was freedom and indiscriminate carnage his watchword. The seizure of Jerusalem, and the massacre of its inhabitants, was with him, a chief purpose, and seemed to be his ultimatum; for farther, he gave no clue to his design—possessed of that, he would have thought his object attained.—But a frolick captured Andre, and a frolick saved Jerusalem—Nat's object was to commence his butcheries, as soon as the inhabitants of the county were asleep, by that means allowing himself full time, to despatch the citizens on his route; and arrive at this place before day—but several of his party getting beastly drunk, at their dinner on Sunday, delayed until very late in the night his purpose— the seizure however of this place, would have had little other effect than supplying the band with arms, and ammunition. I must here advert to a trifling incident, to show how hellish was their purpose. With a scarcity of powder, they made many of their recruits, mix it with their brandy; thinking thereby, to excite them more highly. But before their progress was arrested, the practice of drinking had been entirely suppressed.

RICHMOND *ENQUIRER,* SEPTEMBER 30, 1831

The Southampton Tragedy

The following letters from a friend in Southampton, present several new facts and views of the late insurrection, and are worthy of all reliance. The writer has had the best opportunities of scanning the scenes themselves, as well as the evidence given on the trials of the Banditti.

Jerusalem, Sept. 21st, 1831

"Your letter of the 13th was received, a few days ago, on my return from Greensville Superior Court.—There has been very little variation in the evidence submitted to the Court, in the course of the trials for the late insurrection, and with the exception of one witness, a woman belonging to Mr. Solomon Parker, there has been nothing elicited that goes to prove a concert, beyond the day before the insurrection broke out. She states, however, that she has heard the subject discoursed about among her master's slaves, and some of the neighbouring ones, for the last eighteen months; and that at a meeting held at the meeting-house, in May and August last, some eight or ten expressed their determination to unite in the scheme. Several were tried, some six or eight days ago in this county, upon her unsupported testimony and were all acquitted; whilst in Sussex, five or six were convicted upon the same testimony. She is again to be introduced here, on the trial of three or four others and may, perhaps, obtain more credit with the Court. She is about 16 or 17 years of age, and said to be of very good character. It has been contended that under our set of Assembly, the testimony of a slave or free negro, unless supported by pregnant circumstances, is insufficient to convict in any case.—You will thus perceive that we have, as yet, had no sufficient reason to believe that there was a "concert or general plan" among the Blacks. I have no doubt, however, that the subject has been pretty generally discussed among them, and the minds of many prepared to co-operate in the design. . . .

"To return to the subject of your inquires, I am led to believe, from all that I can learn, that Nat Turner has been revolving this plan of mischief and disruption, 'in a mind capacious of such things,' for years. Pretending to be divinely inspired, more than four years ago, he announced to the Blacks, that he should baptize himself on a particular day, and that whilst in the water, a dove would be seen to descend from Heaven and perch on his head,—thus endeavoring to collect a great crowd, perhaps with a similar design to that he afterwards effected. This assemblage was prevented; but he, in company with a white man did actually baptize himself. From that day until the awful tragedy of the 22nd, he has used every means in his power, to acquire an ascendancy over the minds of the slaves. A dreamer of dreams, and a would be Prophet, he used all the arts familiar to such pretenders, to deceive, delude, and overawe their minds.—Whether these arts were practiced only in his own immediate neighbourhood, or, as some say, were extended to a distance, I have not been able to ascertain, with any certainty. Some allege that he had never left the vicinity of his master's dwelling whilst others think that he had even visited the Metropolis of the State, in his character of Preacher and Prophet."

RICHMOND *WHIG*, NOVEMBER 7, 1831

Southampton Co. Va. Oct. 31, 1831

"It is with great pleasure I announce to you the apprehension of the negro Nat Turner. You may be assured there is no mistake in this. I have lived near him for years, I know him well, and had the gratification of seeing him yesterday carried from house to house in the neighborhood, where the females, who made such narrow escapes from him and his gang, expressed a curiosity to see him.—We have been convinced for several weeks that he was still amongst us. On last Thursday Mr. Nat. Francis (brother to Mrs. Travis, who was Nat's mistress) was riding through his fields examining the condition of his fodder stacks, when to his astonishment, Nat stepped out from between two of the stacks, which stood almost touching each other, with a smiling countenance, and without showing any hostile intention. Mr. F. immediately drew a pistol, when Nat drew his sword, the only weapon he had Mr. Francis fired, but without effect; (we found after taking him that the load passed through his hat). Nat ran off, carrying with him a ham of bacon, and leaving another together with some sweet potatoes and his shoes in the den, which was very ingeniously contrived. By drawing out fodder from the bottom of both stacks, he lay with his head under one, and his feet under the other. Since that time the exertions of the neighborhood have been unremitting. Nothing of importance was discovered until yesterday, when Mr. Ben. Phipps discovered some brush wood collected in a manner to excite suspicion; on removing it he found the opening of a newly dug cave, in which the Captain was concealed. Mr. Phipps called for assistance, but none of the company were within hearing. Nat told him he would give up, and by Mr. Phipps' order, handed out his sword and crawled out, when he was taken in custody and held till some of the company came up and assisted in securing him. The firing and rejoicing was so great, as very soon to collect a large concourse of people from the surrounding country, who joined in the general expression of joy.

"Mr. Phipps is a worthy man, though in indigent circumstances; the reward offered, which no doubt is wholly his own, could not have fallen into more deserving hands.

"Nat seems very humble; willing to answer any questions, indeed quite communicative, and I am disposed to think tells the truth. I heard him speak more than an hour. He readily avowed his motive; confessed that he was the prime instigator of the plot, that he alone opened his master's doors and struck his master the first blow with a hatchet. He clearly verified the accounts which have been given of him. He is a shrewd, intelligent fellow; he insists strongly upon the revelations which he received, as he understood them, urging him on, and pointing to this enterprize: he had taken up the impression, that he could change the aspect of the weather, and produce a drought or a rain, by the efficacy of prayer; that he was in particular favor with Heaven, and that he had often mentioned it to his few associates, that he knew he should come to some great, or some very bad end.—His account of the plot exactly corresponds with that of the other leading men who were apprehended. He denies that any, except himself and five or six others, knew anything of it. He also says that a day in July was fixed upon, but that when the time arrived he dreaded to commence it. He seems even now, to labor, under as perfect a state of fanatical delusion as ever wretched man suffered. He does not hesitate to say, that even now he thinks he was right, but admits he may possibly have been deceived. Nevertheless, he seems of the opinion that if his time were to go over again, he must necessarily act in the same way.

"He denies ever having been out of the county since the insurrection, and says that he intended to lie by till better times arrived."

RICHMOND *ENQUIRER*, NOVEMBER 8, 1831

The Bandit—Taken

In addition to the details which we have extracted from the Petersburg and Norfolk papers, we lay before our readers the following Letters, which have been addressed to this city. The first is from the pen of the gentlemen to whom we have been so much indebted for the previous details of this murderous insurrection. We place full confidence in his statements. No man can read this account, without setting Nat Turner down as a wild fanatic or a gross imposter—but without possessing a single quality of a Hero or a General—without spirit, without courage, and without sagacity.—We are happy however, that he is taken; as it will extinguish in the minds of the ignorant wretches the delusions which his pretensions may have created; and as it may enable the citizens of Southampton better to understand the plans and extent of the insurrection, from the confessions of its leader:

Extracts of Letters

Southampton, Nov. 1

"Nat Turner is at last safely lodged in jail. He was apprehended in a cave, near the residence of his late master, on Sunday about 12 o'clock and brought to Jerusalem on Monday, where I heard him examined by the magistrates, and saw him committed to the custody of the "four walls." . . .

". . . A more gloomy fanatic you have never heard of. He gave, apparently with great candour, a history of the operations of his mind for many years past; of the sights he saw; the spirit he conversed with; of his prayers, fastings, and watchings, and of his supernatural powers and gifts in curing diseases, controlling the weather, etc. These he considered for a long time only as a call to superior righteousness; and it was not until rather more than a year ago that the idea of emancipating the blacks entered his mind. How this idea came or in what manner it was connected with his signs, etc. I could not get him to explain in a manner at all satisfactory—notwithstanding I examined him closely upon this point, he always seemed to mystify. He does not, however, pretend to conceal that he was the author of the design, and that he imparted it to five or six others, all of whom seemed prepared with ready minds and hands to engage in it. These were they who rendezvoused in the field near Travis's. He says their only arms were hatchets and axes at the commencement—that he entered Travis's house by an upper window, passed through his chamber, and going though the outer door into the yard to his followers, told them that the work was now open to them. One of them, Hark, went into the house and brought out three guns:—they then commenced their horrid butchery! he, Nat, giving the first blow, with a hatchet, both to his master and mistress, as they lay asleep in bed. He says that indiscriminate massacre was not their intention after they obtained foothold, and was resorted to in the first instance to strike terror and alarm. Women and children would afterwards have been spared, and men too who ceased to resist. . . ."

ANOTHER.—"Nat, the ringleader of the late insurrection, was apprehended by Mr. Benj. Phipps, on Sunday last, and has been committed to jail. He is making a voluntary confession, of the motives which induced him to commence the insurrection, to Mr. Thomas B. Gray, who intends publishing them in pamphlet form, for the satisfaction of the public."

2
Trial and Execution[1]

At a court of Oyer and Terminer summoned and held for the County of Southampton on Saturday the fifth day of November 1831, for the trial of Nat alias Nat Turner, a negro man slave late the property of Putnam Moore an infant, charged with conspiring to rebel and making insurrection. . . .

For reasons appearing to the Court it is ordered that the Sheriff summon a sufficient additional guard to repel any attempt that may be made to rescue Nat alias Nat Turner from the custody of the Sheriff.

The prisoner Nat alias Nat Turner was set to the Bar in custody of the Jailor of the County, and William C. Parker is by the Court assigned Counsel for the prisoner in his defence, and Meriwether B. Brodnax attorney for the Commonwealth filed an Information against the prisoner, who upon his arraignment pleaded not guilty, and Levi Waller being sworn as a witness stated that on the morning of the 22nd day of August last between 9 and 10 o'clock he heard that the negroes had risen and were murdering the whites and were *coming*. Witness sent his son Thos. to the schoolhouse he living about a quarter of a mile off to let it be known that his children to come home. Mr. Crocker the school master came with witnesses children. Witness told him to go to the house and load the guns but before the guns were loaded Mr. Crocker came to the still where witness was and said they were in sight. Witness retreated and concealed himself in the corner of the fence in the weeds on the opposite side of the house. Several negroes pursued him, but he escaped them by falling among the weeds over the fence. One negro rode up and looked over, but did not observe him. The attention of the party he thinks were called off from him by some of the party going in pursuit of another, which he thinks they took for him but who turned out to be his blacksmith. Witness then retreated into the swamp which was not far off. After remaining some time witness again approached the house. Before he retreated he saw several of his family murdered by the negroes. Witness crept up near the house to see what they were doing and concealed himself by getting in the plum orchard behind the garden. The negroes were drinking. Witness saw prisoner whom he knew very well, mounted (he thought on Dr. Musgrave's horse). States that the prisoner seemed to command the party. Made Peter Edwards negro man Sam who seemed disposed to remain, mount his horse and go with them. Prisoner gave command

[1] From *Minute Book*, Southampton County, Virginia, 1830–35, Southhampton County Courthouse, Courtland, Virginia (microfilm copy, Archives Branch, Virginia State Library).

to the party to "go ahead" when they left his house. Witness states that he cannot be mistaken in the identity of the prisoner.

James Trezvant being sworn said that Mr. James W. Parker and himself were the Justices before whom the prisoner was examined previous to his commitment. That the prisoner at the time was in confinement but no threats or promises were held out to him to make any disclosures. That he admitted that he was one of the insurgents engaged in the late insurrection and the chief among them. That he gave to his master and mistress Mr. Travis and his wife the first blow before they were dispatched. That he killed Miss Peggy Whitehead. That he was with the insurgents from their first movement to their dispersion on the Tuesday morning after the insurrection took place. That he gave a long account of the motives which led him finally to commence the bloody scene which took place. That he pretended to have had intimations by signs and omens from God that he should embark on the desperate attempt. That his comrades and even he was impressed with a belief that he could by the imposition of his hands cure diseases. That he related a particular instance in which it was believed that he had in that manner effected a cure upon one of his comrades. And that he went on to detail a medley of incoherent and confused opinions about his communications with God, his command over the clouds, etc., etc. which he had been entertaining as far back as 1828.

The Court after hearing the testimony and from all the circumstances of the case are unanimously of the opinion that the prisoner is guilty in manner and form as in the Information against him alleged and it being demanded of him if any thing for himself he had or knew to say why the Court to judgement and execution against him of and upon the premises should not proceed, he said he had nothing but what he had before said. Therefore it is considered by the Court that he be taken hence to the Jail from whence he was taken, therein to remain until Friday the 11th day of November instant, on which day between the hours of ten o'clock in the forenoon and four o'clock in the afternoon he is to be taken by the Sheriff to the usual place of execution and then and there be hanged by the neck until he be dead. And the Court value the said slave to the sum of three hundred and seventy-five dollars.

Ordered that William C. Parker be allowed the sum of ten dollars as a fee for defending Nat alias Nat Turner late the property of Putnam Moore an infant.

THE LIBERATOR (BOSTON), NOVEMBER 26, 1831

We learn, says the Petersburg Intelligencer, by a gentleman from Southampton, that the fanatical murderer, Nat Turner, was executed, according to his sentence, at Jerusalem, on Friday last, [November 11] about 1 o'clock. He exhibited the utmost composure throughout the whole ceremony; and although assured that he might, if he thought proper, address the immense crowd assembled on the occasion, declined availing himself of the privilege, and told the sheriff in a firm voice, that he was ready. Not a limb nor a muscle was observed to move. His body, after death, was given over to the surgeons for dissection.

3

The *Confessions* of Nat Turner[1]

On November 1, 1831, the day after Turner's capture, Thomas Gray, a local lawyer, began questioning him in the Jerusalem jail. Gray's purpose was to obtain a first-hand account of Turner's motives and actions in order to satisfy "public curiosity" and put to rest "a thousand idle, exaggerated and mischievous reports" which had "greatly excited the public mind." The resulting document, The Confessions of Nat Turner, is by far the most important source of information about the Southampton insurrection. The question immediately arises, however, how much of the Confessions was Turner's and how much Gray's. According to an affidavit by a number of persons who were present when the Confessions were read back to him, Turner freely acknowledged it to be a "full, free, and voluntary" statement. On the other hand, one contemporary newspaper commented that in some portions, the language seemed too "eloquent and even classically expressed," and voiced fears that the document would give Turner "a character for intelligence which he does not deserve and should not receive." Certainly some statements, like Turner's assertion that "we found no more victims to gratify our thirst for blood," seem implausible; and the summary of Turner's trial at the end of the Confessions differs in some respects from the actual transcript. Yet despite the fact that Turner's words were filtered through the pen of a white slaveholder and racist, historians have accepted the Confessions as authentic, and in most particulars, it does not contradict what independent evidence is available about the rebellion.

By the end of November, 1831, a Baltimore printer had released 50,000 copies of the Confessions. The Virginia press expressed its strong disapproval. "Too much importance has already been given to the miserable wretch," commented the Alexandria Phenix Gazette; others warned that the Confessions would incite the slaves to new rebellions. Today the pamphlet is extremely rare. There is evidence that its sale was forbidden in parts of the South, and that many copies were destroyed by state and local authorities.

[1] From *The Confessions of Nat Turner, the Leader of the Late Insurrection in Southampton, Va. As fully and voluntarily made to Thomas R. Gray* . . . (Baltimore, 1831).

DISTRICT OF COLUMBIA, TO WIT:

Be it remembered, That on this tenth day of November, Anno Domini, eighteen hundred and thirty-one, Thomas R. Gray of the said District, deposited in this office the title of a book, which is in the words as following:

"The Confessions of Nat Turner, the leader of the late insurrection in Southampton, Virginia, as fully and voluntarily made to Thomas R. Gray, in the prison where he was confined, and acknowledged by him to be such when read before the Court of Southampton; with the certificate, under seal, of the Court convened at Jerusalem, November 5, 1831, for his trial. Also, an authentic account of the whole insurrection, and with lists of the whites who were murdered, and of the negroes brought before the Court of Southampton, and there sentenced, &. the right whereof he claims as proprietor, in conformity with an Act of Congress, entitled "An act to amend the several acts respecting Copy Rights."

	EDMUND J. LEE, Clerk of the District. In testimony that the above is a true copy, from the record of the District Court
[Seal.]	for the District of Columbia, I, Edmund J. Lee, the Clerk thereof, have hereunto set my hand and affixed the seal of my office, this 10th day of November, 1831.

EDMUND J. LEE, C. D. C.

TO THE PUBLIC

The late insurrection in Southampton has greatly excited the public mind, and led to a thousand idle, exaggerated and mischievous reports. It is the first instance in our history of an open rebellion of the slaves, and attended with such atrocious circumstances of cruelty and destruction, as could not fail to leave a deep impression, not only upon the minds of the community where this fearful tragedy was wrought, but throughout every portion of our country, in which this population is to be found. Public curiosity has been on the stretch to understand the origin and progress of this dreadful conspiracy, and the motives which influence its diabolical actors. The insurgent slaves had all been destroyed, or apprehended, tried and executed, (with the exception of the leader,) without revealing any thing at all satisfactory, as to the motives which governed them, or the means by which they expected to accomplish their object. Every thing connected with the sad affair was wrapt in mystery, until Nat Turner, the leader of this ferocious band, whose name has resounded throughout our widely extended empire, was captured. This "great Bandit" was taken by a single individual, in a cave near the residence of his late owner, on Sunday, the thirtieth of October, without attempting to make the slightest resistance, and on the following day safely lodged in the jail of the County. His captor was Benjamin Phipps, armed with a shot gun well charged. Nat's only weapon was a small light sword which he immediately surrendered, and begged that his life might be spared. Since his confinement, by permission of the Jailor, I have had ready access to him, and finding that he was willing to make a full and free confession of the origin, progress and consummation of the insurrectory movements of the slaves of which he was the contriver and head; I determined for the gratification of public curiosity to commit his statements to writing, and publish them, with little or no variation, from his own words. That this is a faithful record of his confessions, the annexed certificate of the County Court of Southampton, will attest. They certainly bear one stamp of truth and sincerity. He makes no attempt (as all the other insurgents who were examined did,) to exculpate himself, but frankly acknowledges his full participation in all the guilt of the transaction. He was not only the contriver of the conspiracy, but gave the first blow towards its execution.

It will thus appear, that whilst every thing upon the surface of society wore a calm and peaceful aspect; whilst not one note of preparation was heard to warn the devoted inhabitants of woe and death, a gloomy fanatic was revolving in the recesses of his own dark, bewildered, and overwrought mind, schemes of indiscriminate massacre to the whites. Schemes too fearfully executed as far as his fiendish band proceeded in their desolating march. No cry for mercy penetrated their flinty bosoms. No acts of remembered kindness made the least impression upon these remorseless murderers. Men, women and children, from hoary age to helpless infancy were involved in the same cruel fate. Never did a band of savages do their work of death more unsparingly. Apprehension for their own personal safety seems to have been the only principle of restraint in the whole course of their bloody proceedings. And it is not the least remarkable feature in this horrid transaction, that a band actuated by such hellish purposes, should have resisted so feebly, when met by the whites in arms. Desperation alone, one would think, might have led to greater efforts. More than twenty of them attacked Dr. Blunt's house on Tuesday morning, a little before day-break, defended by two men and three boys. They fled precipitately at the first fire; and their future plans of mischief, were entirely disconcerted and broken up. Escaping thence, each individual sought his own safety either in concealment, or by returning home, with the hope that his participation might escape detection, and all were shot down in the course of a few days, or captured and brought to trial and punishment. Nat has survived all his followers, and the gallows will speedily close his career. His own

account of the conspiracy is submitted to the public, without comment. It reads an awful, and it is hoped, a useful lesson, as to the
operations of a mind like his, endeavoring to grapple with things
beyond its reach. How it first became bewildered and confounded, and
finally corrupted and led to the conception and perpetration of the
most atrocious and heart-rending deeds. It is calculated also to demonstrate the policy of our laws in restraint of this class of our population, and to induce all those entrusted with their execution, as well
as our citizens generally, to see that they are strictly and rigidly enforced. Each particular community should look to its own safety,
whilst the general guardians of the laws, keep a watchful eye over all.
If Nat's statements can be relied on, the insurrection in this county
was entirely local, and his designs confided but to a few, and these in
his immediate vicinity. It was not instigated by motives of revenge or
sudden anger, but the results of long deliberation, and a settled purpose of mind. The offspring of gloomy fanaticism, acting upon materials but too well prepared for such impressions. It will be long
remembered in the annals of our country, and many a mother as she
presses her infant darling to her bosom, will shudder at the recollection of Nat Turner, and his band of ferocious miscreants.

Believing the following narrative, by removing doubts and conjec-
tures from the public mind which otherwise must have remained,
would give general satisfaction, it is respectfully submitted to the
public by their ob't serv't,

T. R. GRAY

JERUSALEM, SOUTHAMPTON, VA. NOV. 5, 1831

We the undersigned, members of the Court convened at Jerusalem, on Saturday, the 5th day of Nov. 1831, for the trial of Nat,
alias Nat Turner, a negro slave, late the property of Putnam Moore,
deceased, do hereby certify, that the confessions of Nat, to Thomas
R. Gray, was read to him in our presence, and that Nat acknowledged
the same to be full, free, and voluntary; and that furthermore, when
called upon by the presiding Magistrate of the Court, to state if he
had any thing to say, why sentence of death should not be passed upon
him, replied he had nothing further than he had communicated to
Mr. Gray. Given under our hands and seals at Jerusalem, this 5th day
of November, 1831.

JEREMIAH COBB,	[Seal.]
THOMAS PRETLOW,	[Seal.]
JAMES W. PARKER,	[Seal.]
CARR BOWERS,	[Seal.]
SAMUEL B. HINES,	[Seal.]
ORRIS A. BROWNE,	[Seal.]

STATE OF VIRGINIA, SOUTHAMPTON COUNTY, TO WIT:

I, James Rochelle, Clerk of the County Court of Southampton in the State of Virginia, do hereby certify, that Jeremiah Cobb, Thomas Pretlow, James W. Parker, Carr Bowers, Samuel B. Hines, and Orris A. Browne, esqr's are acting Justices of the Peace, in and for the County aforesaid, and were members of the Court which convened at Jerusalem, on Saturday the 5th day of November, 1831, for the trial of Nat *alias* Nat Turner, a negro slave, late the property of Putnam Moore, deceased, who was tried and convicted, as an insurgent in the late insurrection in the county of Southampton aforesaid, and that full faith and credit are due, and ought to be given to their acts as Justices of the peace aforesaid.

[Seal.]   In testimony whereof, I have hereunto set my hand and caused the seal of the Court aforesaid, to be affixed this 5th day of November, 1831

JAMES ROCHELLE,

C. S. C. C.

CONFESSION

Agreeable to his own appointment, on the evening he was committed to prison, with permission of the jailer, I visited NAT on Tuesday the 1st November, when, without being questioned at all, he commenced his narrative in the following words:—

SIR,—You have asked me to give a history of the motives which induced me to undertake the late insurrection, as you call it—To do so I must go back to the days of my infancy, and even before I was born. I was thirty-one years of age the 2nd of October last, and born the property of Benj. Turner, of this county. In my childhood a circumstance occurred which made an indelible impression on my mind, and laid the ground work of that enthusiasm, which has terminated so fatally to many, both white and black, and for which I am about to atone at the gallows. It is here necessary to relate this circumstance —trifling as it may seem, it was the commencement of that belief which has grown with time, and even now, sir, in this dungeon, helpless and forsaken as I am, I cannot divest myself of. Being at play with other children, when three or four years old, I was telling them something, which my mother overhearing, said it had happened before I was born—I stuck to my story, however, and related some things which went, in her opinion, to confirm it—others being called on were greatly astonished, knowing that these things had happened, and caused them to say in my hearing, I surely would be a prophet, as the

Lord had shewn me things that had happened before my birth. And my father and mother strengthened me in this my first impression, saying in my presence, I was intended for some great purpose, which they had always thought from certain marks on my head and breast— [a parcel of excrescences which I believe are not at all uncommon, particularly among negroes, as I have seen several with the same. In this case he has either cut them off or they have nearly disappeared]— My grandmother, who was very religious, and to whom I was much attached—my master, who belonged to the church, and other religious persons who visited the house, and whom I often saw at prayers, noticing the singularity of my manners, I suppose, and my uncommon intelligence for a child, remarked I had too much sense to be raised, and if I was, I would never be of any service to any one as a slave—To a mind like mine, restless, inquisitive and observant of every thing that was passing, it is easy to suppose that religion was the subject to which it would be directed, and although this subject principally occupied my thoughts—there was nothing that I saw or heard of to which my attention was not directed—The manner in which I learned to read and write, not only had great influence on my own mind, as I acquired it with the most perfect ease, so much so, that I have no recollection whatever of learning the alphabet—but to the astonishment of the family, one day, when a book was shewn to me to keep me from crying, I began spelling the names of different objects—this was a source of wonder to all in the neighborhood, particularly the blacks—and this learning was constantly improved at all opportunities—when I got large enough to go to work, while employed, I was reflecting on many things that would present themselves to my imagination, and whenever an opportunity occurred of looking at a book, when the school children were getting their lessons, I would find many things that the fertility of my own imagination had depicted to me before; all my time, not devoted to my master's service, was spent either in prayer, or in making experiments in casting different things in moulds made of earth, in attempting to make paper, gunpowder, and many other experiments, that although I could not perfect, yet convinced me of its practicability if I had the means.[1] I was not addicted to stealing in my youth, nor have ever been—Yet such was the confidence of the negroes in the neighborhood, even at this early period of my life, in my superior judgment, that they would often carry me with them when they were going on any roguery, to plan for them. Growing up among them, with this confidence in my superior judgment, and when this, in their opinions, was perfected by Divine inspiration, from the circumstances already alluded to in

---

[1] When questioned as to the manner of manufacturing those different articles, he was found well informed on the subject.

my infancy, and which belief was ever afterwards zealously inculcated by the austerity of my life and manners, which became the subject of remark by white and black.—Having soon discovered to be great, I must appear so, and therefore studiously avoided mixing in society, and wrapped myself in mystery, devoting my time to fasting and prayer—By this time, having arrived to man's estate, and hearing the scriptures commented on at meetings, I was struck with that particular passage which says: "Seek ye the kingdm of Heaven and all things shall be added unto you." I reflected much on this passage, and prayed daily for light on this subject—As I was praying one day at my plough, the spirit spoke to me, saying "Seek ye the kingdom of Heaven and all things shall be added unto you." *Question*—what do you mean by the Spirit. *Ans.* The Spirit that spoke to the prophets in former days—and I was greatly astonished, and for two years prayed continually, whenever my duty would permit—and then again I had the same revelation, which fully confirmed me in the impression that I was ordained for some great purpose in the hands of the Almighty. Several years rolled round, in which many events occurred to strengthen me in this my belief. At this time I reverted in my mind to the remarks made of me in my childhood, and the things that had been shewn me—and as it had been said of me in my childhood by those by whom I had been taught to pray, both white and black, and in whom I had the greatest confidence, that I had too much sense to be raised, and if I was, I would never be of any use to any one as a slave. Now finding I had arrived to man's estate, and was a slave, and these revelations being made known to me, I began to direct my attention to this great object, to fulfil the purpose for which, by this time, I felt assured I was intended. Knowing the influence I had obtained over the minds of my fellow servants, (not by the means of conjuring and such like tricks—for to them I always spoke of such things with contempt) but by the communion of the Spirit whose revelations I often communicated to them, and they believed and said my wisdom came from God. I now began to prepare them for my purpose, by telling them something was about to happen that would terminate in fulfilling the great promise that had been made to me— About this time I was placed under an overseer, from whom I ran-away—and after remaining in the woods thirty days, I returned, to the astonishment of the negroes on the plantation, who thought I had made my escape to some other part of the country, as my father had done before. But the reason of my return was, that the Spirit appeared to me and said I had my wishes directed to the things of this world, and not to the kingdom of Heaven, and that I should return to the service of my earthly master—"For he who knoweth his Master's will, and doeth it not, shall be beaten with many stripes, and thus have I chastened you." And the negroes found fault, and murmured against me, saying that if they had my sense they would not serve any master in the world. And about this time I had a vision—and I saw white spirits and black spirits engaged in battle, and the sun was darkened—the thunder rolled in the Heavens, and blood flowed in streams—and I heard a voice saying, "Such is your luck, such you are called to see, and let it come rough or smooth, you must surely bare it." I now withdrew myself as much as my situation would permit, from the intercourse of my fellow servants, for the avowed purpose of serving the Spirit more fully—and it appeared to me, and reminded me of the things it had already shown me, and that it would then reveal to me the knowledge of the elements, the revolution of the planets, the operation of tides, and changes of the seasons. After this revelation in the year of 1825, and the knowledge of the elements being made known to me, I sought more than ever to obtain true holiness before the great day of judgment should appear, and then I began to receive the true knowledge of faith. And from the first steps of righteousness until the last, was I made perfect; and the Holy Ghost was with me, and said, "Behold me as I stand in the Heavens"—and I looked and saw the forms of men in different attitudes—and there were lights in the sky to which the children of darkness gave other names than what they really were—for they were the lights of the Savior's hands, stretched forth from east to west, even as they were extended on the cross on Calvary for the redemption of sinners. And I wondered greatly at these miracles, and prayed to be informed of a certainty of the meaning thereof—and shortly afterwards, while laboring in the field, I discovered drops of blood on the corn as though it were dew from heaven—and I communicated it to many, both white and black, in the neighborhood—and I then found on the leaves in the woods hieroglyphic characters, and numbers, with the forms of men in different attitudes, portrayed in blood, and representing the figures I had seen before in the heavens. And now the Holy Ghost had revealed itself to me, and made plain the miracles it had shown me—For as the blood of Christ had been shed on this earth, and had ascended to heaven for the salvation of sinners, and was now returning to earth again in the form of dew—and as the leaves on the trees bore the impression of the figures I had seen in the heavens, it was plain to me that the Savior was about to lay down the yoke he had borne for the sins of men, and the great day of judgment was at hand. About this time I told these things to a white man, (Etheldred T. Brantley) on whom it had a wonderful effect—and he ceased from his wickedness, and was attacked immediately with a cutaneous eruption, and blood oozed from the pores of his skin, and after praying and fasting nine days, he was healed, and the Spirit appeared to me again, and said, as the Savior had been baptised so should we be also—and when the white people would not let us be baptised by the church, we went down into the water together, in the sight of many who reviled us, and were baptised by the Spirit—After this I rejoiced greatly, and gave thanks to God. And on the 12th of May, 1828, I heard a loud noise in the heavens, and the Spirit instantly appeared to me and said the Serpent was loosened, and Christ had laid down the yoke he had borne for the sins of men, and that I should take it on and fight against the Serpent, for the time was fast approaching when the first should be last and the last should be first. *Ques.* Do you not find yourself mistaken now? *Ans.* Was not Christ crucified? And by signs in the heavens that it would make known to me when I should commence the great work—and until the first sign appeared, I should conceal it from the knowledge of men—And on the appearance of the sign, (the eclipse of the sun last February) I should arise and prepare myself, and slay my enemies with their own weapons. And immediately on the sign appearing in the heavens, the seal was removed from my lips, and I communicated the great work laid out for me to do, to four in whom I had the greatest confidence, (Henry, Hark, Nelson, and Sam)—It was intended by us to have begun the work of death on the 4th July last—Many were the plans formed and rejected by us, and it affected my mind to such a degree, that I fell sick, and the time passed without our coming to any determination how to commence—Still forming new schemes and rejecting them, when the sign appeared again, which determined me not to wait longer.

Since the commencement of 1830, I had been living with Mr. Joseph Travis, who was to me a kind master, and placed the greatest confidence in me; in fact, I had no cause to complain of his treatment to me. On Saturday evening, the 20th of August, it was agreed between Henry, Hark and myself, to prepare a dinner the next day for the men we expected, and then to concert a plan, as we had not yet determined on any. Hark, on the following morning, brought a pig, and Henry brandy, and being joined by Sam, Nelson, Will and Jack, they prepared in the woods a dinner, where, about three o'clock, I joined them.

Q. Why were you so backward in joining them?

A. The same reason that had caused me not to mix with them for years before.

I saluted them on coming up, and asked Will how came he there, he answered, his life was worth no more than others, and his liberty as dear to him. I asked him if he thought to obtain it? He said he would, or lose his life. This was enough to put him in full confidence. Jack, I knew, was only a tool in the hands of Hark, it was quickly agreed we should commence at home (Mr. J. Travis') on that night, and until we had armed and equipped ourselves, and gathered sufficient force, neither age nor sex was to be spared, (which was invariably adhered to). We remained at the feast, until about two hours in the night, when we went to the house and found Austin; they all went to the cider press and drank, except myself. On returning to the house, Hark went to the door with an axe, for the purpose of breaking it open, as we knew we were strong enough to murder the family, if they were awaked by the noise; but reflecting that it might create an alarm in the neighborhood, we determined to enter the house secretly, and murder them whilst sleeping. Hark got a ladder and set it against the chimney, on which I ascended, and hoisting a window, entered and came down stairs, unbarred the door, and removed the guns from their places. It was then observed that I must spill the first blood. On which, armed with a hatchet, and accompanied by Will, I entered my master's chamber, it being dark, I could not give a death blow, the hatchet glanced from his head, he sprang from the bed and called his wife, it was his last word, Will laid him dead, with a blow of his axe, and Mrs. Travis shared the same fate, as she lay in bed. The murder of this family, five in number, was the work of a moment, not one of them awoke; there was a little infant sleeping in a cradle, that was forgotten, until we had left the house and gone some distance, when Henry and Will returned and killed it; we got here, four guns that would shoot, and several old muskets, with a pound or two of powder. We remained some time at the barn, where we paraded; I formed them in a line as soldiers, and after carrying them through all the manoeuvres I was master of marched them off to Mr. Salathul Francis', about six hundred yards distant. Sam and Will went to the door and knocked. Mr. Francis asked who was there, Sam replied it was him, and he had a letter for him, on which he got up and came to the door; they immediately seized him, and dragging him out a little from the door, he was dispatched by repeated blows on the head; there was no other white person in the family. We started from there for Mrs. Reese's, maintaining the most perfect silence on our march, where finding the door unlocked, we entered, and murdered Mrs. Reese in her bed, while sleeping; her son awoke, but it was only to sleep the sleep of death, he had only time to say who is that, and he was no more. From Mrs. Reese's we went to Mrs. Turner's, a mile distant, which we reached about sunrise, on Monday morning. Henry, Austin, and Sam, went to the still, where, finding Mr. Peebles, Austin shot him, and the rest of us went to the house; as we approached, the family discovered us, and shut the door. Vain hope! Will, with one stroke of his axe, opened it, and we entered and found Mrs. Turner and Mrs. Newsome in the middle of a room, almost frightened to death. Will immediately killed Mrs. Turner, with one blow of his axe. I took Mrs. Newsome by the hand, and with the sword I had when I was apprehended, I struck her several blows over the head, but not being able to kill her, as the sword was dull. Will turning around and discovering it, despatched her also. A general destruction of property and search for money and ammunition, always succeeded the murders. By this time my company amounted to fifteen, and nine men mounted, who started for Mrs. Whitehead's, (the other six were to go through a by way to Mr. Bryant's, and rejoin us at Mrs. Whitehead's,) as we approached the house we discovered Mr. Richard Whitehead standing in the cotton patch, near the lane fence; we called him over into the lane, and Will, the executioner, was near at hand, with his fatal axe, to send him to an untimely grave. As we pushed on to the house, I discovered some one run round the garden, and thinking it was some of the white family, I pursued them, but finding it was a servant girl belonging to the house, I returned to commence the work of death, but they whom I left, had not been idle; all the family were already murdered, but Mrs. Whitehead and her daughter Margaret. As I came round to the door I saw Will pulling Mrs. Whitehead out of the house, and at the step he nearly severed her head from her body, with his broad axe. Miss Margaret, when I discovered her, had concealed herself in the corner, formed by the projection of cellar cap from the house; on my approach she fled, but was soon overtaken, and after repeated blows with a sword, I killed her by a blow on the head, with a fence rail. By this time, the six who had gone by Mr. Bryant's, rejoined us, and informed me they had done the work of death assigned them. We again divided, part going to Mr. Richard Porter's, and from thence to Nathaniel Francis', the others to Mr. Howell Harris', and Mr. T. Doyle's. On my reaching Mr. Porter's, he had escaped with his family. I understood there, that the alarm had already spread, and I immediately returned to bring up those sent to Mr. Doyle's, and Mr. Howell Harris'; the party I left going on to Mr. Francis', having told them I would join them in that neighborhood. I met these sent to Mr. Doyle's and Mr. Harris' returning, having met Mr. Doyle on the road and killed him; and learning from some who joined them, that Mr. Harris was from home, I immediately pursued the course taken by the party gone on before; but knowing they would complete the work of death and pillage, at Mr. Francis' before I could get there, I went to Mr. Peter Edwards', expecting to find them there, but they had been here also. I then went to Mr. John T. Barrow's, they had been here and murdered him. I pursued on their track to Capt. Newit Harris', where I found the greater part mounted, and ready to start; the men now amounting to about forty, shouted and hurraed as I rode up, some were in the yard, loading their guns, others drinking. They said Captain Harris and his family had escaped, the property in the house they destroyed, robbing him of money and other valuables. I ordered them to mount and march instantly, this was about nine or ten o'clock, Monday morning. I proceeded to Mr.

Levi Waller's, two or three miles distant. I took my station in the rear, and as it was my object to carry terror and devastation wherever we went, I placed fifteen or twenty of the best armed and most relied on, in front, who generally approached the houses as fast as their horses could run; this was for two purposes, to prevent escape and strike terror to the inhabitants—on this account I never got to the houses, after leaving Mrs. Whitehead's, until the murders were committed, except in one case. I sometimes got in sight in time to see the work of death completed, viewed the mangled bodies as they lay, in silent satisfaction, and immediately started in quest of other victims —Having murdered Mrs. Waller and ten children, we started for Mr. William Williams'—having killed him and two little boys that were there; while engaged in this, Mrs. Williams fled and got some distance from the house, but she was pursued, overtaken, and compelled to get up behind one of the company, who brought her back, and after showing her the mangled body of her lifeless husband, she was told to get down and lay by his side, where she was shot dead. I then started for Mr. Jacob Williams, where the family were murdered—Here he found a young man named Drury, who had come on business with Mr. Williams—he was pursued, overtaken and shot. Mrs. Vaughan was the next place we visited—and after murdering the family here, I determined on starting for Jerusalem—Our number amounted now to fifty or sixty, all mounted and armed with guns, axes, swords and clubs—On reaching Mr. James W. Parker's gate, immediately on the road leading to Jerusalem, and about three miles distant, it was proposed to me to call there, but I objected, as I knew he was gone to Jerusalem, and my object was to reach there as soon as possible; but some of the men having relations at Mr. Parker's it was agreed that they might call and get his people. I remained at the gate on the road, with seven or eight; the others going across the field to the house, about half a mile off. After waiting some time for them, I became impatient, and started to the house for them, and on our return we were met by a party of white men, who had pursued our blood-stained track, and who had fired on those at the gate, and dispersed them, which I knew nothing of, not having been at that time rejoined by any of them—Immediately on discovering the whites, I ordered my men to halt and form, as they appeared to be alarmed—The white men, eighteen in number, approached us in about one hundred yards, when one of them fired, (this was against the positive orders of Captain Alexander P. Peete, who commanded, and who had directed the men to reserve their fire until within thirty paces)—And I discovered about half of them retreating, I then ordered my men to fire and rush on them; the few remaining stood their ground until we approached within fifty yards, when they fired and retreated. We pursued and overtook some of them who we thought we left dead; (they were not killed) after pursuing them about two hundred yards, and rising a little hill, I discovered they were met by another party, and had halted, and were reloading their guns, (this was a small party from Jerusalem who knew the negroes were in the field, and had just tied their horses to await their return to the road, knowing that Mr. Parker and family were in Jerusalem, but knew nothing of the party that had gone in with Captain Peete; on hearing the firing they immediately rushed to the spot and arrived just in time to arrest the progress of these barbarous villains, and save the lives of their friends and fellow citizens). Thinking that those who retreated first, and the party who fired on us at fifty or sixty yards distant, had all fallen back to meet others with ammunition. As I saw them reloading their guns, and more coming up than I saw at first, and several of my bravest men being wounded, the others became panick struck and squandered over the field; the white men pursued and fired on us several times. Hark had his horse shot under him, and I caught another for him as it was running by me; five or six of my men were wounded, but none left on the field; finding myself defeated here I instantly determined to go through a private way, and cross the Nottoway river at the Cypress Bridge, three miles below Jerusalem, and attack that place in the rear, as I expected they would look for me on the other road, and I had a great desire to get there to procure arms and ammunition. After going a short distance in this private way, accompanied by about twenty men, I overtook two or three who told me the others were dispersed in every direction. After trying in vain to collect a sufficient force to proceed to Jerusalem, I determined to return, as I was sure they would make back to their old neighborhood, where they would rejoin me, make new recruits, and come down again. On my way back, I called at Mrs. Thomas's, Mrs. Spencer's, and several other places, the white families having fled, we found no more victims to gratify our thirst for blood, we stopped at Maj. Ridley's quarter for the night, and being joined by four of his men, with the recruits made since my defeat, we mustered now about forty strong. After placing out sentinels, I laid down to sleep, but was quickly roused by a great racket; starting up, I found some mounted, and others in great confusion; one of the sentinels having given the alarm that we were about to be attacked, I ordered some to ride round and reconnoitre, and on their return the others being more alarmed, not knowing who they were, fled in different ways, so that I was reduced to about twenty again; with this I determined to attempt to recruit, and proceed on to rally in the neighborhood, I had left. Dr. Blunt's was the nearest house, which we reached just before day; on riding up the yard, Hark fired a gun. We expected Dr. Blunt and his family were at Maj. Ridley's, as I knew there was a company of men there;

the gun was fired to ascertain if any of the family were at home; we were immediately fired upon and retreated, leaving several of my men. I do not know what became of them, as I never saw them afterwards. Pursuing our course back and coming in sight of Captain Harris', where we had been the day before, we discovered a party of white men at the house, on which all deserted me but two, (Jacob and Nat), we concealed ourselves in the woods until near night, when I sent them in search of Henry, Sam, Nelson, and Hark, and directed them to rally all they could, at the place we had had our dinner the Sunday before, where they would find me, and I accordingly returned there as soon as it was dark and remained until Wednesday evening, when discovering white men riding around the place as though they were looking for some one, and none of my men joining me, I concluded Jacob and Nat had been taken, and compelled to betray me. On this I gave up all hope for the present; and on Thursday night after having supplied myself with provisions from Mr. Travis's, I scratched a hole under a pile of fence rails in a field, where I concealed myself for six weeks, never leaving my hiding place but for a few minutes in the dead of night to get water which was very near; thinking by this time I could venture out, I began to go about in the night and eaves drop the houses in the neighborhood; pursuing this course for about a fortnight and gathering little or no intelligence, afraid of speaking to any human being, and returning every morning to my cave before the dawn of day. I know not how long I might have led this life, if accident had not betrayed me, a dog in the neighborhood passing by my hiding place one night while I was out, was attracted by some meat I had in my cave, and crawled in and stole it, and was coming out just as I returned. A few nights after, two negroes having started to go hunting with the same dog, and passed that way, the dog came again to the place, and having just gone out to walk about, discovered me and barked, on which thinking myself discovered, I spoke to them to beg concealment. On making myself known they fled from me. Knowing then they would betray me, I immediately left my hiding place, and was pursued almost incessantly until I was taken a fortnight afterwards by Mr. Benjamin Phipps, in a little hole I had dug out with my sword, for the purpose of concealment, under the top of a fallen tree. On Mr. Phipps' discovering the place of my concealment, he cocked his gun and aimed at me. I requested him not to shoot and I would give up, upon which he demanded my sword. I delivered it to him, and he brought me to prison. During the time I was pursued, I had many hair breadth escapes, which your time will not permit you to relate. I am here loaded with chains, and willing to suffer the fate that awaits me.

I here proceeded to make some inquiries of him, after assuring him of the certain death that awaited him, and that concealment would only bring destruction on the innocent as well as guilty, of his own color, if he knew of any extensive or concerted plan. His answer was, I do not. When I questioned him as to the insurrection in North Carolina happening about the same time, he denied any knowledge of it; and when I looked him in the face as though I would search his inmost thoughts, he replied, "I see sir, you doubt my word; but can you not think the same ideas, and strange appearances about this time in the heaven's might prompt others, as well as myself, to this undertaking." I now had much conversation with and asked him many questions, having forborne to do so previously, except in the cases noted in parenthesis; but during his statement, I had, unnoticed by him, taken notes as to some particular circumstances, and having the advantage of his statement before me in writing, on the evening of the third day that I had been with him, I began a cross examination, and found his statement corroborated by every circumstance coming within my own knowledge or the confessions of others who had been either killed or executed, and whom he had not seen nor had any knowledge since 22d of August last, he expressed himself fully satisfied as to the impracticability of his attempt. It has been said he was ignorant and cowardly, and that his object was to murder and rob for the purpose of obtaining money to make his escape. It is notorious, that he was never known to have a dollar in his life; to swear an oath, or drink a drop of spirits. As to his ignorance, he certainly never had the advantages of education, but he can read and write, (it was taught him by his parents,) and for natural intelligence and quickness of apprehension, is surpassed by few men I have ever seen. As to his being a coward, his reason as given for not resisting Mr. Phipps, shews the decision of his character. When he saw Mr. Phipps present his gun, he said he knew it was impossible for him to escape as the woods were full of men; he therefore thought it was better to surrender, and trust to fortune for his escape. He is a complete fanatic, or plays his part most admirably. On other subjects he possesses an uncommon share of intelligence, with a mind capable of attaining anything; but warped and perverted by the influence of early impressions. He is below the ordinary stature, though strong and active, having the true negro face, every feature of which is strongly marked. I shall not attempt to describe the effect of his narrative, as told and commented on by himself, in the condemned hole of the prison. The calm, deliberate composure with which he spoke of his late deeds and intentions, the expression of his fiend-like face when excited by enthusiasm, still bearing the stains of the blood of helpless innocence about him; clothed with rags and covered with chains; yet daring to raise his manacled hands to heaven, with a spirit soaring above the attributes of man; I looked on him and my blood curdled in my veins.

I will not shock the feelings of humanity, nor wound afresh the bosoms of the disconsolate sufferers in this unparalleled and inhuman massacre, by detailing the deeds of their fiend-like barbarity. There were two or three who were in the power of these wretches, had they known it, and who escaped in the most providential manner. There were two whom they thought they left dead on the field at Mr. Parker's, but who were only stunned by the blows of their guns, as they did not take time to re-load when they charged on them. The escape of a little girl who went to school at Mr. Waller's, and where the children were collecting for that purpose, excited general sympathy. As their teacher had not arrived, they were at play in the yard, and seeing the negroes approach, she ran up on a dirt chimney, (such as are common to log houses,) and remained there unnoticed during the massacre of the eleven that were killed at this place. She remained on her hiding place till just before the arrival of a party, who were in pursuit of the murderers, when she came down and fled to a swamp, where, a mere child as she was, with the horrors of the late scene before her, she lay concealed until the next day, when seeing a party go up to the house, she came up, and on being asked how she escaped, replied with the utmost simplicity, "The Lord helped her." She was taken up behind a gentleman of the party, and returned to the arms of her weeping mother. Miss Whitehead concealed herself between the bed and the mat that supported it, while they murdered her sister in the same room, without discovering her. She was afterwards carried off, and concealed for protection by a slave of the family, who gave evidence against several of them on their trial. Mrs. Nathaniel Francis, while concealed in a closet heard their blows, and the shrieks of the victims of these ruthless savages; they then entered the closet, where she was concealed, and went out without discovering her. While in this hiding place, she heard two of her women in a quarrel about the division of her clothes. Mr. John T. Baron, discovering them approaching his house, told his wife to make her escape, and scorning to fly, fell fighting on his own threshold. After firing his rifle, he discharged his gun at them, and then broke it over the villain who first approached him, but he was overpowered, and slain. His bravery, however, saved from the hands of these monsters, his lovely and amiable wife, who will long lament a husband so deserving of her love. As directed by him, she attempted to escape through the garden, when she was caught and held by one of her servant girls, but another coming to her rescue, she fled to the woods, and concealed herself. Few indeed, were those who escaped their work of death. But fortunate for society, the hand of retributive justice has overtaken them; and not one that was known to be concerned has escaped.

The Commonwealth,	Charged with making insurrection, and plotting
vs.	to take away the lives of divers free white per-
Nat Turner	sons,

&c. on the 22d of August, 1831.

The court composed of ——, having met for the trial of Nat Turner, the prisoner was brought in and arraigned, and upon his arraignment pleaded *Not guilty;* saying to his counsel, that he did not feel so.

On the part of the Commonwealth, Levi Waller was introduced, who being sworn, deposed as follows: (*agreeably to Nat's own Confession.*) Col. Trezvant[2] was then introduced, who being sworn, narrated Nat's Confession to him, as follows: (*his Confession as given to Mr. Gray.*) The prisoner introduced no evidence, and the case was submitted without argument to the court, who having found him guilty, Jeremiah Cobb, Esq. Chairman, pronounced the sentence of the court, in the following words: "Nat Turner! Stand up. Have you anything to say why sentence of death should not be pronounced against you?

Ans. I have not. I have made a full confession to Mr. Gray, and I have nothing more to say.

Attend then to the sentence of the Court. You have been arraigned and tried before this court, and convicted of one of the highest crimes in our criminal code. You have been convicted of plotting in cold blood, the indiscriminate destruction of men, of helpless women, and of infant children. The evidence before us leaves not a shadow of doubt, but that your hands were often imbrued in the blood of the innocent; and your own confession tells us that they were stained with the blood of a master; in your own language, "too indulgent." Could I stop here, your crime would be sufficiently aggravated. But the original contriver of a plan, deep and deadly, one that never can be effected, you managed so far to put it into execution, as to deprive us of many of our most valuable citizens; and this was done when they were asleep, and defenseless; under circumstances shocking to humanity. And while upon this part of the subject, I cannot but call your attention to the poor misguided wretches who have gone before you. They are not few in number—they were your bosom associates; and the blood of all cries aloud, and calls upon you, as the author of their misfortune. Yes! You forced them unprepared, from Time to Eternity. Borne down by this load of guilt, your only justification is, that you were led away by fanaticism. If this be true, from my soul I pity you; and while you have my sympathies, I am, nevertheless called upon to pass the sentence of the court. The time between this and your execution, will necessarily be very short; and your only hope must be in another world. The judgment of the court is, that you be taken hence to the jail from whence you came, thence to the place of execution, and on Friday next, between the hours of 10 A.M. and 2 P.M. be hung by the neck until you are dead! dead! dead! and may the Lord have mercy upon your soul.

[2] The committing Magistrate.

A List of Persons Murdered in the Insurrection, on the 21st and 22nd of August, 1831

Joseph Travers and wife and three children, Mrs. Elizabeth Turner, Hartwell Prebles, Sarah Newsome, Mrs. P. Reese and son William, Trajan Doyle, Henry Bryant and wife and child, and wife's mother, Mrs. Catharine Whitehead, son Richard and four daughters and grandchild, Salathiel Francis, Nathaniel Francis' overseer and two children, John T. Barrow, George Vaughan, Mrs. Levi Waller and ten children, William Williams, wife and two boys, Mrs. Caswell Worrell and child, Mrs. Rebecca Vaughan, Ann Eliza Vaughan, and son Arthur, Mrs. John K. Williams and child, Mrs. Jacob Williams and three children, and Edwin Drury—amounting to fifty-five.

A List of Negroes Brought before the Court of Southampton, with Their Owner's Names, and Sentence

Daniel,	Richard Porter,	Convicted.
Moses,	J. T. Barrow,	Do.
Tom,	Caty Whitehead,	Discharged.
Jack and Andrew,	Caty Whitehead,	Con. and transported.
Jacob,	Geo. H. Charlton,	Disch'd without trial.
Isaac,	Do.,	Convi. and transported.
Jack,	Everett Bryant,	Discharged.
Nathan,	Benj. Blunt's estate,	Convicted.
Nathan, Tom, and	Nathaniel Francis,	Convicted and transported.
Davy, (boys),	Elizabeth Turner,	Convicted.
Davy,	Thomas Ridley,	Do.
Curtis,	Do.,	Do.
Stephen,	Benjamin Edwards,	Convicted and transp'd.
Hardy and Isham,	Nathaniel Francis,	Convicted.
Sam,	Joseph Travis' estate,	Do.
Hark,	Do.,	Do. and transported.
Moses, (a boy),	Levi Waller,	Convicted.
Davy,	Jacob Williams,	Do.
Nelson,	Edm'd Turner's estate,	Do.
Nat,	Wm. Reese's estate,	Do.
Dred,	Nathaniel Francis,	Do.
Arnold, Artist, (free),		Discharged.
Sam,	J. W. Parker,	Acquitted.
Ferry and Archer,	J. W. Parker,	Disch'd without trial.
Jim,	William Vaughan,	Acquitted.
Bob,	Temperance Parker,	Do.
Davy,	Joseph Parker,	
Daniel,	Solomon D. Parker	Disch'd without trial.
Thomas Haithcock, (free),		Sent on for further trial.
Joe,	John C. Turner,	Convicted.
Lucy,	John T. Barrow,	Do.
Matt,	Thomas Ridley,	Acquitted.
Jim,	Richard Porter,	Do.
Exum Artes, (free),		Sent on for further trial.
Joe,	Richard P. Briggs,	Disch'd without trial.

Bury Newsome, (free),		Sent on for further trial.
Stephen,	James Bell,	Acquitted.
Jim and Isaac,	Samuel Champion,	Convicted and trans'd.
Preston,	Hannah Williamson,	Acquitted.
Frank,	Solomon D. Parker,	Convi'd and transp'd.
Jack and Shadrach,	Nathaniel Simmons,	Acquitted.
Nelson,	Benj. Blunt's estate,	Do.
Sam,	Peter Edwards,	Convicted.
Archer,	Arthur G. Reese,	Acquitted.
Isham Turner, (free),		Sent on for further trial.
Nat Turner,	Putnam Moore, dec'd.,	Convicted.

AMERICANS REACT TO THE INSURRECTION

4

Virginia Reactions

As news of the insurrection spread through Virginia, it produced two very different kinds of reactions. On the one hand, the newspapers of the state, in order to dispel rumors and allay fears, insisted that the rebellion was an isolated, irrational event, and that most of the slaves were well-treated and loyal. But letters poured into the office of Governor John Floyd, telling of hysteria and rumors of insurrection throughout the state, complaining that even where there was no rebellion, the slaves were unusually surly and unruly, and demanding arms for local militia and vigilante groups. Floyd, who felt the danger was greatly exaggerated, and who was disgusted by the excessive fear in many communities, expressed his view of the revolt in a letter to South Carolina's Governor James Hamilton in November. He believed the plot had been more widespread than had been reported, but that it originated not with the mass of the slaves, but with black preachers and outside agitators from the North.

FREDERICKSBURG *VIRGINIA HERALD*, SEPTEMBER 3, 1831

We copy from the Richmond papers some further particulars of the tragical scenes which have lately occurred in Southampton. It is almost impossible to imagine the degree of infatuation which must have possessed the perpetuators of such crimes—there appears to have been no cause to stir up a spirit of revenge; so far from it, the masters of these deluded wretches are represented to have been of the most kind and indulgent character. What possible motive could have thus led them to commit such barbarities—to hurry themselves to such speedy and inevitable destruction? From the painful contemplation of such savage ferocity, the mind turns with pleasure to the noble conduct of the slaves of Mr. Blunt, who protected their master at the hazard of their own lives, and who have thus laid him under a weight of obligation which he can never cease to feel. So striking an example of faithful attachment and of generous devotion to duty, should never be forgotten.

RICHMOND *WHIG*, SEPTEMBER 8, 1831

In the N. York Journal of Commerce, we find the following letter written from Richmond.

THE INSURRECTION IN VIRGINA.—The Editors of the Journal of Commerce have been favored with the following interesting letter, dated Richmond, Aug. 28th, 1831.

Yours of the 25th, is received. Until today, the opinion has prevailed that the disturbance among the negroes was confined to a number of runaway slaves, in and about the Dismal swamp; and that nothing like a concerted plan of an insurrection was thought of by others.

Our artillery company you will have heard, had returned home. The company of horse were also on their way home. But we learn the Governor received an express last night from the section of country where the murders took place, which induced him to send forward an express to meet the company of horse, and order them to return to the country of insurrectionists again. It is also said that the Governor has received one or two expresses since morning, and that the last accounts are, that several more families have been murdered; that insurrections had broke out in Hallifax, N. C.,—in Surry and Nansemond, Va.,—that a mistake was made by some of the Negroes, and that *this day,* instead of last Sunday, was the day on which the murders were to have been committed. Our City has out a small patrol at night, but people *to-day* seem to be of opinion that stronger measures should be taken. A very intelligent citizen says that at least four hundred men should be under arms to-night, as reports are that threats of insurrection have been made near this city. The reports, which no doubt have been founded upon nothing, in many instances, nevertheless, *cause some alarm.* We can now conceive that the murders at Southampton, could not have been so much an affair of runaway negroes, as was at first supposed; and the question arises, if the slaves in that county would murder the whites, whether they are not as ready to do it in any *other county* in the State; and whether the report that may spread among the slaves in other parts of the State, may not *excite* those to insurrection that never thought of such a thing before. We are of opinion that these occurrences will cause considerable excitement among our citizens for some time, although no further damage may be done; and we are not without fears that more damage will arise before the slaves are learnt what their best interest is.

If they attempt any harm in towns, they would most likely resort to *fire* to aid them; and good destroyed by such, would not be paid for by insurers. For this reason we should not, just at this time, care to have goods sent to us on which we might have to make advances. . . .

GEORGE M. COOKE TO GOVERNOR JOHN FLOYD[1]

Stafford Co., September 13, 1831

Sir,

The excitement produced in this portion of the country by the late disturbances in Southampton and its neighborhood, has made it my duty to bring to your notice the defenceless condition of the white population and the danger to which they are exposed.

The militia are without arms in every county of my brigade, comprising the counties of Fauquir, Prince William, Stafford and King George, in all which there is an over grown slave population: in this county we are peculiarly distracted in reference to that people.

The stone quarries worked in Stafford employ a large number of negroes say 100 men, in the immediate neighborhood of which on a single estate there are as many more and in the improvement of the Rappahannock river a large number are constantly employed so that, if any design should be suggested concert would be easy.

Since the affair of Southampton we conceive, that in the deportment of our slaves a manifest degree of impudence is to be discovered. They have circulating amongst them a high spirit of rebellion. The owners are in progress to learn the source from whence it has sprung.

I ask leave to suggest the propriety of immediately arming such portion of the militia of these counties as the situation of the population may seem to require, and particularly the county of Stafford whose peculiar population and location demands attention. Should it be deemed expedient to arm the whole militia and I incline to that opinion the arms might be distributed at the discretion of the commandant of the regt. in each county. It will be peculiarly proper to arm the cavalry. For the strength and description of the militia of my Brigade I refer you to the adjt. Genl. Having frequent and urgent calls on me upon this subject, I should be pleased to hear from you as early as your attention can be brought to the subject of this letter.

Very respectfully
your obt svt
Geo. M. Cooke

GOVERNOR JOHN FLOYD TO GOVERNOR JAMES HAMILTON, NOVEMBER 19, 1831[2]

Sir,

I received your letter yesterday, and with great pleasure will state my impressions freely.

[1] From *Executive Papers*, Governor John Floyd, Archives Branch, Virginia State Library.

[2] From John Floyd Papers, Library of Congress.

I will notice this affair in my annual message, but shall only give a very careless history of it, as it appears to be public.

I am fully persuaded the spirit of insubordination which has, and still manifests itself in Virginia, had its origin among, and emanated from, the Yankee population, upon their first arrival amongst us, but most especially the Yankee pedlars and traders.

The course has been by no means a direct one. They began first by making them religious; their conversations were of that character, telling the blacks, God was no respecter of persons; the black man was as good as the white; that all men were born free and equal; that they can not serve two masters; that the white people rebelled against England to obtain freedom; so have the blacks a right to do.

In the meantime, I am sure without any purpose of this kind, the preachers, especially Northern, were very assiduous in operating upon our population. Day and night they were at work and religion became, and is, the fashion of the times. Finally our females and of the most respectable were persuaded that it was piety to teach negroes to read and write, to the end that they might read the Scriptures. Many of them became tutoresses in Sunday Schools and pious distributors of tracts from the New York Society.

At this point more active operations commenced; our magistrates and laws became more inactive; large assemblies of negroes were suffered to take place for religious purposes. Then commenced the efforts of the black preachers. Often from the pulpits these pamphlets and papers were read, followed by the incendiary publications of Walker, Garrison and Knapp of Boston; these too with songs and hymns of a similar character were circulated, read and commented upon, we resting in apathetic security until the Southampton affair.

From all that has come to my knowledge during and since this affair, I am fully convinced that every black preacher, in the whole country east of the Blue Ridge, was in the secret, that the plans as published by those northern prints were adopted and acted upon by them, that their congregations, as they were called knew nothing of this intended rebellion, except a few leading, and intelligent men, who may have been head men in the church. The mass were prepared by making them aspire to an equal station by such conversations as I have related as the first step.

I am informed that they had settled the form of government to be that of the white people, whom they intended to cut off to a man, with this difference that the preachers were to be their governors, generals and judges. I feel fully justified to myself, in believing the northern incendiaries, tracts, Sunday Schools, religion and reading and writing has accomplished this end.

I shall in my annual message recommend that laws be passed to confine the slaves to the estates of their masters, prohibit negroes from preaching, absolutely to drive from this state all free negroes, and to substitute the surplus revenue in our treasury annually for slaves, to work for a time upon our railroads, etc., and then sent out of the country, preparatory, or rather as the first step to emancipation. This last point will of course be tenderly and cautiously managed, and will be urged or delayed as your state and Georgia may be disposed to co-operate.

In relation to the extent of this insurrection I think it greater than will ever appear. The facts will as now considered, appear to be these: It commenced with Nat and nine others on Sunday night, two o'clock, we date it Monday morning before day, and ceased by the dispersion of the negroes on Tuesday morning at ten o'clock. During this time the negroes had murdered sixty-one persons and traversed a distance of twenty miles, and increased to about seventy men. They spared but one family and that one was so wretched as to be in all respects upon a par with them. All died bravely indicating no reluctance to lose their lives in such a cause.

I am with consideration and respect. Your obedient servant,

JOHN FLOYD.

5

Southern Reactions

Hysteria and rumors of new slave rebellions were by no means confined to Virginia; on the contrary, they occurred in virtually every slave state. The most extensive alarms took place in North Carolina where slaves and free blacks in many communities were rounded up, and some executed, after reports that an army of blacks had burned the town of Wilmington and was marching on Raleigh, the state capital. The state's Governor, Montfort Stokes, later insisted that the reports from his state had been completely erroneous, and expressed his regret that some innocent slaves had been put to death. In South Carolina, where the Vesey plot had been suppressed nine years earlier, newspapers made mention of important news from Virginia, but refused to publish even meagre details for fear of arousing the slaves. Many white readers must have been mystified about what exactly was going on. Nonetheless, as news of the Turner revolt filtered down to South Carolina, the same rumors and alarms appeared as in other states, and the authorities were forced to issue statements denying that any slave rebellion had occurred in South Carolina. By 1832, the South's fears had waned, but there were several more insurrection panics before the Civil War. The most notable were those in 1856, sparked by fears of the election of John C. Fremont as president, and in 1859, in the aftermath of John Brown's raid.

NORTH CAROLINA: WASHINGTON, D.C. NATIONAL INTELLIGENCER, SEPTEMBER 19, 1831

Commotion in North Carolina

The feelings of the inhabitants of Washington were much excited, on Saturday, by the reports brought by the Mail of that morning of outrages committed by the Blacks in the lower counties of North Carolina. These rumors became exaggerated in proportion to their distance from the scene of action; and, among the less informed of the geography and physical character of the country, produced great though vague alarm. Much of this was dissipated by the mail of yesterday morning; but enough yet remains to constitute a cause of deep regret and some solicitude. We publish the accounts from authentic sources which have reached us. The extract of a private letter, at the close of them, is the latest.

Raleigh, Sept. 14

Another Insurrection!—For the last twenty-four hours this City has been in a state of considerable excitement, in consequence of the reception of intelligence from such a source as leaves no doubt of its truth, that the Slaves of Duplin and Sampson counties, in this State, have risen in rebellion against the Whites, and have committed many horrid butcheries. Some accounts include New Hanover and Bladen also, but the probability as to these is not so strong. We are, as yet, entirely in the dark as to the number of the insurgents, the extent of their murders, the names of their victims, or their ultimate destination. Our town, however, has been put in a state of complete defence, for the purpose either of suppressing disturbances at home or of meeting danger from abroad.

At a meeting of the citizens held at the Court House, on Tuesday afternoon a *Senior Volunteer Association* was formed, composed altogether of individuals exempt from military duty, the command of which was assigned to Thomas G. Scott, Esq. Other measures of defence were also adopted, calculated to add to the security of our citizens.

An express having arrived from Johnston county, requesting a supply of ammunition, the Commissioners of the City had a meeting and immediately ordered a full supply of powder, lead, and flints, to be despatched to Smithfield, where it is understood that the Militia of the County are embodied.

The most recent account states the number of families murdered at *seventeen!* We are in momentary expectation of particulars. . . .

Observer Office, Fayetteville

Sept. 14, 3 P.M.

Two of the gentlemen who went from this place to Clinton on Monday night, have this moment returned; there being no danger, though the existence of the plot is clearly established. We have procured from one of them the following statement, drawn up by himself yesterday at Clinton. It is worthy of entire reliance.

On Sunday, the 4th inst. the first information of the contemplated rising of the blacks was sent from South Washington. The disclosure was made by a free mulatto man to Mr. Usher, of Washington, who sent the information to Mr. Kelly of Duplin. It appears from the mulatto's testimony, that Dave, a slave belonging to Mr. Morissey, of Sampson, applied to him to join the conspirators; stated that the negroes in Sampson, Duplin, and New Hanover, were regularly organized and prepared to rise on the 4th of October. Dave was taken up, and on this testimony convicted. After his conviction, he made a confession of the above to his master, and, in addition, gave the names of the four principal ringleaders in Sampson and Duplin, and several in Wilmington, named several families which they intended to murder. Their object was to march by two routes to Wilmington, spreading destruction and murder on their way. At Wilmington they expected to be reinforced by 2000 to supply themselves with arms and ammunition, and then return. Three of the ringleaders in Duplin have been taken, and Dave and Jim executed. There are 23 negroes in jail in Duplin county, all of them no doubt concerned in the conspiracy. Several have been whipped, and some released. In Sampson 25 are in jail, all concerned directly or indirectly in the plot. The excitement among the people in Sampson is very great, and increasing; they are taking effectual measures to arrest all suspected persons. A very intelligent negro preacher named David was put on his trial to-day, and clearly convicted by the testimony of another negro. The people were so much enraged, that they scarcely could be prevented from shooting him on his passage from the Court house to the jail. All the confessions made induce the belief that the conspirators were well-organized, and their plans well understood in Duplin, Sampson, Wayne, New Hanover, and Lenoir. Nothing had transpired to raise even a suspicion that they extended into Cumberland or Bladen, except that Jim confessed that Nat, Col. Wright's negro, (who has been missing since the discovery of the plot,) had gone to Bryant Wright's, in the neighborhood of Fayetteville, to raise a company to join the conspirators. The rumors respecting a large force having been seen collected together are unfounded, though there seems no doubt but that small armed bands have been seen. I cannot believe that any danger is to be apprehended, where the citizens are so constantly on the watch, and pursue such rigorous measures toward the offenders. The militia are assembled in ample force.

The Raleigh Star of Thursday last says—"We understand that about 21 negroes have been committed to jail in *Edenton,* on a charge of having been concerned in concerting a project of rebellion."

(Edenton is 100 miles from Southampton county, Virginia, and near 200 miles from Duplin and Sampson counties, in North Carolina.)

Private Correspondence

Raleigh, N. C., Sept. 15, 1831

"As I promised, I write again to-day, and am glad that I am able to say, that our excitement has in a great measure subsided. We learn, from Fayetteville, that there have been disturbances in Sampson and Duplin, but cannot ascertain particulars. It is now even doubtful, whether any white family has been killed, though the statement, current yesterday, that seventeen families were murdered, was communicated to the Governor by an official despatch from Gen. Whitfield of Lenoir. The Newbern stage, this evening, will give us the particulars, we expect. In the mean time, we keep up, at night, a vigilant watch. Business has resumed its usual course, and several families of the country which flocked in here, have returned. Things look so well, that, unless some additional information is received this evening, I shall not think it necessary to write again to-morrow, but leave you to infer good news from the absence of all intelligence.

"Yesterday, every free negro in the city, without exception, was arrested, and underwent an examination before the Committee of Vigilance constituted at our town meeting. Those who could not give a satisfactory account of their mode of subsistence, were either imprisoned for the moment, or ordered to leave the place forthwith. Every kitchen in the town was diligently searched, and, I am happy to say, that nothing was found on any one, likely to bring them into trouble."

NORTH CAROLINA: GOVERNOR MONTFORT STOKES TO GOVERNOR JAMES HAMILTON [1]

This is Stokes's reply to Governor Hamilton's request, in a letter of November 14, 1831, for information concerning "the causes, extent, and character of the late disturbances among a portion of the black population of your state."

November 18, 1831

Sir,

I have this day received your favour of the 14th Inst; on the subject of the late disturbances among the slaves, and as you request a speedy reply I lose not a moment in answering it.

There has been no insurrection of slaves in North Carolina. After the insurrection in Southampton County in Virginia, there existed much excitement in the lower counties of this state, adjoining the Virginia line, and many negroes were arrested and imprisoned upon charges for conspiracy. But in that section of the state, the whole of these suspected slaves have been discharged for the want of proof of their guilt.

In the South Eastern counties on Cape Fear and Pedee Rivers about ten or twelve negroes have been convicted for conspiracy to raise an insurrection, and most of them have been executed. I have no doubt, but the news of the Virginia insurrection prompted the restless and unruly among the slaves, in a few instances, to make a similar attempt

[1] From Governor Montfort Stokes, *Letterbook,* in the North Carolina Department of Archives and History. Used by permission of the North Carolina Department of Archives and History.

in this state; but nothing like a concerted or extensive plan has been discovered; and, I am afraid, that among the negroes condemned and executed, some, who were innocent, have suffered. I am led to this conclusion from the circumstance, that in places, where the excitement had subsided, the prisoners were all acquitted. . . .

I am, sir, your obed. servt.

M. Stokes

SOUTH CAROLINA: CHARLESTON *MERCURY*, AUGUST 29, 30, 1831

[August 29:] We take this mode to acknowledge the receipt of a letter from North Carolina upon a subject highly important and interesting not only to the people of this city, but of the whole Southern country. We thank the writer for his polite attention. The information communicated has been disposed of in the manner which we deem best calculated to answer his humane and philanthropic purpose.

[August 30:] We acknowledge the receipt of a second letter from our North Carolina correspondent, upon the very painful and revolting subject at which we hinted yesterday. We again thank him for his kindness, and for the trouble he has taken to communicate detailed and accurate information. We cannot publish his letters, nor anything indeed relating to their subject matter, for very obvious reasons; but we shall use them in the only effective way in which they can be used, and we trust that he will continue to oblige us by imparting all such additional information as it may be in his power to afford.

SOUTH CAROLINA: CHARLESTON *COURIER*, OCTOBER 4, 1831

As many idle and unfounded reports, from Checaw, Pee Dee, and Georgetown, have been in circulation for two or three days past, it may be proper to state, that official letters were received in town yesterday, by the proper authorities, stating that there was not the least foundation whatever, for these various exaggerated statements, and that all was quiet, in the various places above named.

6

The Slaves and Nat Turner

The reaction of the slaves to news of the Turner insurrection is, of course, almost impossible to ascertain. We know that a "slave grapevine" existed, which transmitted information throughout the South. This was how, for example, blacks in the slave states learned of the Emancipation Proclamation during the Civil War. We also know that the story of Nat Turner was incorporated into slave folklore and song, and was handed down from generation to generation. But only a few pieces of written evidence are available which describe the way slaves reacted to the insurrection in 1831. These come from fugitive slave narratives written in the North by blacks who were able to escape from bondage. And they focus not so much on Turner himself, as on the panic among the whites that followed the rebellion, the savage retribution upon innocent blacks, and the suppression of black preachers in the aftermath of the rebellion.

EXCERPT FROM A SLAVE SONG [1]

You mought be rich as cream
And drive you coach and four-horse team,
But you can't keep de world from moverin' round
Nor keep Nat Turner from gainin' ground

And your name it mought be Caesar sure
And got you cannon can shoot a mile or more,
But you can't keep de world from moverin' round
Nor Nat Turner from gainin' ground.

RECOLLECTIONS OF CHARITY BOWERY [2]

Lydia Maria Child, a leading New York abolitionist, published in 1839 a report of her conversation with Charity Bowery, a sixty-five-year-old former slave woman who lived in North Carolina at the time of the Turner insurrection.

---

[1] Cited in William Styron, "This Quiet Dust," *Harper's* (April, 1965), 135.
[2] From Lydia Maria Child, "Charity Bowery," *The Liberty Bell* (Boston, 1839), pp. 41–42.

In the course of my conversations with this interesting woman, she told me much about the patrols, who, armed with arbitrary power, and frequently intoxicated, break into the houses of the colored people, and subject them to all manner of outrages. But nothing seemed to have excited her imagination so much as the insurrection of Nat Turner. The panic that prevailed throughout the Slave States on that occasion of course reached her ear in repeated echoes, and the reasons are obvious why it should have awakened intense interest. It was in fact a sort of Hegira to her mind, from which she was prone to date all important events in the history of her limited world.

"On Sundays," said she, "I have seen the negroes up in the country going away under large oaks, and in secret places, sitting in the woods with spelling books. The brightest and best men were killed in Nat's time. Such ones are always suspected. All the colored folks were afraid to pray in the time of the old Prophet Nat. There was no law about it; but the whites reported it round among themselves that, if a note was heard, we should have some dreadful punishment; and after that, the low whites would fall upon any slaves they heard praying, or singing a hymn, and often killed them before their masters or mistresses could get to them."

RECOLLECTIONS OF HENRY "BOX" BROWN [3]

Brown, who became an instant celebrity among abolitionists when he escaped from slavery by placing himself in a wooden carton and mailing himself to Philadelphia, published his reminiscences in 1849.

After the lapse of about a year and a half from the time I commenced living in Richmond, a strange series of events transpired. I did not then know precisely what was the cause of these scenes, for I could not get any very satisfactory information concerning the matter from my master, only that some of the slaves had undertaken to kill their owners; but I have since learned that it was the famous Nat Turner's insurrection that caused all the excitement I witnessed. Slaves were whipped, hung, and cut down with swords in the streets, if found away from their quarters after dark. The whole city was in the utmost confusion and dismay; and a dark cloud of terrific blackness, seemed to hang over the heads of the whites. So true is it, that "the wicked flee when no man pursueth." Great numbers of the slaves were locked in the prison, and many were "half hung," as it was termed; that is, they were suspended to some limb of a tree, with a rope about their necks, so adjusted as not to quite strangle them, and

[3] From *Narrative of Henry Box Brown* (Boston, 1849), pp. 37–40.

then they were pelted by the men and boys with rotten eggs. This half-hanging is a refined species of cruelty, peculiar to slavery, I believe.

Among the cruelties occasioned by this insurrection, which was however some distance from Richmond, was the forbidding of as many as five slaves to meet together, except they were at work, and the silencing of all colored preachers. One of that class in our city, refused to obey the imperial mandate, and was severely whipped; but his religion was too deeply rooted to be thus driven from him, and no promise could be extorted from his resolute soul, that he would not proclaim what he considered the glad tidings of the gospel. (Query. How many white preachers would continue their employment, if they were served in the same way?) It is strange that more insurrections do not take place among the slaves; but their masters have impressed upon their minds so forcibly the fact, that the United States Government is pledged to put them down, in case they should attempt any such movement, that they have no heart to contend against such fearful odds; and yet the slaveholder lives in constant dread of such an event.

The rustling of

——————— the lightest leaf,
That quivers to the passing breeze,

fills his timid soul with visions of flowing blood and burning dwellings; and as the loud thunder of heaven rolls over his head, and the vivid lightning flashes across his pale face, straightway his imagination conjures up terrible scenes of the loud roaring of an enemy's cannon, and the fierce yells of an infuriated slave population, rushing to vengeance. There is no doubt but this would be the case, if it were not for the Northern people, who are ready, as I have been often told, to shoot us down, if we attempt to rise and obtain our freedom. I believe that if the slaves could do as they wish, they would throw off their heavy yoke immediately, by rising against their masters; but ten millions of Northern people stand with their feet on their necks, and how can they arise? How was Nat Turner's insurrection suppressed, but by a company of United States troops, furnished the governor of Virginia at his request, according to your Constitution?

RECOLLECTIONS OF HARRIET JACOBS [4]

Fear of Insurrection

Not far from this time Nat Turner's insurrection broke out; and the news threw our town into great commotion. Strange that they

[4] From [Harriet Jacobs], *Incidents in the Life of a Slave Girl*, ed. Lydia Maria Child (Boston, 1861), pp. 97–104.

should be alarmed, when their slaves were so "contented and happy"! But so it was.

It was always the custom to have a muster every year. On that occasion every white man shouldered his musket. The citizens and the so-called country gentlemen wore military uniforms. The poor whites took their places in the ranks in every-day dress, some without shoes, some without hats. This grand occasion had already passed; and when the slaves were told there was to be another muster, they were surprised and rejoiced. Poor creatures! They thought it was going to be a holiday. I was informed of the true state of affairs, and imparted it to the few I could trust. Most gladly would I have proclaimed it to every slave; but I dared not. All could not be relied on. Mighty is the power of the torturing lash.

By sunrise, people were pouring in from every quarter within twenty miles of the town. I knew the houses were to be searched; and I expected it would be done by country bullies and the poor whites. I knew nothing annoyed them so much as to see colored people living in comfort and respectability; so I made arrangements for them with especial care. I arranged every thing in my grandmother's house as neatly as possible. I put white quilts on the beds, and decorated some of the rooms with flowers. When all was arranged, I sat down at the window to watch. Far as my eye could reach, it rested on a motley crowd of soldiers. Drums and fifes were discoursing martial music. The men were divided into companies of sixteen, each headed by a captain. Orders were given, and the wild scouts rushed in every direction, wherever a colored face was to be found.

It was a grand opportunity for the low whites, who had no negroes of their own to scourge. They exulted in such a chance to exercise a little brief authority, and show their subserviency to the slaveholders; not reflecting that the power which trampled on the colored people also kept themselves in poverty, ignorance, and moral degradation. Those who never witnessed such scenes can hardly believe what I know was inflicted at this time on innocent men, women, and children, against whom there was not the slightest ground for suspicion. Colored people and slaves who lived in remote parts of the town suffered in an especial manner. In some cases the searchers scattered powder and shot among their clothes, and then sent other parties to find them, and bring them forward as proof that they were plotting insurrection. Every where men, women, and children were whipped till the blood stood in puddles at their feet. Some received five hundred lashes; others were tied hands and feet, and tortured with a bucking paddle, which blisters the skin terribly. The dwellings of the colored people, unless they happened to be protected by some influential white person, who was nigh at hand, were robbed of clothing and every thing else the marauders thought worth carrying away. All day long these unfeeling wretches went round, like a troop of demons, terrifying and tormenting the helpless. At night, they formed themselves into patrol bands, and went wherever they chose among the colored people, acting out their brutal will. Many women hid themselves in woods and swamps, to keep out of their way. If any of the husbands or fathers told of these outrages, they were tied up to the public whipping post, and cruelly scourged for telling lies about white men. The consternation was universal. No two people that had the slightest tinge of color in their faces dared to be seen talking together.

I entertained no positive fears about our household, because we were in the midst of white families who would protect us. We were ready to receive the soldiers whenever they came. It was not long before we heard the tramp of feet and the sound of voices. The door was rudely pushed open; and in they tumbled, like a pack of hungry wolves. They snatched at every thing within their reach. Every box, trunk, closet, and corner underwent a thorough examination. A box in one of the drawers containing some silver change was eagerly pounced upon. When I stepped forward to take it from them, one of the soldiers turned and said angrily, "What d'ye foller us fur? D'ye s'pose white folks is come to steal?"

I replied, "You have come to search; but you have searched that box, and I will take it, if you please."

At that moment I saw a white gentleman who was friendly to us; and I called to him, and asked him to have the goodness to come in and stay till the search was over. He readily complied. His entrance into the house brought in the captain of the company, whose business it was to guard the outside of the house, and see that none of the inmates left it. This officer was Mr. Litch, the wealthy slaveholder whom I mentioned, in the account of neighboring planters, as being notorious for his cruelty. He felt above soiling his hands with the search. He merely gave orders; and, if a bit of writing was discovered, it was carried to him by his ignorant followers, who were unable to read.

My grandmother had a large trunk of bedding and table cloths. When that was opened, there was a great shout of surprise; and one exclaimed, "Where'd the damned niggers git all dis sheet an' table clarf?"

My grandmother, emboldened by the presence of our white protector, said, "You may be sure we didn't pilfer 'em from *your* houses."

"Look here, mammy," said a grim-looking fellow without any coat, "you seem to feel mighty gran' 'cause you got all them 'ere fixens. White folks oughter have 'em all."

His remarks were interrupted by a chorus of voices shouting, "We's got 'em! We's got 'em! Dis 'ere yaller gal's got letters!"

There was a general rush for the supposed letter, which, upon examination, proved to be some verses written to me by a friend. In packing away my things, I had overlooked them. When their captain informed them of their contents, they seemed much disappointed. He inquired of me who wrote them. I told him it was one of my friends. "Can you read them?" he asked. When I told him I could, he swore, and raved, and tore the paper into bits. "Bring me all your letters!" said he, in a commanding tone. I told him I had none. "Don't be afraid," he continued, in an insinuating way. "Bring them all to me. Nobody shall do you any harm." Seeing I did not move to obey him, his pleasant tone changed to oaths and threats. "Who writes to you? half free niggers?" inquired he. I replied, "O, no; most of my letters are from white people. Some request me to burn them after they are read, and some I destroy without reading."

An exclamation of surprise from some of the company put a stop to our conversation. Some silver spoons which ornamented an old-fashioned buffet had just been discovered. My grandmother was in the habit of preserving fruit for many ladies in the town, and of preparing suppers for parties; consequently she had many jars of preserves. The closet that contained these was next invaded, and the contents tasted. One of them, who was helping himself freely, tapped his neighbor on the shoulder, and said, "Wal done! Don't wonder de niggers want to kill all de white folks, when dey live on 'sarves" [meaning preserves]. I stretched out my hand to take the jar, saying, "You were not sent here to search for sweetmeats."

"And what *were* we sent for?" said the captain, bristling up to me. I evaded the question.

The search of the house was completed, and nothing found to condemn us. They next proceeded to the garden, and knocked about every bush and vine, with no better success. The captain called his men together, and, after a short consultation, the order to march was given. As they passed out of the gate, the captain turned back, and pronounced a malediction on the house. He said it ought to be burned to the ground, and each of its inmates receive thirty-nine lashes. We came out of this affair very fortunately; not losing any thing except some wearing apparel.

Towards evening the turbulence increased. The soldiers, stimulated by drink, committed still greater cruelties. Shrieks and shouts continually rent the air. Not daring to go to the door, I peeped under the window curtain. I saw a mob dragging along a number of colored people, each white man, with his musket upraised, threatening instant death if they did not stop their shrieks. Among the prisoners was a respectable old colored minister. They had found a few parcels of shot in his house, which his wife had for years used to balance her scales. For this they were going to shoot him on Court House Green.

What a spectacle was that for a civilized country! A rabble, staggering under intoxication, assuming to be the administrators of justice!

The better class of the community exerted their influence to save the innocent, persecuted people; and in several instances they succeeded, by keeping them shut up in jail till the excitement abated. At last the white citizens found that their own property was not safe from the lawless rabble they had summoned to protect them. They rallied the drunken swarm, drove them back into the country, and set a guard over the town.

The next day, the town patrols were commissioned to search colored people that lived out of the city; and the most shocking outrages were committed with perfect impunity. Every day for a fortnight, if I looked out, I saw horsemen with some poor panting negro tied to their saddles, and compelled by the lash to keep up with their speed, till they arrived at the jail yard. Those who had been whipped too unmercifully to walk were washed with brine, tossed into a cart, and carried to jail. One black man, who had not fortitude to endure scourging, promised to give information about the conspiracy. But it turned out that he knew nothing at all. He had not even heard the name of Nat Turner. The poor fellow had, however, made up a story, which augmented his own sufferings and those of the colored people.

The day patrol continued for some weeks, and at sundown a night guard was substituted. Nothing at all was proved against the colored people, bond or free. The wrath of the slaveholders was somewhat appeased by the capture of Nat Turner. The imprisoned were released. The slaves were sent to their masters, and the free were permitted to return to their ravaged homes. Visiting was strictly forbidden on the plantations. The slaves begged the privilege of again meeting at their little church in the woods, with their burying ground around it. It was built by the colored people, and they had no higher happiness than to meet there and sing hymns together, and pour out their hearts in spontaneous prayer. Their request was denied, and the church was demolished. They were permitted to attend the white churches, a certain portion of the galleries being appropriated to their use. There, when every body else had partaken of the communion, and the benediction had been pronounced, the minister said, "Come down, now, my colored friends." They obeyed the summons, and partook of the bread and wine, in commemoration of the the meek and lowly Jesus, who said, "God is your Father, and all ye are brethren."

RECOLLECTIONS OF JAMES L. SMITH [5]

Smith was a skilled slave shoemaker in Virginia at the time of the rebellion. His narrative gives us insights into both the "invisible institution"—the slave church—and the folk memory of Nat Turner.

. . . While learning the shoe-maker's trade, I was about eighteen years old. At this time I became deeply interested in my soul's salvation; the white people held a prayer meeting in Fairfield one evening in a private house; I attended the meeting that evening, but was not permitted to go in the same room, but only allowed to go in an adjoining room. While there I found peace in believing, and in this happy state of mind I went home rejoicing and praising the Lord for what he had done for me. A few Sabbath's following, I united with the Church in Fairfield. Soon after I was converted I commenced holding meetings among the people, and it was not long before my fame began to spread as an exhorter. I was very zealous, so much so that I used to hold meetings all night, especially if there were any concerned about their immortal soul.

I remember in one instance that having quit work about sundown on a Saturday evening, I prepared to go ten miles to hold a prayer meeting at Sister Gould's. Quite a number assembled in the little cabin, and we continued to sing and pray till daybreak, when it broke. All went to their homes, and I got about an hour's rest while Sister Gould was preparing breakfast. Having partaken of the meal, she, her daughter and myself set out to hold another meeting two miles further; this lasted till about five o'clock, when we returned. Then I had to walk back ten miles to my home, making in all twenty-four miles that day. How I ever did it, lame as I was, I cannot tell, but I was so zealous in the work that I did not mind going any distance to attend a prayer meeting. I actually walked a greater part of the distance fast asleep; I knew the road pretty well. There used to be a great many run-aways in that section, and they would hide away in the woods and swamps, and if they found a person alone as I was, they would spring out at them and rob them. As this thought came into my head during my lonely walk, thinks I, it won't do for me to go to sleep, and I began to look about me for some weapon of defence; I took my jackknife from my pocket and opened it; now I am ready to stab the first one that tackles me, I said; but try as I would, I commenced to nod, nod, till I was fast asleep again. The long walk and the exertion of carrying on the meeting had nearly used me up.

[5] From *Autobiography of James L. Smith* (Norwich, Conn., 1881), pp. 26–30.

The way in which we worshiped is almost indescribable. The singing was accompanied by a certain ecstasy of motion, clapping of hands, tossing of heads, which would continue without cessation about half an hour; one would lead off in a kind of recitative style, others joining in the chorus. The old house partook of the ecstasy; it rang with their jubilant shouts, and shook in all its joints. It is not to be wondered at that I fell asleep, for when I awoke I found I had lost my knife, and the fact that I would now have to depend on my own muscle, kept me awake till I had reached the neighborhood of my home. . . .

When Nat. Turner's insurrection broke out, the colored people were forbidden to hold meetings among themselves. Nat. Turner was one of the slaves who had quite a large army; he was the captain to free his race. Notwithstanding our difficulties, we used to steal away to some of the quarters to have our meetings. . . .

7
Reactions in the North

Northern newspapers devoted much less attention to the Southampton insurrection than might be expected; most contented themselves with reprinting an account or two from the Richmond press, and with brief editorial comments. Newspapers at this time were almost exclusively organs of political parties, and they devoted much more space to such political controversies as the nullification crisis and the coming presidential election, than to Nat Turner. Aside from the abolitionist press, few northern papers used the occasion for vigorous attacks on slavery. The general reaction ranged from mild criticism of slavery, usually coupled with endorsements of colonization, to denunciations of the rebels and pledges of northern military assistance if it ever became necessary. Small wonder that a number of southern newspapers assured their readers that the northern reaction was proof of the strength of the ties of Union, and the weakness of the abolitionists in the free states.

NEW YORK *JOURNAL OF COMMERCE*, CITED IN *THE LIBERATOR*, SEPTEMBER 10, 1831.

INSURRECTION IN VIRGINIA—Viewed in all its bearings, this in one of the most distressing occurrences which has ever taken place in this country. Nothing can exceed the savage atrocity of the negroes, in the execution of their purposes, whatever they may have been. The mind shrinks with horror from the spectacle, when it contemplates whole families murdered, without regard to age or sex, and weltering in their gore. It is not strange if under such circumstances the whites should be wrought up to a high pitch of excitement, and shoot down without mercy not only the perpetrators, but all who are suspected of participation in the diabolical transaction. We do not say that they have gone too far in this matter. When the lives of a whole community are in jeopardy, severe measures are not only justifiable, but necessary. And yet the second scene of the tragedy is not without its horrors. No man can contemplate the slaughter of so many human beings as will perish by the white man's hand in consequence of the insurrection, without the most painful emotions. Some of them no doubt deserve to die; others may be comparatively or altogether innocent.

We cannot imagine what infatuation could have seized the minds of these negroes, that they should even dream of success in attempting to recover their freedom by violence and bloodshed. Do they not know that in addition to the forces of the white population among whom they are placed, the whole strength of the General Government is pledged to put down such insurrection? that if necessary, a million of men could be marched, on short notice, from the non-slaveholding States, to defend their brethren in the South? For, much as we abhor slavery; much as it is abhorred throughout the Northern and Eastern States; there is not a man of us who would not run to the relief of our friends in the South, when surrounded by the horrors of a servile insurrection.

It has been said that the leaders of this band of murderers are white men. It seems incredible. Who or what can they be? Monsters in human shape, undoubtedly; by whatever other names they may be called. But we shall know more on this head hereafter, together with the motives which prompted the insurrection.

NEW YORK *DAILY SENTINEL*, SEPTEMBER 17, 1831

The Daily Sentinel, *organ of the New York Workingmen's Party, was one of the most outspoken newspapers in the North in its denunciation of slavery and the South after the Turner insurrection.*

DARING OUTRAGE OF VIRGINIA SLAVITES—It becomes our *duty to-day* to record the particulars of an outrage more daring than any we remember to have heard of in this country, and one of more unjustifiable atrocity than any committed by the poor degraded ignorant blacks in Virginia, some of whom have been put to death, for their unsuccessful attempt to emancipate themselves.

No one laments more the occurence of such scenes as the Southampton massacre than the writer of this paragraph, and no one is more desirous of preventing the recurrence of such scenes; but we believe that the only effectual method of preventing their recurrence is to speak the truth in relation to what has taken place, even though we are certain that it may prove unpalatable. Of what were the Southampton negroes guilty? Of putting to death men, women, and children. For what object? Plunder? No—there is no evidence that such was their object. On the contrary, almost all the accounts concur in stating that they expected to emancipate themselves, and they no doubt thought that their only hope of doing so was to put to death, indiscriminately, the whole race of those who held them in bondage. If such were their impressions, were they not justifiable in doing so? Undoubtedly they were, if freedom is the birthright of man, as the declaration of independence tells us. If their ideas respecting their chance of success were absurd, and their plans chimerical, it is attributable to their ignorance. But who kept them in ignorance? Those who have suffered so dearly by its effects. Would the blacks have attempted their foolish project, if they had possessed even the mere rudiments of a common education? Never. They were in a state of brutal ignorance, and however absurd or cruel were their proceedings, if their object was to obtain their freedom, those who kept them in slavery and ignorance alone are answerable for their conduct. They were deluded, but their cause was *just*.

Now let us look at the conduct of the slaveholders. They say the evil of slavery was entailed upon them—that they deplore its existence, and desire its removal, and so forth. We readily grant that the evil is not of their own choosing, and no one, we believe, will contend that they are responsible for it, *as they found it*. But have they done what they could and should do for eradicating the evil of slavery?—Have they diminished the number of slaves? Have they prepared for the present generation, or made provision for preparing the next, to enjoy freedom? The answer to each of these questions involves them in guilt. The number of slaves in proportion to the number of freemen is increasing! and instead of preparing them for the enjoyment of freedom, and providing means for their gradual emancipation, Virginia—yes, the state which gave birth to the immortal Jefferson, the author of the declaration that declares that *all* men are born *free and equal*—that declaration which no slaveholder dare dispute the truth of—Virginia! at the last session of its legislature, passed a law making it penal for a slaveholder to teach his own slaves to read and write!!— . . .

ALBANY *ARGUS*, SEPTEMBER 22, 1831

As organ of the "Regency," the Democratic machine of New York State, which, through its leader, Martin Van Buren, had close political ties with southern Democrats, the Argus *felt a special need to reassure the South about northern intentions.*

We publish all the accounts on this engrossing subject [rumors of insurrection in North Carolina] that have come to hand. Although they abound in exaggerations, the natural effect of a feverish and excited state of the public mind, they show at least that there is too much cause for active and vigorous precautionary measures. So far, these seem to have been taken. If, however, the rising shall prove to be extensive or formidable, and the danger real, we know with how much alacrity the men of the North will come to the aid of their fellow citizens of the South. The cause is a common one; and the claim upon us, although less direct, is not the less the claim of humanity and patriotism.

COLUMBUS *OHIO STATE JOURNAL*, OCTOBER 20,1831

Insurrectionary Movements

Since the suppression of the late Negro insurrection in Southampton county, Va., it appears that similar outrages have been attempted by the slaves and free colored people in different parts of North and South Carolina, Louisiana, Delaware, and the Eastern Shore of Maryland, and although the designs of the poor wretches concerned therein have been for the most part discovered and frustrated before much actual mischief has been done, yet the frequency of their late attempts has occasioned no little alarm in those parts of the union which have most to fear from a servile war. Whether these almost simultaneous movements in sections of the country far removed from each other are the result of accident or of something like a preconcerted plan for a general insurrection of the slaves about this union does not fully appear. The latter supposition, however, is not altogether improbable; and although every man possessed of common sense will at once see that an attempt of this kind, however well matured, must ultimately result in the total extermination of at least all those engaged in it, if not of the entire colored population, yet, it is evident that it would inevitably occasion the loss of many valuable lives, and be productive of a vast amount of misery, before it could be suppressed.

A southern paper, speaking of these movements, and of the probability of their frequent recurrence so long as slavery shall be tolerated among us, suggests, whether it would not be right and expedient, after the National Debt shall have been paid, to apply the surplus revenue to the general emancipation of the slaves, and their removal beyond our territorial limits; and without intending to express an opinion, either as the expediency or the feasibility of such a measure, we must say that it appears to us to be worthy of serious consideration. We believe that the people of these United States ought no longer to shut their eyes to the dreadful evils of slavery, and the consequences which, sooner or later, must inevitably result from it; and that the time has fully arrived when some plan should be devised for the removal of this curse from among us. We shall probably recur to the subject in a future number.

FREDERICKSBURG *ARENA*, CITED IN ALEXANDRIA *PHENIX GAZETTE*, SEPTEMBER 9, 1831

It is gratifying to state that the language held by our Editorial brethren of the North, in relation to the late disastrous occurrences, is entirely unobjectionable. We have seen no taunts, no cant, no complacent dwelling upon the superior advantages of the non-slaveholding states; on the contrary, there has been a burst of generous sympathy, an unequivocal expression of horror at the scenes enacted by the deluded wretches. We have no doubt, that should it ever be necessary, the citizens of the United States would promptly fly to the assistance of their Southern brethren—we speak of the vast majority—fanatics there are, doubtless, who so far from thus acting would not very much scruple to foment disaffection and excite servile insurrection.

8
The Abolitionist Response

Nat Turner's insurrection occurred at a time of transition for the antislavery movement in the United States. The appearance of David Walker's Appeal *in 1829, and William Lloyd Garrison's* The Liberator, *which began publication on January 1, 1831, signaled the emergence of a new, militant breed of abolitionist who scorned colonization and demanded immediate abolition. At the same time, however, the Garrisonians were self-proclaimed pacifists who rejected the use of violence in the antislavery struggle and believed that "moral suasion" could convince the nation to abandon the sin of slavery. Garrison's initial reaction to the news from Southampton was twofold—he condemned the violence of Turner and his followers, but viewed the rebellion as a form of retribution for the nation's sins; and he warned that unless speedy steps were taken to eradicate slavery, more insurrections would surely follow. As reports reached Boston of further outbreaks in the South, Garrison for a time seemed to exult at the violence, and went to the verge of justifying it as vengeance for the wrongs done black people in this country. Other abolitionists, such as an anonymous white resident of Albany, urged the slaves on and even offered armed aid to the rebels. Most abolitionists, however, continued to recoil with horror from violence, and during the 1830s many used the Turner rebellion as an example of what the nation could expect if it did not quickly mend its ways.*

THE LIBERATOR, SEPTEMBER 3, 1831

The Insurrection

What we have so long predicted,—at the peril of being stigmatized as an alarmist and declaimer,—has commenced its fulfilment. The first step of the earthquake, which is ultimately to shake down the fabric of oppression, leaving not one stone upon another, has been made. The first drops of blood, which are but the prelude to a deluge from the gathering clouds, have fallen. The first flash of the lightning, which is to smite and consume, has been felt. The first wailings of a bereavement, which is to clothe the earth in sackcloth, have broken upon our ears.

In the first number of the Liberator, we alluded to the hour of vengeance in the following lines:

> Wo if it come with storm, and blood, and fire,
>   When midnight darkness veils the earth and sky!
> Wo to the innocent babe—the guilty sire—
>   Mother and daughter—friends of kindred tie!
>   Stranger and citizen alike shall die!
> Red-handed Slaughter his revenge shall feed,
>   And Havoc yell his ominous death-cry,
> And wild Despair in vain for mercy plead—
> While hell itself shall shrink and sicken at the deed!

Read the account of the insurrection in Virginia, and say whether our prophecy be not fulfilled. What was poetry—imagination—in January, is now a bloody reality. "Wo to the innocent babe—to mother and daughter!" Is it not true? Turn again to the record of slaughter! Whole families have been cut off—not a mother, not a daughter, not a babe left. Dreadful retaliation! "The dead bodies of white and black lying just as they were slain, unburied"—the oppressor and the oppressed equal at last in death—what a spectacle!

True, the rebellion is quelled. Those of the slaves who were not killed in combat, have been secured, and the prison is crowded with victims destined for the gallows!

> Yet laugh not in your carnival of crime
> Too proudly, ye oppressors!

You have seen, it is to be feared, but the beginning of sorrows. All the blood which has been shed will be required at your hands. At your hands alone? No—but at the hands of the people of New England and of all the free states. The crime of oppression is national. The south is only the agent in this guilty traffic. But, remember! the same causes are at work which must inevitably produce the same effects; and when the contest shall have again begun, it must be again a war of extermination. In the present instance, no quarters have been asked or given.

But we have killed and routed them now—we can do it again and again—we are invincible! A dastardly triumph, well becoming a nation of oppressors. Detestable complacency, that can think, without emotion, of the extermination of the blacks! We have the power to kill *all*—let us, therefore, continue to apply the whip and forge new fetters!

In his fury against the revolters, who will remember their wrongs! What will it avail them, though the catalogue of their sufferings, dripping with warm blood fresh from their lacerated bodies, be held up to extenuate their conduct? It is enough that the victims were black —that circumstance makes them less precious than the dogs which have been slain in our streets! They were black—brutes, pretending to be men—legions of curses upon their memories! They were black —God made them to serve us!

Ye patriotic hypocrites! ye panegyrists of Frenchmen, Greeks, and Poles! ye fustian declaimers for liberty! ye valiant sticklers for equal rights among yourselves! ye haters of aristocracy! ye assailants of monarchies! ye republican nullifiers! ye treasonable disunionists! be dumb! Cast no reproach upon the conduct of the slaves, but let your lips and cheeks wear the blisters of condemnation!

Ye accuse the pacific friends of emancipation of instigating the slaves to revolt. Take back the charge as a foul slander. The slaves need no incentives at our hands. They will find them in their stripes —in their emaciated bodies—in their ceaseless toil—in their ignorant minds—in every field, in every valley, on every hill-top and mountain, wherever you and your fathers have fought for liberty—in your speeches, your conversations, your celebrations, your pamphlets, your newspapers—voices in the air, sounds from across the ocean, invitations to resistance above, below, around them! What more do they need? Surrounded by such influences, and smarting under their newly made wounds, is it wonderful that they should rise to contend—as other "heroes" have contended—for their lost rights? It is *not* wonderful.

In all that we have written, is there aught to justify the excesses of the slaves? No. Nevertheless, they deserve no more censure than the Greeks in destroying the Turks, or the Poles in exterminating the Russians, or our fathers in slaughtering the British. Dreadful, indeed, is the standard erected by worldly patriotism!

For ourselves, we are horror-struck at the late tidings. We have exerted our utmost efforts to avert the calamity. We have warned our countrymen of the danger of persisting in their unrighteous conduct. We have preached to the slaves the pacific precepts of Jesus Christ. We have appealed to christians, philanthropists and patriots, for their assistance to accomplish the great work of national redemption through the agency of moral power—of public opinion—of individual duty. How have we been received? We have been threatened, proscribed, vilified and imprisoned—a laughing stock and a reproach. Do we falter, in view of these things? Let time answer. If we have been hitherto urgent, and bold, and denunciatory in our efforts,—hereafter we shall grow vehement and active with the increase of danger. We shall cry, in trumpet tones, night and day,—Wo to this guilty land, unless she speedily repent of her evil doings! The blood of millions of her sons cries aloud for redress! IMMEDIATE EMANCIPATION can alone save her from the vengeance of Heaven, and cancel the debt of ages!

WILLIAM LLOYD GARRISON TO LAROY SUTHERLAND[1]

September 8, 1831

Dear Sir,

I labor under very signal obligations to you for your disclosures, relative to my personal safety. These do not move me from my purpose the breadth of a hair. Desperate wretches exist at the south, no doubt, who would assassinate me for a sixpence. Still, I was aware of this peril when I began my advocacy of African rights. Slaveholders deem me their enemy; but my aim is simply to benefit and save them, and not to injure them. I value their bodies and soul, at a high price, though I abominate their crimes. Moreover, I do not justify the slaves in their rebellion; yet I do not condemn *them,* and applaud similar conduct in *white men.* I deny the right of any people to fight for liberty, and so far am a Quaker in principle. Of all men living, however, our slaves have the best reason to assert their rights by violent measures, inasmuch as they are more oppressed than others.

My duty is plain—my path without embarrassment. I shall still continue to expose the criminality and danger of slavery, be the consequences what they may to myself. I hold my life at a cheap rate: I know it is in imminent danger: but if the assassin take it away, the Lord will raise up another and better advocate in my stead.

Again thanking you for your friendly letter, I remain, in haste,

Yours, in the best of bond,
Wm. Lloyd Garrison

THE LIBERATOR, SEPTEMBER 24, 1831

BLOOD! BLOOD!! BLOOD!!!
Another Insurrection!

North Carolina is thrown into a high fever! The Avenger is abroad, scattering desolation and death in his path! An insurrection has broken out among the slaves near Wilmington, the town is reported to be burnt, and *seventeen families murdered!!* At the last accounts, the insurgents were slaying and burning all before them, and women and children were flying in every direction almost distracted. . . .

We have no room for particulars—not even for comments. So much for oppression! so much for the happiness of the slaves! so much for the security of the South! Where now are our white boasters of liberty?

[1] From William Lloyd Garrison Papers, Boston Public Library. Used by permission of the Boston Public Library.

where the Polish shouters? where the admirers of those who die for liberty? Let the blood which is now flowing rest upon the advocates of war—upon the heads of the oppressors and their apologists. Yea, God will require it at their hands. MEN MUST BE FREE!

"Hath not" a slave "hands, organs, dimensions, *senses, affections, passions,*—hurt with the same weapons, subject to the same diseases, healed by the same means, warmed and cooled by the same summer and winter, as his master is? If you lash him, does he not bleed? If you wrong him, shall he not revenge?"

ALBANY *AFRICAN SENTINEL AND JOURNAL OF LIBERTY,* OCTOBER 1, 1831

This obscure, short-lived antislavery newspaper was published in Albany by the free black, Stephen Meyers. The following article is a comment on the Albany Argus *article of September 22, 1831, included above; "Mr. Croswell" is the editor of the* Argus.

Is it true, as stated in the above article by Mr. Croswell that the men of the north will fly with alacrity "to the aid of their fellow citizens of the south?" We believe not. "The cause is a common one," adds Mr. Croswell: but how will he make out this to be the case? New York by abolishing slavery has shown that the cause is not a "common one." The freemen of the north profess to be republican.— Mr. Croswell professes to be a republican; but a republican cannot be either a slave holder or a friend to slave holding. We might with equal propriety style the *devil* a *christian* as to style a *slave holder* a *republican.* The writer of this article is a white man—and a white man who will never raise his pen, his voice, or his arm to quench the spirit of liberty, in the bosoms either of blacks or whites. The slaves have a perfect right derived from God Almighty, to their freedom. They have done vastly wrong in the late insurrection, in killing women and children; but still it is not to be wondered at. Their struggle for freedom is the same in principle as the struggle of our fathers in '76. I hope they may achieve their liberty eventually by fair and honorable means, in a brave and manly conflict with their masters. In short they should refrain from assailing women and children, and conduct on the true principles of heroism. I shall, for one, wish them success whenever the battle may come.—*Fiat justitia, ruat coelum,* is the maxim of our common law. *Let Justice be done, tho' heaven falls,* is the plain English of it. The maxim is a just one and applies to the present cause. Mr. Croswell may perhaps think he will incite all the South in favor of Van Buren, by talking of "a common cause" between Southern *slave holders*, and Northern *Republicans*—but he will never find Northern *Republicans* ready to draw the sword against men who are struggling for their rights, though their skins may not be so white as his own delicate complexion. For one northern Republican, I wish universal emancipation to slaves, whether black or white, and never will I raise my arm to support tyranny and oppression. We wish success to the Poles; and have not the slaves in this country as good a right to be free as the slaves in Poland? If the *Poles* deserve freedom, so do the *Africans*—the cause of one is the cause of the other—and may heaven succor both, is the wish of . . . A.N.R.

JAMES FORTEN TO WILLIAM LLOYD GARRISON [2]

James Forten, the wealthy, free black sailmaker of Philadelphia, was a pioneer abolitionist who helped finance Garrison's early antislavery activities.

October 20, 1831

My Dear Sir,

Many thanks for your friendly letter. It was truly cheering to find, that the recent efforts against us have not damped the ardour of your spirits, but that you are still urging onward unintimidated by the many threats of personal violence from the South, indeed we have felt not a little uneasy on your account for they certainly seem to have the will, if not the power, to stop the thunderings of the Liberator, which sounds so loudly in their ears, the cause of the oppressed—how fearfully true have been its predictions, the late tragedy in Virginia has clearly shown, and yet with all these facts, and dreadful they really are, before them, that they should still close their eyes and seek to find the cause from without, when all the materials are so plentiful within. How eagerly therefore do they seize upon the Liberator, as a pretext, and would willingly screen themselves, by holding it forth, as one of the prominent agents, if not the sole cause of the late disturbance. This insurrection in the south, will be the means of bringing the evils of slavery more prominently before the public, and the urgent sense of danger, if nothing else, will lead to something more than mere hopes and wishes, with which many who have professed themselves friends to emancipation, have remained satisfied. Indeed we live in stirring times, and every day brings news of some fresh effort for liberty, either at home or abroad—onward, onward, is indeed the watchword. . . . Your subscribers at the south I suppose

[2] From William Lloyd Garrison Papers, Boston Public Library. Used by permission of the Boston Public Library.

will be afraid to receive the paper any longer, on account of the recent disturbances—this will be a loss, but we must try to make it up by our exertions elsewhere. With the sincerest wishes for the continued prosperity of the Liberator, and its persevering Editor

I remain ever my Dear Sir,

Most truly yours

James Forten

9
The Attack on the Abolitionists

For both northern and southern defenders of slavery, the abolitionists were an easy scapegoat for the Southampton rebellion. Demands were raised for the suppression of the Liberator and the prosecution of its editor; and vigilante committees organized throughout the South to destroy "incendiary publications" and drive out northerners suspected of antislavery views.

WASHINGTON, D.C., *NATIONAL INTELLIGENCER,* SEPTEMBER 15, 1831

Incendiary Publications

The excitement produced a few months since, in the Southern country, by the discovery of several copies of the notorious "Walker Pamphlet," is doubtless still fresh in the recollection of most of our readers. Notwithstanding the pointed rebukes which the publishers of that inflammatory production received from many of the well disposed and reflecting part of our northern brethren, it appears that some misguided and deluded fanatics are still bent on exciting our colored population to scenes at which the heart sickens on the bare recital, and which instead of improving their moral or physical condition, cannot fail to overwhelm the actors in ruin, and curtail the privileges of all the others. Let them view the first fruits of their diabolical projects in the Southampton massacre, and pause—an awful retribution awaits them. A letter from a gentleman in Washington City, dated 29th ult. to the Postmaster at this place, says

"An incendiary paper, 'The Liberator,' is circulated openly among the free blacks of this city; and if you will search, it is very probably you will find it among the slaves of your county. It is published in Boston or Philadelphia by a white man, with the avowed purpose of inciting rebellion in the South; and I am informed, is to be carried through your country by secret agents, who are to come amongst you under the pretext of pedling, etc. Keep a sharp look out for the villains, and if you catch them, by all that is sacred, you ought to barbecue them. Diffuse this information amongst whom it may concern." Tarborough Free Press.

The existence of the production above referred to and the fact of its transmission in great numbers through the medium of the Post Office, are beyond doubt; though we do not believe in secret agents being employed to circulate it, simply, because the vocation would be too dangerous for even the most desperate man to undertake.

No one knows better than we do the sincerity with which the intelligent population of New England abhor and reprobate the incendiary publications which are *intended by their authors* to lead to precisely such results (as concerns the whites) as the Southampton Tragedy. But, we appeal to the people of New England, if not in behalf of the innocent women and children of the whites, then in behalf of the blacks, whose utter extermination will be the necessary result of any general commotion, whether they will continue to permit their humanity to lie under the reproach of approving or even tolerating the atrocities among them which have already caused the plains of the South to be manured with human flesh and blood. To be more specific in our object, we now appeal to the worthy Mayor of the City of Boston, whether no law can be found to prevent the publication, within the City over which he presides, of such diabolical papers as we have seen a sample of here in the hands of slaves, and of which there are many in circulation to the South of us. We have no doubt whatever as to the feelings of Mr. Otis on this subject, or those of his respectable constituents. We know they would prompt him and them to arrest the instigator of human butchery in his mad career. We know the difficulty which surrounds the subject, because the nuisance is not a nuisance, technically speaking, within the limits of the State of Massachusetts. But, surely, surely if the Courts of Law have no power, public opinion has, to interfere, until the intelligent Legislators of Massachusetts can provide a durable remedy for this most appalling grievance. The crime is as great as that of poisoning the waters of life to a whole community. The destroying angel, visiting the South, would hardly move with a more desolating step than the deluded fanatic or mercenary miscreant who scatters abroad these pestilential sheets. We know nothing of the man: we desire not to have him unlawfully dealt with: we can even conceive of his motive being good in his own opinion: but it is the motive of the man who cuts the throat of your wife and children, in the hope of accomplishing what is an impossibility, and which, if it were not so, would be, of itself, a tremendous evil. There are citizens of Boston who know what slavery is—who have measured the breadth and depth of the evil—who know how much injustice has been done on this subject by well-meaning persons in the Middle and Eastern States to the People of the South in this particular. We call upon them to step forward, and with that pen they wield so ably, vindicate the cause of humanity, as it is outraged by the publications to which we refer. We intreat them to awaken the People to the truth and the whole truth, on this subject.

Our readers in the Middle and Eastern States may be assured we do not speak thus earnestly on light grounds. The subject is too grave to be trifled with. By all which they hold dear we conjure the real friends of humanity not to delude themselves into the belief that we overrate the evil of which we speak, but to desist from countenancing, even by silence, these incendiary undertakings. Let them be frowned down by universal consent.

NEW YORK *DAILY SENTINEL*, SEPTEMBER 17, 1831

The Daily Sentinel, *an outspoken critic of slavery, published the diary of a New York lawyer who was driven out of Virginia in the days immediately following the Turner rebellion.*

August 30th (Tuesday) . . . Called on Mr. Herthorn at 12 o'clock A.M. Had a conversation on slavery. Maintained that the blacks, as men, were entitled to their freedom, and *ought* to be emancipated. Mr. Herthorn, his clerk, and a country doctor were the only persons present. The doctor assumed that the blacks were not men, and that they ought all to be exterminated. "They had declared war first," he said, "let them be hunted like wild beasts." . . . The fellow asked me "how I dared express myself as I had just done before blacks." I told him that I had not done so, and would not do it for fear they might misunderstand me, and think I approved of their killing women and children, which I condemned as much as any man; and this, I said, was proved last Friday, when an alarm was given at 11 o'clock at night, and five hundred of them said to be coming down the Halifax road. I was one of the first to fly to arms. . . .

31st (Wednesday). I was fast asleep at 6 o'clock this morning when Mr. Carter entered my bed-room, and informed me that some of the inhabitants were determined to mob me for what I had said the day before. He advised me to leave town immediately. I could scarcely credit what he was telling me, till he told me that it was a serious business—that my life was in danger, and repeated his earnest advice that I should leave Petersburg immediately. The mayor had received an anonymous letter the evening before, in which it was stated, that, although the blacks had not succeeded in their recent attempt, they would ultimately, and very soon, overcome the white population of the State of Virginia. The Mayor thought I was the author of this note, which was no doubt written by one of the actors in this morning's atrocious assault on my person.

I agreed to leave Petersburg at 8 o'clock. This was told to the leaders of the mob, who expressed themselves satisfied, and promised to let me depart in peace. I made my preparations, ordered the coachman of the Richmond stage to call for me, and after parting with my worthy landlord and landlady, got into the coach, which was yet to stop at Powell's hotel, Bolingbroke Street. When we arrived there I saw a party of fifteen or twenty men coming down Bolingbroke Street. They looked into the coach, saw that I was there, and walked off towards the bridge leading to Richmond. I guessed their purpose, and as soon as they were at a distance I told the driver that I had forgotten something, but would be back in a few minutes. I ran to Mr. Carter's. . . . The doors were locked, and he went out to request the assistance of the civil authorities. But these, it seems, did not think it worth their while to interfere. A mob soon assembled in the street. . . . At last the ruffians forced themselves into the house, in spite of Mr. Carter's exertions to keep them out. . . .

The drawing room was first visited by the bloodthirsty republicans! I heard Mrs. Carter exclaim, "Oh! what do you want? what are you going to do?" "Do not be alarmed, Madam, we will not hurt you." And not finding me in the drawing room, they ascended the staircase leading to the place where I was. A little hesitation prevailed at that moment, for I heard one of them cry out, "Well! who comes with me? God damn! will none come?" As soon as they made their appearance at the foot of the stair case, I put down the musket I still held in my hand, and said, "here I willingly give up my life." They rushed on me. One dragged me down by one arm, another took hold of me by the other arm, and a third held me behind by the collar of my coat. As they were dragging me along, a pistol was fired behind me, whether at me I cannot tell. There were about a hundred or a hundred and fifty persons in the street, as near as I could judge. I expected to be murdered before the house, but the executioners led me towards the bridge. My idea at that time was, that they intended to drown me in the river. I made several attempts to speak, and told them a few plain and severe truths, the force of which they felt, and therefore did all they could to prevent my being heard. "Do not let him speak," was vociferated from the mob. "Knock him down if he does not hold his tongue," was often repeated; but whenever I had an opportunity, I made my voice heard. I asked them whether this was the country in which "all men were born free and equal"—in which "the freedom of speech" was guaranteed to every one; and, also, whether this was their reward for my flying to arms, last Friday, in defence of the helpless —of their wives, and of their children? . . .

. . . Another altercation followed, which, fortunately for me, terminated in favor of those who were for mercy. Never can I forget a young man who stood near me with my clothes in his hands, and who strongly opposed this intended cruelty. I saw grief and compassion written in his countenance, and I am glad I had an opportunity of shaking him by the hand as he handed me my clothes. I am not sure I know his name, although I believe it to be C. C.; but never can I forget his face, nor will ever my heart cease to remember the proofs of sympathy and kindness he gave me on this occasion.

I was now allowed to dress, and ordered to take immediately the road to Richmond. A line was drawn with a stick, and I was told that if ever I passed that line, it would fare "worser" with me.

I took my departure, scarcely believing in my escape from these Virginian brigands; and notwithstanding the soreness I felt all over my lacerated body, I walked on as fast as possible. The sun, which was on my back all the way, caused me to suffer excruciating pains. After marching 5 or 6 miles, my feet began also to feel sore, so that it was with difficulty I reached the half-way house. The landlord knew already part of my story, which had been related to him by the coachman, who drove the 8 o'clock coach. Here I learnt that a party of men, the same that passed me in Bolingbroke Street, had stopped the stage on the other side of the bridge, from Petersburg to Richmond; that they looked in, and not finding me, said, "he is not here," and ran back towards the town.

The landlord advised me not to show my wounds to any one; but I assured him, that far from being ashamed, I felt proud of them.

NEW YORK *MORNING COURIER AND ENQUIRER,* OCTOBER 3, 1831

Edited by James Watson Webb, the Courier and Enquirer *was one of the most rabidly antiblack, antiabolitionist papers of the North.*

Slave Insurrection in Southampton County, Virginia

The horrible atrocities committed by the Blacks upon the unoffending women and children of Southampton County, in the late insurrection, it is hoped, will induce the dangerous enthusiasts to whose endeavors these inhuman murders may justly be, in a great measure, ascribed, to pause and reflect on the probable, nay certain consequence of persevering in the same means to render the slaves of the South dissatisfied and ungovernable.

The first lesson inculcated upon these ignorant people, by those whose endeavors are ostensibly directed to the amelioration of their condition, is that of hatred to the Whites. They are told that the white man has been the cruel, inexorable oppressor of themselves and their forefathers from generation to generation; and that the same fate awaits their posterity. Every species of inflammatory declamation is resorted to, in painting the imaginary horrors of the situation, and their sufferings exaggerated by all the powers of rhetoric and poetry. Instead of teaching them to avail themselves of the means of happiness in their power, and to accommodate their minds to the cheerful performance of those duties which circumstances beyond their control or that of their masters, have entailed upon them, every means is resorted to for the purpose of stimulating them to disobedience, disaffection, and ultimate vengeance.

Hence the relation between master and slave, instead of being what it ought, and might be—an exchange of kindness, protection and maintenance on the one hand, and respect, obedience and service on the other—degenerates into moody obstinacy, unwilling labours or downright refusal on the side of the slave, and consequent fear, jealousy, and coercion on that of the master. A state of things is thus produced, fatal alike to the happiness of both, and a road to mutual antipathies, and mutual injuries opened, the termination of which must be a bloody and unrelenting struggle for mutual extermination.

Here let us pause and ask these rampant philanthropists, to whom we will pay the compliment of believing it possible they *may* be serious, a few questions. What do they mean, and where do they intend to stop in their mad career? Do they mean to array the black skin against the white? Do you mean, by preaching up the equality of the two races, to blend them with each other in a mongrel breed of crisp-haired mulattoes—or do they mean by promising the blacks the certain aid of an avenging Diety, to incite them to a bloody war, in which, as in the insurrection of Southampton County, neither sex nor age, nor unoffending weakness will be spared? Again we say, let us know what they mean, and where they intend to stop?

Admitting the first to be their intention, we would ask of the white man if he is ready to barter away the noble prerogative of being the master piece of nature: the first, the Wisest, the greatest and the most beautiful of all the race of created animals, and sink himself to the level of a mulish compound, neither one thing or the other? Is he ready to mix the pure blood of ages with a race, on which all history has placed the indelible stamp of inferiority, and become the assassin of his own high rank in the creation? If he is—so be it—the question is settled.

But if he is not—and we trust to his honest pride that he is not—what then? Why then the inevitable result of the mischievous labors of these dangerous fanatics is easy to be calculated. It has been exemplified on a small scale in the County of Southampton. Its history is written by anticipation in the blood of innocent white women and children—in the sacrifice of the white man and his posterity. Look at St. Domingo—look at the island of Jamaica—look any where that the slave has ever got the upper hand, and we shall see the same uniform results—indiscriminate rapine, indiscriminate massacre. . . .

The situation of the Southern states at this moment is one of deep interest, and cannot but excite the commiseration of all who have the happiness of our common country at heart—not that they are unable or unprepared to defend themselves against their slaves, but that the wild notions of liberty which fiends in human shape have inculcated, are calculated to produce insurrection after insurrection, massacre after massacre, and execution after execution. The people of the South can and will protect themselves, but in doing so, blood will flow freely, and humanity shudders at the picture which is presented to the mind. Under these circumstances, does it not become the duty of the General Government to interfere, not to put down, but prevent insurrection? The property in slaves is guaranteed to their masters by the Constitution of the United States, and the government is as much bound to protect it, as they are to build fortifications for the protection of our commercial cities, and the property of their inhabitants. Let the government then concentrate a large portion of our little army in the Southern states, and so distribute them that the slaves shall feel that to attempt an insurrection will be attended with certain punishment. We repeat, the South can protect themselves, but it is necessary that insurrections should be *prevented* instead of being put down, and this can only be done by the presence of regular troops. . . .

CHARLESTON *MERCURY*, CITED IN WASHINGTON, D.C. *GLOBE*, OCTOBER 11, 1831

The "Vigilance Association of Columbia," composed of gentlemen of the first respectability, offer a reward of $1,500 for the apprehension and prosecution to conviction, of any white person who may be detected in distributing or circulating within the State the newspaper, called "the Liberator," printed in Boston, or the pamphlet called "Walker's Pamphlet," or any other publication of a seditious tendency.

10

Virginians Demand Action by the State Legislature

In the aftermath of the rebellion, some Virginians demanded the enactment of new repressive laws and the strict enforcement of those already on the books to ensure the safety of the white population. Others petitioned the legislature for the removal of free blacks from the state. At the same time, pent-up resentments against both blacks and slavery, not normally given political expression, were articulated, as in the petition of about 260 women of Augusta County, asking action to end slavery, and the petition of citizens of Culpeper County, expressing the resentments and problems of white laborers.

RICHMOND *COMPILER,* CITED IN NEW YORK *DAILY SENTINEL,* OCTOBER 11, 1831

The black missionaries must be prevented from travelling about. The black preachers must be disbanded. All unlawful meetings must be suspended and the laws for that purpose should be enforced. Slaves must be confined to their own plantations—not permitted to go off, but upon urgent considerations. The attendance of large collections of blacks from distant places at some central point must be restricted —for these meetings are a *point d'appui,* where they may give and receive information, form plans, and communicate signs and watchwords.

Further still.—The laws forbidding schools and education, must be enforced, as they *have been* in this city—since the law of the last Legislature [barring the education of blacks] was to go into force.

Further.—Regular patrols ought to be established in the counties and cities. Arms ought to be distributed among the whites, where necessary, and proper means taken to preserve them, to prevent their being stolen and lost. Uniform companies ought to be encouraged, and a good corps of cavalry especially organized in the towns and counties.

In fine, every means ought to be taken, to give a more effective organization to the one part, and to prevent concert and communication in the other.

Here many persons might stop, but others would go *further still,* and ask, if some means had not better be devised for striking a gradual stroke at the root of the evil.

LEGISLATIVE PETITION, AUGUSTA COUNTY, JANUARY 19, 1832 [1]

To the Hon. the General Assembly of the State of Virginia, the memorial of the subscribing females of the County of Augusta humbly represents, that although it is unexampled, in our beloved State, that females should interfere in its political concerns, and although we feel all the timidity incident to our sex in taking this step, yet we hold our right to do so to be unquestionable and feel ourselves to be irresistably impelled to the exercise of that right by the most potent considerations and the perilous circumstances which surround us. We pretend not to conceal from you, our fathers and brothers, our protectors by your investment with the political powers of the land, the fear which agitates our bosoms, and the dangers which await us, as revealed by recent tragical deeds. Our fears, we admit, are great; but we do not conceed that they are the result of blind and unreflecting cowardice; we do not conceed that they spring from superstitious timidity of our sex. Alas! We are timid indeed; but we appeal to your manly reason, to your more mature wisdom to attest the justice, propriety, of our fears, when we call to your recollection the late slaughter of our sisters and little ones, in certain parts of our land, and the strong probability that the slaughter was but a partial execution of a widely projected scheme of carnage. We know not, we can not know the night, or the unguarded moment, by day or by night which is pregnant with our distruction, and that of our husbands, and brothers, and sisters, and children; but we do know that we are, at any moment exposed to the means of extinction of all that is dear to us in life. The bloody monster that threatens us is warmed and cherished on our own hearths. O hear our prayer, and remove it, ye protectors of our persons, ye guardians of our peace!

Tell us not of the labors and hardships which we shall endure when our bondservants shall be removed from us. They have no terrors for us. Those labors, hardships, can not be greater or so great as those we now endure in providing for and ruling the faithless beings who are subjected to us. Our fears were they greater, still they are in our esteem, less than the small dust in the balance, compared with the burden of our fears and dangers. But what have we to fear from these causes, more than the females of other countries? Are they of the East and of the West, of England and of France, more "cumbered with much serving" than we are? Are they less enlightened, or less accomplished? However we may be flattered, we will not be argued out of our senses, and persuaded into a belief which is contradicted by experience, and the testimony of sober facts. Many, very

[1] From *Legislative Petitions*, Archives Branch, Virginia State Library.

many of our sisters and brothers have fled to other lands, from the
evils we experience, and they send us back the evidences of their con-
tentment and prosperity. They lament not their labors and hardships,
but exult in their deliverance from servitude to their quondam slaves;
and we too would fly—we, too, would exult in similar deliverance
were our destiny otherwise ordered than it is. That destiny is in your
hands, and we implore your high agency in ordering it for the best.
We would enjoy such exultation on our native soil. Do not slight our
importunities. Do not disregard our fears. Our destiny is identified
with yours. If we perish, alas! What will become of you and your offspring? We are no political economists; but our domestic employ-
ments, our engagement in rearing up the children of our husbands and
brothers, our intimate concern with the interests and prosperity of
society, we presume, can not but inform us of the great and elementary
principles of that science. Indeed, it is impossible that that science can
have any other basis than the principles that are constantly developing themselves to us in our domestic relations. What is a nation but a
family on a large scale? Our fears teach us to reflect and reason. And
our reflections and reasonings have taught us that the peace of our
homes, the prosperity of future generations call aloud and imperiously
for some decisive and efficient measure—and that measure can not,
we believe be efficient, or of much benifit, if it have not, for its ultimate object, the extinction of slavery from amongst us.

Without, therefore, entering upon a detail of facts and arguments,
we implore you, by the urgency of our fears, by the love we bear you,
as our fathers, and brothers, by our anxieties for the little ones around
us, by our estimate of domestic and public weal, by present danger, by
the prospects of the future, by our female virtues, by the patriotism
which glows in our bosoms, by our prayers to Almighty God, not to
let the powers with which you are invested lie dormant, but that you
exert it for the deliverance of yourselves, of us, of the children of the
land of future ages, from the most direct curse which can befall a
people. Signalize your legislation by this mighty deed. This we pray;
and in duty bound will ever pray.

LEGISLATIVE PETITION, CULPEPER COUNTY, DECEMBER 9, 1831 [2]

To the General Assembly of Virginia.

Your memorialists, citizens of the county of Culpeper, actuated by
a deep sense of the necessity that exists to prevent if practicable the
migration of the labouring class of the white population of Virginia,
and believing the subject to be one of vital importance to the peace,
happiness and prosperity of the state, generally, they deem it worthy

---

[2] From *Legislative Petitions*, Archives Branch, Virginia State Library.

of the consideration of your honourable body. Your memorialists have in common with their fellow citizens, deeply lamented the tragical occurence which has been acted by a portion of the black population of Virginia, which circumstance has as your memorialists verily believe, engendered to a certain extent, restless and insurrectionary feelings with the slaves throughout this Commonwealth. Your memorialists reside in a remote part of the Commonwealth from the scene of the late disturbance, yet with the slaves amongst them, there is evidently an unfavourable impression made upon them, growing out of that occurence, and other incidental causes, not the least of which is the unprecedented migration of the labouring class of our citizens this fall to the western states. Your memorialists verily believe that there has been a greater migration of that class this fall, from their immediate vicinity than for the last ten years previous, and from reports they believe such removal to have been general. Your memorialists in submitting this subject which they propose to lay before you, conceive that they are discharging what they believe to be a duty to the community, themselves and posterity, and that its importance will merit, and will receive from your honourable body a deliberate consideration. The object of your memorialists is to [?] it of you, and interposition of your power, and authority, to stay as far as practicable the migration of the white population east of the Blue ridge, which they believe you can do, by a judicious course of legislation to a very great extent. It must be known to many of your body, that the mechanick trades and arts are fast falling into the hands of the black population. Your memorialists venture to assert that the time is near at hand, without your interposition, when the most common and useful trades will be professed and carried on by slaves. Within the knowledge of your memorialists the blacksmith's trade is at present almost exclusively carried on by slaves, that the trades of stonemason, plasterer, painter, bricklayer, miller, carpenter, and cooper and not uncommon the trades of tanner, carrier, shoe and boot maker, distiller and in fine handicrafts of all kinds are executed by slaves; the effect of which is to throw out of employ the white mechanick; and to degrade his profession, depressing at the same time his labour below its fair value, and to cause him to be impoverished, and finally drive him from his home and native state, to find in the west an assylum where he will be appreciated according to his honesty, industry and ingenuity. We your memorialists many of whom are slave holders and some of us holding mechanick slaves, in common with our fellow citizens have not until recent circumstances transpired thought of the impolicy and impropriety of our slaves acquiring trades; but upon taking a view of our present and probably future situation, we are decidedly impressed with the belief that it is a course frought with great danger, and viewing the innumerable evils which result from slavery, many of which we shall forbear to enumerate and confine ourselves to the single remark that its effects upon the morals of our people are highly injurious, and that its corrupting influence is in no instance more marked, than in the increasing illicit trade and traffick existing between the slaves and the poor and dependent part of our white people, that the necessary trades being much monopolised by the slaves, produces and fosters in a great measure such connection. Believing as we do, that the publick weal would be promoted, a class of citizens highly useful and meritorious in time of peace and peril restored and retained amongst us, We your memorialists, pray your honourable body to pass a law for the encouragement and protection of the white mechanick, by *prohibiting* any slave, free negro or mulatto, being placed as an apprentice in any manner whatsoever to learn a trade or art, under severe and onerous penalties upon the owner of such slave, or servant, as well as upon the white person who may undertake to teach such slave, free negro, or mulatto his art or trade. And your memorialists, as in duty bound will ever pray.

11

Nat Turner and the Virginia Debate on Slavery

Certainly the most remarkable consequence of the Southampton insurrection was the Virginia debate on slavery, of January and February, 1832. This was the last time that the slavery question and the possibility of emancipation were freely discussed in the southern press and debated in a southern legislature. Governor Floyd, who had become convinced of the need for some action against slavery, at the last minute decided to omit a guarded invitation to emancipation from his message to the legislature in December. But suddenly in January, slavery was openly attacked in the press and legislature, and plans for gradual emancipation and colonization commanded the support of a large minority of the House of Delegates. The opponents of slavery argued mainly from the ruinous economic effects of the institution on Virginia and the danger of further rebellions, while slavery's defenders insisted that the rights of property could not be violated and denied that slavery was the cause of the state's economic woes. One interesting aspect of the debate was the way in which each side interpreted the Turner revolt. The proslavery forces tended to minimize it, arguing that most of the slaves were contented and that the rebellion was actually a "petty affair," while the antislavery men stressed the danger of further outbreaks and recalled vividly the panic that had swept the white population in the fall of 1831.

GOVERNOR FLOYD'S MESSAGE TO THE LEGISLATURE, DECEMBER 6, 1831[1]

Fellow-Citizens of the Senate and of the House of Delegates:

You are again assembled under circumstances calculated to inspire the community with a just expectation, that your deliberations will be followed by measures equal in energy and decision, to the crisis in which your country is placed: an expectation which I am sure will not be disappointed. The deep interest which the citizens in every

[1] From *Journal of the Senate, of the Commonwealth of Virginia, Begun and Held in the Capitol, in the City of Richmond, on Monday the Fifth Day of December, in the Year One Thousand Eight Hundred and Thirty One* (Richmond, 1831), pp. 7–15.

part of this Commonwealth have felt, and manifested, in relation to occurrences of a grave and distressing character, which have taken place since your adjournment, new, unexpected, and heretofore unknown to the State—together with the anxiety felt in the future fate of some of the great subjects which were agitated at your last session, and the unpleasant aspect of our Federal relations, all conspire to cause the people to turn their eyes upon you at this time, with profound and fixed attention. You alone possess the power of accomplishing all the great objects which the public desire, and much of the future welfare of this Republic, depends upon your present deliberations—deliberations which doubtless will be first turned to the melancholy subject which has filled the country with affliction, and one of the fairest counties in the Commonwealth with mourning.

Whilst we were enjoying the abundance of the last season, reposing in the peace and quiet of domestic comfort and safety—we were suddenly aroused from that security by receiving information, that a portion of our fellow-citizens had fallen victims to the relentless fury of assassins and murderers, even whilst wrapped in profound sleep and that, those bloody deeds had been perpetrated in a spirit of wantonness and cruelty, unknown to savage warfare even in their most revolting form.

In August last, a banditti of slaves, consisting of but few at first, and not at any time exceeding a greater number than seventy, rose upon some of the unsuspecting and defenceless inhabitants of Southampton, and under circumstances of the most shocking and horrid barbarity, put to death sixty-one persons, of whom, the greater number were women and helpless children.—Much of this bloody work was done on Monday morning, and on the day following, about ten o'clock, the last murder was committed.—The citizens of that and the adjacent counties, promptly assembled, and all real danger was speedily terminated.

The conspiracy was at first believed to be general: wherefore, I was induced to call into service, a force sufficient to crush at a single blow all opposing power, whatever might be its strength.—To this end, detachments of light infantry from the 7th and 54th regiments, and from the 4th regiment of cavalry and 4th light artillery, under Captains Harrison and Richardson, were ordered to repair to the scene of action with all possible speed, and report to Brigadier General Eppes, who had been desired to assume the command, and call out his brigade. Arms and ammunition were amply furnished and thrown into all the counties which were suspected of disaffection.—Two regiments in Brunswick and Greensville, were called into service by their commanding officers, under the law vesting them with power to do so, for such purposes: These troops being within the brigade commanded by Brigadier General William H. Broadnax, that officer assumed the command of, and remained in the field, until the danger had passed.

It gives me great pleasure to communicate to the General Assembly, the high satisfaction I feel in bearing testimony to the zeal, promptitude and dispatch, with which every officer discharged his duty, and the cheerful alacrity with which every citizen obeyed the call of the law.

Though the call upon the light troops was so promptly obeyed, yet before their arrival, the revolt was subdued, and many of these deluded fanatics were either captured or were placed beyond the possibility of escape; some had already been immolated by an excited people.

I feel the highest gratification in adding, that the readiest aid was afforded by Commodore Elliott of the United States Navy, and a detachment of sailors from the ship Natchez, under his command, who, notwithstanding they had just returned from a long and distant cruise, repaired to the scene of action with a highly creditable alacrity.— Much is also due to Colonel House, then commanding officer at Fortress Monroe, for the promptitude with which he detached a part of his force to our aid, under the command of Lieutenant Colonel Worth, to whom similar praise is due, as likewise to the officers and soldiers under his command, for the promptitude with which they also repaired to our assistance, so soon as it came to their knowledge: all necessity for their co-operation had ceased before they reached their point of destination, but they are not the less entitled to commendation on that account.

All of those who participated in the bloody tragedy, have expiated their crimes by undergoing public execution, whilst some who had been condemned have been reprieved for reasons which were deemed satisfactory.—There is much reason to believe the spirit of insurrection was not confined to Southampton; many convictions have taken place elsewhere, and some few in distant counties. From the documents which I herewith lay before you, there is too much reason to believe those plans of treason, insurrection and murder, have been designed, planned and matured by unrestrained fanatics in some of the neighbouring States, who find facilities in distributing their views and plans amongst our population, either through the Post Office, or by Agents sent for that purpose throughout our territory.

Upon inspecting these documents, and contemplating that state of things which they are intended to produce, I felt it my duty to open a correspondence with the Governors of some of the neighbouring powers of this confederacy, to preserve as far as possible the good understanding which exists, and which ought to be cherished between the different members of this Union. The result of this correspondence will be made known to you, so soon as it is ascertained.

The most active among ourselves, in stirring up the spirit of revolt, have been the negro preachers. They had acquired great ascendancy over the minds of their fellows, and infused all their opinions, which had prepared them for the development of the final design. There is also some reason to believe, those preachers have a perfect understanding in relation to these plans throughout the Eastern counties— and have been the channels through which the inflammatory papers and pamphlets, brought here by the agents and emisaries from other States, have been circulated amongst our slaves. The facilities thus afforded for plotting treason and conspiracy to rebel and make insurrection, have been great: Through the indulgence of the magistracy and the laws, large collections of slaves have been permitted to take place, at any time through the week, for the ostensible purpose of indulging in religious worship, but in many instances, the real purpose, with the preacher, was of a different character; the sentiments, and sometimes the words of these inflammatory pamphlets, which the meek and charitable of other States have seen cause to distribute as fire-brands in the bosom of our society, have been read. What shall be thought of those fiends, who, having no interest in our community, nevertheless seek to excite a servile war—a war which exhausts itself in the massacre of unoffending women and children on the one side, and on the other, in the sacrifice of all who have borne part in the savage undertaking? Not only should the severest punishment be inflicted upon those disturbers of our peace whenever they or their emisaries are found within our reach, but decisive measures should be adopted to make all their measures abortive. The public good requires the negro preachers to be silenced, who, full of ignorance, are incapable of inculcating any thing but notions of the wildest superstition, thus preparing fit instruments in the hands of the crafty agitators, to destroy the public tranquility.

As the means of guarding against the possible repetition of these sanguinary scenes, I cannot fail to recommend to your early attention, the revision of all the laws intended to preserve in due subordination the slave population of our State. In urging these considerations upon you, let me not be understood as expressing the slightest doubt or apprehension of general results; all communities are liable to suffer from the dagger of the murderer and midnight assassin; and it behoves them to guard against them.

With us the first returning light dispels the danger, and soon witnesses the murderer in chains.

Though means have been taken by those of other States to agitate our community and discontent our slaves and incite them to attempt an unattainable object, some proof is also furnished, that for the class of free people of colour, they have opened more enlarged views, and urge the achievement of a higher destiny, by means, for the present less violent, but not differing in the end from those presented to the slaves. That class of the community, our laws have heretofore treated with indulgent kindness, and many instances of solicitude for their welfare have marked the progress of legislation.—If the slave is confined by law to the estate of his master, as it is advisable he should be, the free people of colour may nevertheless convey all the incendiary pamphlets and papers, with which we are sought to be inundated. This class too, has been the first to place itself in hostile array against any and every measure designed to remove them from amongst us. Though it will be indispensably necessary for them to withdraw from this community, yet in the spirit of kindness, which has ever characterized the Legislature of Virginia, it is submitted, whether as the last benefit which we can confer upon them, it may not be wise to appropriate annually a sum of money to aid in their removal from this Commonwealth.

Whilst recent events had created apprehensions in the minds of a few, some agitation was also more extensively felt; wherefore, it was deemed prudent to arm the militia in a manner calculated to quiet all apprehensions, and arms were accordingly furnished to nearly all the regiments on the Eastern frontier. The want of them, upon this sudden emergency, was so sensibly felt by those in the vicinity of Norfolk, as to induce Commodore Warrington, in command of the Navy Yard in Gosport, to distribute a portion of the public arms under his care. That gallant and patriotic officer, did not hesitate to assume the responsibility of this step, and it is gratifying to perceive that his conduct has met the approbation of the public functionaries.—The policy of disarming the militia, it is believed, was pursued as a measure of economy, as the men and officers had been culpably negligent in their attention to their preservation, so that many were lost, or by neglect become unfit for service. Now, however, the necessity for preserving them is distinctly felt, and a doubt cannot be entertained, that more care will be taken of them in future. I could not weigh the expense incurred by this measure, against the possible sacrifice of life, much less the possible repetition of the scenes of Southampton. . . .

It will be necessary to call your attention to the present condition of our militia, and to recommend a thorough revision of the law on that subject. Much of the strength and efficiency of that kind of force depends upon the promptness with which they can be ready for action, and some knowledge of the first duties of a soldier.

Our light troops might be increased in every battalion and regiment with great advantage to the service, and ought to be encouraged by privileges and exemptions, as they will always be the first called into service, and unlike the infantry of the line, they will be called out by whole companies instead of being detailed for duty as is now the case with the body of the militia. From the dexterity and skill of our citizens in the use of the rifle, and a fondness for that kind of arms, as well as the great care and time it requires to drill a regiment in the rifle exercise, the propriety of organizing them into regiments is suggested.

From the position in which this State is placed, and the attitude occupied by her, it becomes a matter of very serious reflection, whether a force more available than the militia may not be advisable and attainable at a small expense. By a well organized intermediate force, even a foreign war might be sustained without disturbing the quiet operations of the Government, or of the farmer. We have at this time an hundred and thirty-nine regiments full and strong—Were one company to be authorized by law to be raised by voluntary enlistment from each regiment, or such number of regiments as would give the number of men required, and put upon the footing of the Public Guard, you would have a cheap and efficient army ready to perform any and every duty. These soldiers might be permitted to live at home and work their crops as heretofore, but at all times subject to the call of their officers. Some allowances should be made them, and the equipments of a soldier furnished as an inducement to enlist; to be drilled once a month for as many days as the General Assembly should think proper, and whilst on drill, to receive ample pay for their time, but no other pay allowed unless embodied for service, when their pay and allowances should be the same as that received by the Public Guard now in service.

It will be found, on inspection, that many of the public arms now in the Arsenal, need repair, particularly those of the smaller calibre, a part of which, by law, were intended to arm the twenty-first brigade—application has been made for the residue required for that purpose, but has been delayed, until this representation could be made to you: Nor can I refrain from calling your attention to the necessity of providing sword slings, cartouch boxes and holsters, of which at this time the militia are much in want, besides some equipments for the artillery. . . .

RICHMOND *ENQUIRER*, JANUARY 7, 1832

Virginia Legislature

We have different estimates made of the probable duration of the Session. One member tells you, they will be able to adjourn from the 1st to the 15th of February—Another extends it to the end of February—A third, from the 1st to the 10th March. We are inclined to side with the longest livers.—We admit that a business spirit seems to pervade their movements; but it cannot be concealed at the same time, that the great objects of the Session have not been brought forward to the House nor even digested in the Committees.

The law concerning delinquent and forfeited lands is yet to undergo revision.—Some insist upon its modification—others, upon its repeal.

But the two great subjects before the Committees are those which relate to the *colored population* of the State, and to its *Internal Improvements*. Upon neither of these is the Committee yet prepared to report.

It is probable, from what we hear, that the Committee on the colored population will report some plan for getting rid of the free people of color—But is this all that can be done? Are we forever to suffer the greatest evil, which can scourge our land, not only to remain, but to increase in its dimensions? "We may shut our eyes and avert our faces, if we please," (writes an eloquent South Carolinian, on his return from the north a few weeks ago)—"But there it is, the dark and growing evil, at our doors; and meet the question we must, at no distant day. God only knows what it is the part of wise men to do on that momentous and appalling subject. Of *this* I am very sure, that the difference—nothing short of frightful—between all that exists on one side of the Potomac, and all on the other, is owing to *that cause alone*. —The disease is deep-seated—it is at the heart's core—it is consuming, and has all along been consuming our vitals, and I could laugh, if I *could* laugh on such a subject, at the ignorance and folly of the politician, who ascribes that to an act of the government, which is the inevitable effect of the eternal laws of Nature. What is to be done? Oh! my God—I don't know, but something must be done."

Yes—something must be done—and it is the part of no honest man to deny it—of no free press to affect to conceal it. When this dark population is growing upon us; when every new census is but gathering its appalling numbers upon us; when within a period equal to that in which this Federal Constitution has been in existence, those numbers will increase to more than two millions within Virginia;— when our Sister States are closing their doors upon our blacks for sale, and when our whites are moving Westwardly, in greater numbers than we like to hear of—When this, the fairest land on all this Continent, for soil and climate and situation combined, might become a sort of garden spot, if it were worked by the hands of white men alone, *can we, ought we,* to sit quietly down, fold our arms, and say to each other, "Well, well, this thing will not come to the worst in our day. We will leave it to our children and our grandchildren, and great grandchildren, to take care of themselves—and to brave the storm"? Is this to act like wise men? Heaven knows! we are no fanatics—We detest the madness which actuated the *Amis des Noirs.*—But something ought to be done—Means sure, but gradual, systematic, but discreet, ought to be adopted, for reducing the mass of evil, which is pressing upon the South, and will still more press upon her, the longer it is put off.—We ought not to shut our eyes, nor avert our faces. And though we speak almost without a hope, that the Committee or that the Legislature, will do any thing, at the present session, to meet this question, yet we say now, in the utmost sincerity of our hearts, that our wisest men cannot give too much of their attention to this subject —nor can they give it too soon.

RICHMOND *WHIG*, JANUARY 13, 1832

The Great Question

On yesterday, Mr. Goode offered a resolution to discharge the Select Committee from the farther consideration of the branch of enquiry touching abolition, submitted to them. Mr. Randolph offered an amendment, which may be seen under the proper head; and these propositions have at once brought on a debate on the whole question of slavery, and its evils, physical and moral. That debate we shall lay before the reader as speedily as we may, and seldom have we heard one more ably conducted, and never one involving consequences of such deep, vital and enduring import.

When we, who have so long experienced the restraints imposed by public opinion on this subject; who have dared to exercise the freedom of the Press, guaranteed to us by the Godlike fathers of the Republic, but did not, could not, dare to breathe a syllable on a subject ever nearest our hearts, and of transcendent moment to the Country; when we, who know so well at how hopeless and impracticable a distance, even the consideration of the subject was deemed six months ago—when we see the General Assembly of Virginia actually engaged, with open doors, in the discussion of the evils of slavery, and the propriety and practicability of abolition—we can hardly believe the evidence of our own senses. Yet so it is. Short sighted are we all, and none can tell what an hour may bring forth.

We foresee the agitation which is to pervade the Country. We anticipate the alarms which will be sounded, to the slave-holder. We know in advance, the declamation which will be addressed to his fears, his cupidity, and his passions. We are already informed of the unfounded designs charged and circulated. But, we trust the alarmists will fail in producing an excitement beyond what is favorable to an enlightened consideration of the situation of Virginia. We trust they will succeed in alarming no man for the rights and safety of his property—for we venture to say that there is not one man who proposes to disregard its sanctity. Above all, we hope that the alarmists will not succeed in raising a spirit of resistance to the results of legislation, or produce a persuasion that the scope of legitimate legislation does not embrace an enquiry which touches the interest of every citizen of the Commonwealth. Deep interest must and ought to be felt.

SPEECH OF JAMES GHOLSON [2]

Gholson represented Brunswick County in the Piedmont, or central portion of the state.

We are not responsible for the existence of slavery amongst us. It is here; and no reproaches on the one hand, or regrets on the other, can avoid it. But it is the duty of a just, wise and virtuous people to mitigate its evils to the utmost extent of their ability, and to make it subservient to the best purposes of society; and on this ground I challenge investigation, I will not discuss the abstract question of the right of slavery: but I will say that the slaves of Va. are as happy a laboring class as exists upon the habitable globe. They are as well fed, as well clothed, and as well treated. In health, but reasonable labour is required of them—in sickness, they are nursed and attended to. In times of plenty, they live in waste—in times of scarcity, they do not want—they are content to-day, and have no care or anxiety for to-morrow. Cruel treatment of them is discountenanced by society, and until of late, their privileges were daily extending. Among what labouring class will you find more happiness and less misery? Not among the serfs and labouring poor of Europe! No, Sir—Nor among the servants to the North of us.

Our slave population is not only a happy one, but it is a contented, peaceful and harmless one. For the last sixty years, while riots, seditions, rebellions, revolutions, bloodshed, and convulsions, have marked the histories of the fairest nations upon earth—While licentiousness and anarchy, and tyranny and despotism have held their alternate sway—governments been crumbled into atoms, and empires torn from their deep foundations—what has been the history of the internal condition of the State in which we live? Sir, during all this time, we have had one insurrection. And to a faithful history of that, I beg to call the attention of this House for a moment. I do not wish to palliate the horrors of that occurrence; but I wish to show to this House and this people, that none of its characteristics are of such a cast, as to destroy a sense of security, or to attach suspicion to the slave population generally. What is its history, Sir? An ignorant, religious fanatic, conceived the idea of insurrection. He succeeded in involving four or

---

[2] From Richmond *Enquirer*, January 21, 1832.

five others, of his immediate neighborhood, in his designs: They
commence the massacre—they traverse a region of country containing
hundreds of slaves; but neither threats, promises, nor intoxication,
could secure more than from forty to fifty adherents—they remain
embodied something more than twenty-four hours—then disperse
without being forced—are taken without resistance—and are at last
hung on the evidence of persons of their own class and colour. Is
there any thing in this history, Mr. Speaker, to justify the belief that
this whole class of our population is corrupt, treacherous and dangerous? Sir, in opposition to this solitary occurrence of insubordination
I could present to you innumerable instances of the most steadfast
fidelity and devoted loyalty—but it is unnecessary: Suffice it to say,
that I believe it a happy, and, when well regulated, a harmless population.—A chivalrous and high-minded Virginian, while standing in
London; was reproached by a disciple of Wilberforce, with the existence and evils of slavery in Virginia. He indignantly replied, that he
believed, more misery, vice and corruption, existed within ten miles
of the spot on which he stood, than prevailed in the entire slave population of Virginia.

GENERAL WILLIAM H. BRODNAX'S ASSESSMENT OF SLAVERY AND THE REBELLION [3]

*Brodnax, of Dinwiddie County, had taken part in putting
down the Southampton insurrection. He reflects the middle position in the debate—those who admitted that slavery was an evil,
but were extremely wary of precipitous action against it.*

That *slavery in Virginia is an evil,* and a transcendent evil, it
would be idle, and more than idle, for any human being to doubt or
deny. It is a mildew which has blighted in its course every region it
has touched, from the creation of the world. Illustrations from the
history of other countries and other times might be instructive and
profitable, had we the time to review them; but we have evidences
tending to the same conviction nearer at hand and accessible to daily
observation, in the short histories of the different States in this great
Confederacy, which are impressive in their admonitions and conclusive
in their character. That Virginia,—originally the first-rated State in
the Union,—the one which, in better days, led the Counsels and dictated the measures of the Federal Government, had been gradually
razed to the condition of a third-rate state, and was destined soon to
yield precedency to another, among the youngest of her daughters;

[3] From Richmond *Enquirer,* January 24, 1832.

that many of the finest portions, originally of her territory, now (as was so glowingly depicted the other day,) exhibited scenes of widespread desolation and decay; that many of her most valuable citizens are removing to other parts of the world, have certainly been attributed to a variety of causes; but who can doubt that it is principally *slavery* that is at the bottom of all—that this is the *incubus* which paralyzes her energies and retards her every effort at advancement. I presume that every body is prepared to admit and regret the existence of this evil, and that *something* should be done to alleviate or exterminate it, *if any thing* can be done, by means less injurious or dangerous than the evil itself. But, Sir, it is on this point on which so much diversity of opinion exists among us. All *would* remove it, if they could. Some seem to think this immediately and directly attainable, while others conclude that it is a misfortune (not a crime, for we are not responsible for its introduction among us,) which no effort can remove or reduce, and that we must content ourselves to submit to it forever, and avert our eyes from the consequences which are hereafter to follow. While they admit that every hour we delay lessens the possibility of effecting anything, they say that it is already *too late* to make any attempt which will not aggravate the evil. They would treat us like patients affected by chronic diseases believed to be incurable, by endeavoring to divert our minds from the contemplation of our real situation. Believing, however, that there is an entire coincidence of public opinion on the preliminary question involved, I deem it useless to enter into a long abstract discussion of the origin of slavery, or the evil effects which result from it. All will admit its extinction *desirable,* if *attainable*—and cannot, therefore, like my friend from Brunswick, undertake to follow the gentleman from Rockbridge (M. Moore), in the discursive lights he has indulged in, in a general disquisition upon slavery. He translated us occasionally with electrical rapidity, first to China, and then to the Rocky Mountains. He amused us for awhile on Earth, and then mounted up to Heaven, Prometheus-like, to take fire from thence, with which he attempted to slight and confound our Sauls of Tarsus, as he regarded us, as we were journeying to Damascus.

Any scheme for the gradual diminution, or ultimate extermination of the black population of Virginia, should be based, as a substratum, on certain great cardinal principles of justice, morality, and political expediency, about which I had hoped but little diversity of opinion would be found to exist. They are such as lie at the foundation of all civilized society, and on which all free governments must rest. Any action on this subject, without due regard to those polar principles, would not only fail of its intended effects, but would be subversive of the rights of the citizen—and ruinous in its consequences. Among these, I have always regarded the following as axioms, which should never be disregarded, and from which for one, I will never consent to depart:

> Ist. That no emancipation of slaves should ever be tolerated, unaccompanied by their immediate removal from among us.

> 2nd. That no system should be introduced, which is calculated to interfere with, or weaken the *security* of private property, or affect its value—And

> 3d. That not a single slave, or any other property he possesses, should be taken from its owner, *without his own consent*, or an ample compensation for its value. . . .

Sir, it was with unqualified astonishment, that I heard any supposition advanced of the possibility of a successful insurrection by our coloured population. It is true there has been great excitement, and much unpleasant apprehension of danger. I am happy to have learned that all this is to a considerable extent subsiding. It demonstrates certainly, however, the propriety, the necessity of our adopting some measure to re-assure public confidence; and prevent as far as practicable the recurrence of scenes similar to those so often alluded to. I certainly am not without my fears. But not the craven fear I trust; but that which dictates the expediency of looking guardedly at every thing before us, so as to be best prepared to meet or to ward off approaching danger. I do believe, and such must be the deliberate judgment of every reflecting man, that unless something is done in time to obviate it, the day must arrive when scenes of inconceivable horror must inevitably occur, and one of these two races of human beings, will have their throats cut by the other. It is impossible that things can always continue to flow on in their present current, without some radical change in our policy towards the African caste. This consequence must result, unless something can be done to remove or mitigate the tremendous evil.

But when allusions have heretofore been made to this horrible catastrophe, did it enter into the imagination of any body, that *the whites* were to be the ultimate victims?—that any successful general conspiracy ever could occur? No, Sir, I beg you to understand, that however dreadful either alternative would be—however anxious— however painfully solicitous we may be, to provide some efficient measure of prevention, it is not founded on the supposition, by a human being in the region more immediately concerned, that our negroes are ever to exchange conditions with us, or make laws for a subjugated province? The real extent of the danger—and God knows that is bad enough!—is that in insulated neighborhoods, a few misguided fanatics, like Nat Turner—or reckless infatuated desperadoes, like his followers, in total ignorance of the extent of such an enterprise, or of the means necessary to accomplish it, ay, in moments of sudden excitement, make desperate attempts, and commence partial excesses of pillage and massacre. Much mischief—(yes, Sir, as important to the wretched individuals assailed, as if all the world was involved,)—much injury might be inflicted, before the insurgents could be met with and arrested. But, so far from their overwhelming the whites, conquering the country, overturning our political dynasty, and usurping the seats of legislation, *the very act of their embodying, would be the immediate signal for their annihilation.* Sir, I assure you, that whatever little of military information I may possess, confirms and corroborates the obvious view of the subject. The only difficulty consists in finding them. The danger to be apprehended is entirely of a temporary character, and while they advance unseen and unopposed. The idea of a military force invading and conquering any country, without uniting in a mass, or by avoiding the opposing force of the invaded, would be ridiculous. In truth, there was never a single moment, from the commencement to the termination of this celebrated Southampton insurrection, in which ten resolute, well armed men, could not easily have put the whole down. With the relative moral, intellectual and scientific advantages which we possess, the numerical superiority of our slaves would have to become at least twenty to one, before any probable prospect could exist, of a successful general rebellion. Should the disproportion ever become very great, the God of Heaven who governs the universe, only knows what might happen. The only serious apprehension is, that now and then—perhaps after intervals of many years —partial attempts at local insurrection may be made, much mischief may be done in small districts, until, I repeat it, one or the other party will be exterminated. Another attempt soon after the recent one, would, in my judgment, lead the way to an indiscriminate slaughter of all the blacks, whether concerned in it or not. I assure you, Sir, that at the close of that which has passed, and when the public mind was excited almost to frenzy, by seeing the mangled corpses of helpless females and unoffending infants devoured by dogs and vultures before interment could be effected, it was with the greatest difficulty, and at the hazard of personal popularity and esteem, that the coolest and most judicious among us could exert an influence sufficient to restrain an indiscriminate slaughter of the blacks who were suspected. Sir, a few more such efforts! and the whole race will be swept from among us. Who would willingly behold such a spectacle! But, Sir, does the belief that it will be the *blacks* themselves, and not the *whites* who must eventually fall in such a struggle, constitute any reason for our remitting all our exertions to avert it?—Surely not.

JAMES MCDOWELL ON NAT TURNER [4]

McDowell, from Rockbridge County in western Virginia, was a leading antislavery spokesman in the debate. After citing some of the newspaper reports about the rebellion, he went on:

From these and like extracts, which might easily be multiplied, it appears, generally, sir, that to its extent, there never was a bloodier or more shocking massacre than that of Southampton, that besides the sixty-two or sixty-three white persons who were murdered and the forty odd insurgents who were shot in arms or executed afterwards, there were others (how many is not known) who were shot privily (and by whom, I believe is not known) without accusation or trial;— that many died in the field refusing to surrender; that a detachment only of these wretches attacked Dr. Blount's house and were repelled by the "three men and two boys" spoken of; that the insurgents, *recruited others at every house to which they went,* with but few exceptions, and that before they were checked, they had traversed the country a distance of twenty miles spreading desolation and woe around them. It also appears that it was early believed and early made known to the governor and the public as the opinion of the commanding general (General Brodnax,) that there was no general conspiracy and that Nat and his whole force might at any time have been put down by twenty resolute men. And yet sir, notwithstanding this statement such was the general consternation produced by this event and such the conscious insecurity of every neighborhood and family that rapid and vigorous preparations were almost every where making for military defence. Companies were organized—concerts established—military supplies provided—towns and counties far from the place of revolt—far from one another—many of them days and weeks after the revolt had been crushed, were still anxiously calling on the Executive for arms, arms.

Now sir, I ask you, I ask gentlemen, in conscience to say, was this a "petty affair"? I ask you, whether that was a petty affair which startled the feelings of your whole population,—which threw a portion of it into alarm—a portion of it into panic; which wrung out from an affrighted people the thrilling cry, day after day conveyed to your Executive, "we are in peril of our lives, send us arms for defence." Was that a "petty affair" which drove families from their homes, which assembled women and children in crowds and without shelter at

⁴ From *Speech of James McDowell, Jr. (of Rockbridge) in the House of Delegates of Virginia, on the Slave Question* . . . (Richmond, 1832), pp. 28–29.

places of common refuge, in every condition of weakness and infirmity, under every suffering which want and pain and terror could inflict, yet willing to endure all—willing to meet death from famine, death from the climate, death from hardships, any thing rather than risk the horrors of meeting it from a domestic assassin? Was that a "petty affair" which erected a peaceful and confiding portion of the State into a military camp, which outlawed from pity the unfortunate beings whose brothers had offended, which barred every door, penetrated every bosom with fear or suspicion, which so banished the sense of security from every man's dwelling that let a hoof or a horn but break upon the silence of night and an aching throb would be driven to the heart; the husband would look to his weapon and the mother would shudder and weep upon her cradle!

Was it the fear of Nat Turner and his deluded and drunken handful of followers which produced or could produce such effects? Was it this that induced distant counties where the very name Southampton was strange, to arm and equip for a struggle? No sir, it was the suspicion eternally attached to the slave himself, the suspicion that a Nat Turner might be in every family, that the same bloody deed could be acted over at any time and in any place, that the materials for it were spread through the land and always ready for a like explosion. Nothing but the force of this withering apprehension, nothing but the paralyzing and deadening weight with which it falls upon and prostrates the heart of every man who has helpless dependents to protect, nothing but this could have thrown a brave people into consternation, or could have made any portion of this powerful Commonwealth, for a single instant, to have quailed and trembled.

12
Virginia and Other States Strengthen Their Slave Codes

In the end, all that came of the Virginia debate of 1832, so far as the slaves were concerned, was new legal repression. Earlier in 1831, Virginia had barred slaves and free blacks from being instructed in reading and writing. Now black preaching was prohibited, with the effect, according to one historian, of "completely removing Negro preachers as pastors of churches or ministrants at religious ceremonies." Other southern states likewise tightened their slave codes, particularly in the area of slave literacy and preaching, and forbade the circulation of "incendiary publications."

VIRGINIA [1]

[Passed March 15th, 1832.]

1. *Be it enacted by the general assembly,* That no slave, free negro or mulatto, whether he shall have been ordained or licensed, or otherwise, shall hereafter undertake to preach, exhort or conduct, or hold any assembly or meeting, for religious or other purposes, either in the day time, or at night; and any slave, free negro or mulatto, so offending, shall for every such offence, be punished with stripes, at the discretion of any justice of the peace, not exceeding thirty-nine lashes; and any person desiring so to do, shall have authority, without any previous written precept or otherwise, to apprehend any such offender and carry him before such justice.

2. Any slave, free negro or mulatto, who shall hereafter attend any preaching, meeting or other assembly, held or pretended to be held for religious purposes, or other instruction, conducted by any slave, free negro or mulatto preacher, ordained or otherwise; and any slave who shall hereafter attend any preaching in the night time, although conducted by a white minister, without a written permission from his or her owner, overseer or master or agent of either of them, shall

[1] From *Acts Passed at a General Assembly of the Commonwealth of Virginia, Begun and Held at the Capitol, in the City of Richmond* . . . (Richmond, 1832), pp. 20–22.

be punished by stripes at the discretion of any justice of the peace, not exceeding thirty-nine lashes; and may for that purpose be apprehended by any person, without any written or other precept: *Provided,* That nothing herein contained shall be so construed, as to prevent the masters or owners of slaves, or any white person to whom any free negro or mulatto is bound, or in whose employment, or on whose plantation or lot such free negro or mulatto lives, from carrying or permitting any such slave, free negro or mulatto, to go with him, her or them, or with any part of his, her, or their white family to any place of religious worship, conducted by a white minister, in the night time: *And provided also,* That nothing in this, or any former law, shall be so construed, as to prevent any ordained or licensed white minister of the gospel, or any layman licensed for that purpose by the denomination to which he may belong, from preaching, or giving religious instruction to slaves, free negroes and mulattoes, in the day time; nor to deprive any masters or owners of slaves of the right to engage, or employ any free white person whom they may think proper, to give religious instruction to their slaves; nor to prevent the assembling of the slaves of any one master together, at any time for religious devotion.

3. No free negro or mulatto shall hereafter be capable of purchasing or otherwise acquiring permanent ownership, except by descent, to any slave, other than his or her husband, wife or children; and all contracts for any such purchase are hereby declared to be null and void.

4. No free negro or mulatto shall be suffered to keep or carry any firelock of any kind, any military weapon, or any powder or lead; and any free negro or mulatto who shall so offend, shall, on conviction before a justice of the peace, forfeit all such arms and ammunition to the use of the informer; and shall moreover be punished with stripes, at the discretion of the justice, not exceeding thirty-nine lashes. And the proviso to the seventh section of the act, entitled, "an act reducing into one the several acts concerning slaves, free negroes and mulattoes," passed the second day of March, one thousand eight hundred and nineteen, authorizing justices of the peace, in certain cases, to permit slaves to keep and use guns or other weapons, powder and shot; and so much of the eighth section of the said recited act as authorizes the county and corporation courts to grant licenses to free negroes and mulattoes to keep or carry any firelock of any kind, any military weapon, or any powder or lead, shall be, and the same are hereby repealed.

5. No slave, free negro or mulatto, shall hereafter be permitted to sell, give, or otherwise dispose of any ardent or spirituous liquor at or within one mile of any muster, preaching, or other public assembly of black or white persons; and any slave, free negro or

mulatto, so offending, shall be punished by stripes, at the discretion of a justice of the peace, not exceeding thirty-nine.

6. If any slave, free negro or mulatto, shall hereafter wilfully and maliciously assault and beat any white person, with intention in so doing to kill such white person; every such slave, free negro or mulatto, so offending, and being thereof lawfully convicted, shall be adjudged and deemed guilty of felony, and shall suffer death without benefit of clergy.

7. If any person shall hereafter write, print, or cause to be written or printed, any book, pamphlet or other writing, advising persons of colour within this state to make insurrection, or to rebel, or shall knowingly circulate, or cause to be circulated, any book, pamphlet or other writing, written or printed, advising persons of colour in this commonwealth to commit insurrection or rebellion; such person if a slave, free negro or mulatto, shall, on conviction before any justice of the peace, be punished for the first offence with stripes, at the discretion of the said justice, not exceeding thirty-nine lashes; and for the second offence, shall be deemed guilty of felony, and on due conviction, shall be punished with death without benefit of clergy; and if the person so offending be a white person, he or she shall be punished on conviction, in a sum not less than one hundred nor more than one thousand dollars.

8. Riots, routs, unlawful assemblies, trespasses and seditious speeches, by free negroes or mulattoes, shall hereafter be punished with stripes, in the same mode, and to the same extent, as slaves are directed to be punished by the twelfth section of the before recited act. . . .

NORTH CAROLINA [2]

An Act for the Better Regulation of the Conduct of Negroes, Slaves and Free Persons of Color.

Be it enacted by the General Assembly of the State of North Carolina, and it is hereby enacted by the authority of the same, That it shall not be lawful under any pretence for any free negro, slave or free person of color to preach or exhort in public, or in any manner to officiate as a preacher or teacher in any prayer meeting or other association for worship where slaves of different families are collected together; and if any free negro or free person of color shall be thereof duly convicted on indictment before any court having jurisdiction thereof, he shall for each offence receive not exceeding thirty-nine lashes on his bare back; and where any slave shall be guilty of a

[2] From *Acts Passed by the General Assembly of the State of North Carolina, at the Session of 1831–32* (Raleigh, 1832), p. 7.

violation of this act, he shall on conviction before a single magistrate receive not exceeding thirty-nine lashes on his bare back.

II. *And be it further enacted by the authority aforesaid,* That it shall not be lawful for any slave to go at large as a freeman, exercising his or her own discretion in the employment of his or her time; nor shall it be lawful for any slave to keep house to him or herself as a free person, exercising the like discretion in the employment of his or her time; and in case the owner of any slave shall consent or connive at the commission of such offence, he or she so offending shall be subject to indictment, and on conviction be fined in the discretion of the court not exceeding one hundred dollars: *Provided,* that nothing herein shall be construed to prevent any person permitting his or her slave or slaves to live or keep house upon his or her land for the purpose of attending to the business of his or her master or mistress.

ALABAMA [3]

30. From and after the first day of February next, it shall not be lawful for any free person of color to settle within the limits of this state; and should any free person of color, after that time, settle in this state, he, she, or they shall, on notice of this act, depart within thirty days, or shall be liable, on conviction before any justice of the peace, to receive thirty-nine lashes; and any person may arrest any such free person of color, and take him or her before any justice of the peace for trial; and if any such free person of color shall not depart this state within twenty days after the infliction of the punishment last mentioned, he or she shall be liable to be arrested by any person, and be taken before a justice of the peace for trial, and on conviction by such justice, shall be ordered to be sold as a slave for the term of one year for ready money, ten days' notice being given of the time of sale, one half of which, after paying all the expenses of the prosecution, (which shall be to the justice one dollar, the constable two dollars for summoning the witnesses, attending the trial, and selling the said free person of color, and fifty cents a day for each day he may keep such person of color, and fifty cents per day for each witness who may attend the trial,) shall be paid to the informer, and the other half to the state. And if any free person of color shall not depart this state within twenty days after the expiration of said year, he or she shall forfeit his or her freedom; and upon conviction thereof before any circuit court of this state, shall, by order of said court, be sold to the highest bidder, and the proceeds of the sale of said free negro so forfeiting his or her freedom, shall go, one half to the informer, and the other half to the state.

[3] From John G. Aiken, comp., *A Digest of the Laws of the State of Alabama,* 2d ed. (Tuscaloosa, 1836), pp. 396–98.

31. Any person or persons who shall attempt to teach any free person of color, or slave, to spell, read, or write, shall, upon conviction thereof by indictment, be fined in a sum not less than two hundred and fifty dollars, nor more than five hundred dollars.

32. Any free person of color who shall write for any slave, a pass or free-paper, on conviction thereof, shall receive for every such offence, thirty-nine lashes on the bare back, and leave the state of Alabama within thirty days thereafter; and should he or she again return to the state of Alabama, or be found within the same after the time above limited for his or her departure, on conviction of violating this provision of the law, he or she shall forfeit his or her liberty, and be sold as a slave for the term of ten years, by order of any two justices of the peace, before whom he or she may be taken and convicted, ten days' previous notice being given of the time and place of sale: one half of the proceeds of said sale, after paying one dollar each to said justices, and two dollars to the constable for attending the trial, and selling said free person of color, together with all other costs that may accrue, shall be paid to the use of the informer, and the other half to the use of the state. . . .

35. If any free negro or person of color shall be found in company with any slaves in any kitchen, out-house, or negro-quarter, without a written permission from the owner, master, or overseer of said slaves, said free negro or person of color shall, for the first offence, receive fifteen lashes, and for every subsequent offence, thirty-nine lashes, on his or her bare back, which may be inflicted by said master, owner, or overseer, or by any officer or member of any patrol company who may find said free negro or person of color, in any kitchen, out-house, or negro-quarter, associating with slaves without such written permission. . . .

42. If any slave or free person of color shall preach to, exhort, or harangue any slave or slaves, or free persons of color, unless in the presence of five respectable slave-holders, any such slave or free person of color so offending, shall, on conviction before any justice of the peace, receive, by order of said justice of the peace, thirty-nine lashes for the first offence, and fifty lashes for every offence thereafter; and any person may arrest any such slave or free person of color, and take him before a justice of the peace for trial: *Provided,* That the negroes so haranguing or preaching, shall be licensed thereto, by some regular body of professing Christians immediately in the neighborhood, and to whose society or church such negro shall properly belong.

13

The Attack on Freedom of Discussion, and Emergence of the Proslavery Argument

The Virginia debate on slavery, the southern historian Ulrich B. Phillips wrote, was "a blazing indiscretion." He was only echoing what an increasing number of Virginians believed as the debate progressed. The newspapers' newly found freedom of discussion about slavery, and the heated debate in the legislature, it was argued, could only incite the slaves to further outbreaks. Even while the debate was in progress such fears were voiced, particularly by the leading Whig politician Benjamin Leigh, who in a series of letters written under the name "Appomattox" denounced the Virginia press and the antislavery legislators. But the most effective proslavery argument was made by a professor at William and Mary College, Thomas R. Dew, whose Review of the Debates *marked a turning point in the development of proslavery thought. Dew not only denounced the debate as a reckless indulgence, and answered the economic arguments of the antislavery legislators, but for the first time marshalled a coherent defense of the institution as a positive and necessary benefit to society, drawing on arguments from history, the Bible, economics, and racial inferiority. Moreover, Dew effectively demolished the plans of the antislavery forces for emancipation and colonization at state expense, by calculating the immense cost of such a project and pointing to the need for black labor in the state. The only practicable emancipation plan, he insisted, was one that would allow the blacks to remain as citizens after abolition. Dew rightly sensed that the antislavery forces, faced with the alternatives of emancipation without deportation or a continuation of slavery, would choose the latter without hesitation.*

As Virginia's economic situation improved in the 1830s, and the revival of the interstate slave trade drew off some of the state's growing black population, articulate antislavery sentiment disappeared. By 1838, John C. Calhoun could tell the Senate that, throughout the south, where once men had believed slavery to be "a moral and political evil; that folly and delusion are gone; we now see it in its true light, and regard it as the most safe and stable basis for free institutions in the world."

119

THOMAS R. DEW ON NAT TURNER AND THE DANGER OF
SLAVE REBELLION [1]

In our Southern slaveholding country the question of emancipation has never been seriously discussed in any of our legislatures, until
the whole subject, under the most exciting circumstances, was, during
the last winter, brought up for discussion in the Virginia Legislature,
and plans of partial or total abolition were earnestly pressed upon
the attention of that body. It is well known, that during the last summer, in the county of Southampton, in Virginia, a few slaves, led on
by Nat Turner, rose in the night, and murdered in the most inhuman
and shocking manner, between sixty and seventy of the unsuspecting
whites of that county. The news, of course, was rapidly diffused, and
with it, consternation and dismay were spread throughout the State,
destroying, for a time, all feeling of security and confidence, and
even when subsequent development had proved, that the conspiracy
had been originated by a fanatical negro preacher,—(whose confessions prove beyond a doubt mental aberration)—and that this conspiracy embraced but few slaves, all of whom had paid the penalty of
their crimes; still the excitement remained—still the repose of the
commonwealth was disturbed—for the ghastly horrors of the Southampton tragedy could not immediately be banished from the mind—
and *rumor*, too, with her thousand tongues, was busily engaged in
spreading tales of disaffection, plots, insurrections, and even massacres,
which frightened the timid, and harassed and mortified the whole of
the slaveholding population. During this period of excitement,
when reason was almost banished from the mind, and the imagination
was suffered to conjure up the most appalling phantoms, and picture
to itself a crisis in the vista of futurity, when the overwhelming numbers of the blacks would rise superior to all restraint, and involve the
fairest portion of our land in universal ruin and desolation, we are
not to wonder, that even in the lower part of Virginia, many should
have seriously inquired, if this supposed monstrous evil could not be
removed from our bosom? Some looked to the removal of the free
people of color by the efforts of the Colonization Society, as an anti-
dote to all our ills. Some were disposed to strike at the root of the evil
—to call on the General Government for aid, and by the labors of
Hercules, to extirpate the curse of slavery from the land. Others again,
who could not bear that Virginia should stand towards the General
Government (whose unconstitutional action she had ever been fore-
most to resist) in the attitude of a suppliant, looked forward to the

[1] From Thomas R. Dew, *An Essay on Slavery* (Richmond, 1849), pp. 4–6, 99–102.
This is a later edition of Dew's *Review of the Debates in the Virginia Legislature
of 1831 and 1832* (Richmond, 1832).

legislative action of the State as capable of achieving the desired result. In this state of excitement and unallayed apprehension, the Legislature met, and plans for abolition were proposed, and earnestly advocated in debate.

Upon the impropriety of this debate, we beg leave to make a few observations. Any scheme of abolition proposed so soon after the Southampton tragedy, would necessarily appear to be the result of that most inhuman massacre. Suppose the negroes, then, to be really anxious for their emancipation, no matter on what terms, would not the extraordinary effect produced on the Legislature by the Southampton insurrection, in all probability, have a tendency to excite another? And we must recollect, from the nature of things, no plan of abolition could act suddenly on the whole mass of slave population in the State? Mr. Randolph's was not even to commence its operation till 1840. Waiting, then, one year or more, until the excitement could be allayed, and the empire of reason could once more have been established, would surely have been productive of no injurious consequences; and, in the mean time, a Legislature could have been selected, which would much better have represented the views and wishes of their constituents on this vital question. Virginia could have ascertained the sentiments and wishes of other slaveholding States, whose concurrence, if not absolutely necessary, might be highly desirable, and should have been sought after and attended to, at least as a matter of State courtesy. Added to this, the texture of the Legislature was not of that character calculated to ensure the confidence of the people in a movement of this kind. If ever there was a question debated in a deliberative body, which called for the most exalted talent, the longest and most tried experience, the utmost circumspection and caution, a complete exemption from prejudice and undue excitement, where both are apt to prevail, an ardent and patriotic desire to advance the vital interests of the State, uncombined with mere desire for vain and ostentatious display, and with no view to party or geographical divisions, that question was the question of the *abolition* of *slavery* in the Virginia Legislature. "*Grave* and *Reverend* seniors," the very fathers of the Republic, were indeed required for the settlement of a question of such magnitude. It appears, however, that the Legislature was composed of an unusual number of young and inexperienced members, elected in the month of April, previous to the Southampton massacre, and at a time of profound tranquillity and repose, when, of course, the people were not disposed to call from their retirement their most distinguished and experienced citizens.

We are very ready to admit, that in point of ability and eloquence, the debate transcended our expectations. One of the leading political papers in the State remarked—"We have never heard any debate so eloquent, so sustained, and in which so great a number of speakers had appeared, and commanded the attention of so numerous and intelligent an audience." . . . . . . "Day after day, multitudes throng to the capital, and have been compensated by eloquence which would have illustrated Rome or Athens." But however fine might have been the rhetorical display, however ably some isolated points may have been discussed, still we affirm, with confidence, that no enlarged, wise, and practical plan of operations, was proposed by the abolitionists. We will go farther, and assert that their arguments, in most cases, were of a wild and intemperate character, based upon false principles and assumptions of the most vicious and alarming kind; subversive of the rights of property and the order and tranquillity of society; and portending to the whole slaveholding country—if they ever shall be followed out in practice—the most inevitable and ruinous consequences. Far be it, however from us, to accuse the abolitionists in the Virginia Legislature, of any settled malevolent design to overturn or convulse the fabric of society. We have no doubt that they were acting conscientiously for the best; but it often happens that frail, imperfect man, in the too ardent and confident pursuit of imaginary good, runs upon his utter destruction.

We have not formed our opinion lightly upon this subject; we have given to the vital question of abolition the most mature and intense consideration which we are capable of bestowing, and we have come to the conclusion—a conclusion which seems to be sustained by facts and reasoning as irresistible as the demonstration of the mathematician— that every plan of emancipation and deportation which we can possibly conceive, is *totally* impracticable. We shall endeavor to prove, that the attempt to execute these plans can only have a tendency to increase all the evils of which we complain, as resulting from slavery. If this be true, then the great question of abolition will necessarily be reduced to the question of emancipation, with a permission to remain, which we think can easily be shown to be utterly subversive of the interests, security, and happiness, of both the blacks and whites, and consequently hostile to every principle of expediency, morality, and religion. We have heretofore doubted the propriety even of too frequently agitating, especially in a public manner, the question of abolition, in consequence of the injurious effects which might be produced on the slave population. But the Virginia Legislature, in its zeal for discussion, boldly set aside all prudential considerations of this kind, and openly and publicly debated the subject before the world. The seal has now been broken, the example has been set from a high quarter; we shall, therefore, waive all considerations of a prudential character, which have heretofore restrained us, and boldly grapple with the abolitionists on this great question. We fear not the result, so far as truth, justice, and expediency alone are concerned. But we must be permitted to say, that we do most deeply dread the effects of misguided philanthropy, and the marked, and we had like to have said, impertinent intrusion in this matter, of those who have no interest at stake, and who have not that intimate and minute knowledge of the whole subject so absolutely necessary to wise action. . . .

Insecurity of the whites, arising from plots, insurrections, &c. among the blacks. This is the evil, after all, let us say what we will which really operates most powerfully upon the schemers and emancipating philanthropists of those sections where slaves constitute the principal property. Now, if we have shown, as we trust we have, that the scheme of deportation is utterly impracticable, and that emancipation, with permission to remain, will produce all these horrors in *still greater degree*, it follows that this evil of slavery, allowing it to exist in all its latitude would be no argument for legislative action, and therefore we might well rest contented with this issue; but as we are anxious to exhibit this whole subject in its true bearings, and as we do believe that this evil has been most strangely and causelessly exaggerated, we have determined to examine it a moment, and point out its true extent. It seems to us that those who insist most upon it, commit the enormous error of looking upon every slave in the whole slaveholding country as actuated by the most deadly enmity to the whites and possessing all that reckless, fiendish temper, which would lead him to murder and assassinate the moment the opportunity occurs. This is far from being true, the slave, as we have already said, generally loves the master and his family;[1] and few indeed there are, who can coldly plot the murder of men, women, and children; and if they do, there are fewer still who can have the villainy to execute. We can sit down and imagine that all the negroes in the south have conspired to rise on a certain night, and murder all the whites in their respective families, we may suppose the secret to be kept, and that they have the physical power to exterminate, and yet we say the whole is morally impossible. No insurrection of this kind can ever occur where the blacks are as much civilized as they are in the United States. Savages and Koromantyn slaves can commit such deeds, because their whole life and education have prepared them; and they glory in the achievement; but the negro of the United States has imbibed the principles, the sentiments, and feelings of the white; in one word, he is civilized—at least, comparatively; his whole education and course of life are at war with such fell deeds. Nothing, then, but the most subtle and poisonous principles, sedulously infused into his mind, can break his allegiance, and transform him into the midnight murderer. Any man who will attend to the history of the Southampton massacre, must at once see, that the cause of even the partial success of the insurrectionists, was the very circumstance that there

[1] We scarcely know a single family, in which the slaves, especially the domestics, do not manifest the most unfeigned grief at the deaths which occur among the whites.

was no extensive plot, and that Nat, a demented fanatic, was under the impression that heaven had enjoined him to liberate the blacks, and had made its manifestations by loud noises in the air, an eclipse, and by the greenness of the sun. It was these signs which determined *him*, and ignorance and superstition, together with implicit confidence in Nat, determined a few others, and thus the bloody work began. So fearfully and reluctantly did they proceed to the execution, that we have no doubt that if Travis, the first attacked, could have waked whilst they were getting into his house, or could have shot down Nat or Will, the rest would have fled, and the affair would have terminated *in limine.*

We have read with great attention the history of the insurrections in St. Domingo, and have no hesitation in affirming, that to the re-flecting mind, that whole history affords the most complete evidence of the difficulty and almost impossibility of succeeding in these plots, even under the most favorable circumstances. It would almost have been a moral miracle, if that revolution had not succeeded. The French revolution had kindled a blaze throughout the world. The society of the *Amis des Noirs,* (the friends of the blacks,) in Paris, had educated and disciplined many of the mulattoes, who were almost as numerous as the whites in the island. The National Assembly, in its mad career, declared these mulattoes to be equal in all respects to the whites, and gave them the same privileges and immunities as the whites. During the ten years, too, immediately preceding the revolu-tion, more than 200,000 negroes were imported into the island from Africa. It is a well known fact, that newly imported negroes, are al-ways greatly more dangerous than those born among us; and of those importations a very large proportion consisted of Koromantyn slaves, from the Gold Coast, who have all the savage ferocity of the North American Indian.[2] And lastly the whites themselves, disunited, and strangely inharmonious would nevertheless have suppressed the insur-rections, although the blacks and mulattoes were nearly *fifteen-fold* their numbers, if it had not been for the constant and too fatal inter-ference of France. The great sin of that revolution rests on the Na-tional Assembly, and should be an awful warning to every legislature to beware of too much tampering with so delicate and difficult a sub-ject, as an alteration of the fundamental relations of society.

But there is another cause which will render the success of the blacks for ever impossible in the south, as long as slavery exists. It is,

---

[2] It was the Koromantyns who brought about the insurrection in Jamaica, in 1760. They are a very hardy race, and the Dutch, who are a calculating, money-making people, and withal the most cruel masters in the world, have generally preferred these slaves, because they might be forced to do most work; but the consequence of their avarice has been, that they have been more cursed with in-surrections than any other people in the West Indies.

that in modern times especially, wealth and talent must ever rule over mere physical force. During the feudal ages, the vassals never made a settled concerted attempt to throw off the yoke of the lord or landed proprietor, and the true reason was, they had neither property nor talent, and consequently the power, under these circumstances, could be placed no where else than in the hands of the lords; but so soon as the *tiers etat* arose, with commerce and manufactures, there was something to struggle for, and *le crise des revolutions,* (the crisis of revolutions,) was the consequence. No connected, persevering, and well concerted movement, ever takes place, in modern times, unless for the sake of property. Now, the property, talent, concert, and we may add habit, are all with the whites, and render their continued superiority absolutely certain, if they are not meddled with, no matter what may be the disproportion of numbers. We look upon these insurrections in the same light that we do the murders and robberies which occur in society, and in a slaveholding State, they are a sort of substitute for the latter; the robbers and murderers in what are called free States, are generally the poor and needy, who rob for money; negro slaves rarely murder or rob for this purpose; they have no inducement to do it—the fact is, the whole capital of the south is pledged for their maintenance. The present Chief Magistrate of Virginia has informed us that he has never known of but one single case in Virginia where negroes murdered for the sake of money. Now, there is no doubt but that the common robberies and murders for money, take off, in the aggregate, more men, and destroy more property, than insurrections among the slaves; the former are the result of fixed causes eternally at work, the latter of occasional causes which are rarely, *very rarely,* in action. Accordingly, if we should look to the whole of our southern population, and compare the average number of deaths, by the hands of assassins, with the numbers elsewhere, we would be astonished to find them perhaps as few or fewer than in any other population of equal amount on the globe. In the city of London there is, upon an average, a murder or a house-breaking and robbery every night in the year, which is greater than the amount of deaths by murders, insurrections, &c., in our whole southern country; and yet the inhabitant of London walks the streets, and sleeps in perfect confidence, and why should not we who are in fact in much less danger? These calamities in London, very properly give rise to the establishment of a police, and the adoption of precautionary measures; and so they should in our country, and every where else. And if the Virginia Legislature had turned its attention more to this subject during its last session, we think, with all due deference, it would have redounded much more to the advantage of the State than the intemperate discussion which was gotten up.

PART THREE

NAT TURNER IN HISTORY

14

John Brown and Nat Turner

*During the 1830s and 1840s the majority of abolition-
ists, including most black antislavery leaders, continued to reject
violence as a means of freeing the slave. The Declaration of
Sentiments of the American and Foreign Anti-Slavery Society,
for example, explicitly stated, "We reject and entreat the oppressed to reject the use of all carnal weapons for deliverance
from bondage, relying solely upon those which are spiritual and
mighty through God. . . ." Nor did political abolitionists take
a different view. One Liberty party address of 1842 declared,
"Woful as is slavery, and desirable as is liberty, we entreat [the
slaves] to endure the former—rather than take a violent and
bloody hold of the latter."*

*Nonetheless, the 1840s did witness a growing militant spirit,
particularly among black abolitionists. A key document in the
growing acceptance of violence was the fugitive slave Henry H.
Garnet's "Address to the Slaves," delivered at the Buffalo National Negro Convention of 1843, which invoked the memory
of Turner and other slave rebels, and called on the slaves to rise
in rebellion. In 1850, another fugitive slave, Henry Bibb, published a history of the Vesey and Turner rebellions, and included
a collection of abolitionist songs, one of which linked David
Walker, Nat Turner, and others as abolitionist heroes.*

*The 1850s was a decade of violence, beginning with rescues
of fugitive slaves from northern courtrooms, spiraling into civil
war in Kansas and fistfights and beatings in Congress, and end-
ing in John Brown's raid. Under the impact of events, non-
violent abolitionism suddenly seemed to collapse. Even Garrison,
after Brown's raid, told a Boston audience, "I am prepared to
say: 'Success to every slave insurrection at the South.'" It was
therefore inevitable that interest in Turner would grow in the
1850s. In 1855, the first serious work on black history by a black
American, William C. Nell's* Colored Patriots of the American
Revolution, *devoted a short section to Turner, and in the following year, Harriet Beecher Stowe published her novel* Dred,
*which centered on a slave rebellion in North Carolina, and
which included as an appendix Turner's* Confessions.

John Brown's raid, according to his friend and biographer James Redpath, was in part inspired by the example of Turner; and it was not surprising that a parallel between the two men was quickly drawn in late 1859.

AN ABOLITIONIST SONG[1]

The Lovejoy in the song is Elijah P. Lovejoy, the abolitionist editor killed by a mob in 1837.

Set the Captive Free

I hear the cry of millions, of millions, of millions,
I hear the cry of millions— of millions in bonds.
Oh! set the captive free, set him free, set him free,
Oh! set the captive free from his chains. . . .

I hear the voice of Walker, of Walker, of Walker,
I hear the voice of Walker, in words of living truth,
Oh! set the captive free, set him free, set him free,
Oh! set the captive free from his chains.

I hear the voice of Turner, of Turner, of Turner,
I hear the voice of Turner, for Liberty or Death!
Oh! set the captive free, set him free, set him free,
Oh! set the captive free from his chains.

I hear the voice of Lovejoy, of Lovejoy, of Lovejoy,
I hear the voice of Lovejoy, from Alton's bloody plains.
Oh! set the captive free, set him free, set him free,
Oh! set the captive free from his chains. . . .

I hear the voice of thousands, of thousands, of thousands,
I hear the voice of thousands—in spite of John Calhoun,
Oh! set the captive free, set him free, set him free,
Oh! set the captive free from his chains.

[1] From Henry Bibb, *Slave Insurrection in Southampton County, Va., Headed by Nat Turner* (New York, 1850).

NEW YORK *WEEKLY ANGLO–AFRICAN,* OCTOBER 29, DECEMBER 31, 1859 [2]

[October 29] Nat Turner, the Virginia Hero

At a time when the public mind is, to a great extent, centered upon the case of the *man* and the *hero,* John Brown, who has offered himself a sacrifice for the sake of liberty, it is fitting that the people should inform themselves upon that and kindred subjects. In 1830 [sic], Nat Turner made his appearance in an effort to release his race from the trammels of American slavery. That effort was made in the same ancient dominion where the present hero now lingers. It will be interesting, therefore, to listen to the eloquent J. Sella Martin next Wednesday evening, in his lecture on "Nat Turner." That will be an opportunity for seeing what degree of interest the people really take in such a subject, and in what direction their sympathies really run. There seems to have been a providence in the selection of this subject, and the orator who is to set it forth. . . .

[December 31] The Nat Turner Insurrection

There are two reasons why we present our readers with the Confession of Nat Turner. First, to place upon record this most remarkable episode in the history of human slavery, which proves to the philosophic observer, that in the midst of the most perfectly contrived and apparently secure systems of slavery, humanity will out, and engender from its bosom, forces, that will contend against oppression, however unsuccessfully: and secondly, that the two methods of Nat Turner and of John Brown may be compared. The one is the mode in which the slave seeks freedom for his fellows, and the other, the mode in which the white man seeks to set the slave free. There are many points of similarity between these two men: they were both idealists; both governed by their views of the teachings of the Bible; both had harbored for years the purpose to which they gave up their lives; both felt themselves swayed as by some divine, or at least, spiritual, impulse; the one seeking in the air, the earth and the heavens, for signs which came at last; and the other, obeying impulses which he believes to have been fore-ordained from the eternal past; both cool, calm and heroic in prison and in the prospect of inevitable death; both confess with childlike frankness and simplicity the object they had in view—the pure and simple emancipation of their fellow-men; both win from the judges who sentence them, expressions of deep sympathy—and here the par-

---

[2] The *Weekly Anglo-African* was edited by the New York free black, Thomas Hamilton.

allel ceases. Nat Turner's terrible logic could only see the enfranchise-
ment of one race, compassed by the extirpation of the other; and he
followed his gory syllogism with rude exactitude. John Brown, believing that the freedom of the enthralled could only be effected by placing them on an equality with their enslavers, and unable, in the very
effort at emancipation, to tyrannize himself, is moved with compassion
for tyrants as well as slaves, and seeks to extirpate this formidable
cancer, without spilling one drop of christian blood.

These two narratives present a fearful choice to the slaveholders, nay,
to this great nation—which of the two modes of emancipation shall
take place? The method of Nat Turner or the method of John Brown?

Emancipation must take place, and soon. There can be no long
delay in the choice of methods. If John Brown's be not soon adopted
by the free North, then Nat Turner's will be by the enslaved South.

Had the order of events been reversed—had Nat Turner been in John
Brown's place, at the head of these twenty-one men, governed by his
inexorable logic and cool daring, the soil of Virginia and Maryland
and the far South, would by this time be drenched in blood, and the
wild and sanguinary course of these men, no earthly power then could
stay.

The course which the South is now frantically pursuing, will engender in its bosom and nurse into maturity a hundred Nat Turners,
whom Virginia is infinitely less able to resist in 1860, than she was in
1831.

So, people of the South, people of the North! men and brethren,
choose ye which method of emancipation you prefer—Nat Turner's
or John Brown's?

15

Thomas Wentworth Higginson: "This Extraordinary Man"

The first historian to really do justice to Nat Turner, and to investigate other contemporary sources than the Confessions, was Thomas Wentworth Higginson. Higginson, a New England abolitionist who had aided John Brown during the 1850s, was soon to become famous as the commander of a black regiment during the Civil War. His essay, "Nat Turner's Insurrection," published in 1861, is in many ways still the best short account of the Southampton rebellion.

NAT TURNER'S INSURRECTION [1]

During the year 1831, up to the 23d of August, the Virginia newspapers seem to have been absorbed in the momentous problems which then occupied the minds of intelligent American citizens: What Gen. Jackson should do with the scolds, and what with the disreputables? should South Carolina be allowed to nullify? and would the wives of cabinet ministers call on Mrs. Eaton? It is an unfailing opiate to turn over the drowsy files of the Richmond *Enquirer,* until the moment when those dry and dusty pages are suddenly kindled into flame by the torch of Nat Turner. Then the terror flared on increasing, until the remotest Southern States were found shuddering at nightly rumors of insurrection; until far-off European colonies—Antigua, Martinique, Caraccas, Tortola—recognized by some secret sympathy the same epidemic alarms; until the very boldest words of freedom were reported as uttered in the Virginia House of Delegates with unclosed doors; until an obscure young man named Garrison was indicted at common law in North Carolina, and had a price set upon his head by the Legislature of Georgia.

Near the south-eastern border of Virginia, in Southampton County, there is a neighborhood known as "The Cross Keys." It lies fifteen miles from Jerusalem, the county-town, or "court-house," seventy miles from Norfolk, and about as far from Richmond. It is some ten or fifteen miles from Murfreesborough in North Carolina, and about twenty-five from the Great Dismal Swamp. Up to Sunday, the 21st of August, 1831, there was nothing to distinguish it from any other rural, lethargic, slipshod Virginia neighborhood, with the due allotment of

[1] From Thomas Wentworth Higginson, "Nat Turner's Insurrection," *Atlantic Monthly,* VIII (August, 1861), 173–87.

mansion-houses and log huts, tobacco-fields and "old-fields," horses, dogs, negroes, "poor white folks," so called, and other white folks, poor without being called so. One of these last was Joseph Travis, who had recently married the widow of one Putnam Moore, and had unfortunately wedded to himself her negroes also.

In the woods on the plantation of Joseph Travis, upon the Sunday just named, six slaves met at noon for what is called in the Northern States a picnic, and in the Southern a barbecue. The bill of fare was to be simple: one brought a pig, and another some brandy, giving to the meeting an aspect so cheaply convivial that no one would have imagined it to be the final consummation of a conspiracy which had been for six months in preparation. In this plot four of the men had been already initiated,—Henry, Hark or Hercules, Nelson, and Sam. Two others were novices, Will and Jack by name. The party had remained together from twelve to three o'clock, when a seventh man joined them,—a short, stout, powerfully built person, of dark mulatto complexion, and strongly marked African features, but with a face full of expression and resolution. This was Nat Turner.

He was at this time nearly thirty-one years old, having been born on the 2d of October, 1800. He had belonged originally to Benjamin Turner,—from whom he took his last name, slaves having usually no patronymic;—had then been transferred to Putnam Moore, and then to his present owner. He had, by his own account, felt himself singled out from childhood for some great work; and he had some peculiar marks on his person, which, joined to his mental precocity, were enough to occasion, among his youthful companions, a superstitious faith in his gifts and destiny. He had some mechanical ingenuity also; experimentalized very early in making paper, gunpowder, pottery, and in other arts, which, in later life, he was found thoroughly to understand. His moral faculties appeared strong, so that white witnesses admitted that he had never been known to swear an oath, to drink a drop of spirits, or to commit a theft. And, in general, so marked were his early peculiarities that people said "he had too much sense to be raised; and, if he was, he would never be of any use as a slave." This impression of personal destiny grew with his growth: he fasted, prayed, preached, read the Bible, heard voices when he walked behind his plough, and communicated his revelations to the awe-struck slaves. They told him, in return, that, "if they had his sense, they would not serve any master in the world."

The biographies of slaves can hardly be individualized; they belong to the class. We know bare facts; it is only the general experience of human beings in like condition which can clothe them with life. The outlines are certain, the details are inferential. Thus, for instance, we know that Nat Turner's young wife was a slave; we know that she belonged to a different master from himself; we know little more than this, but this is much. For this is equivalent to saying, that, by day or by night, her husband had no more power to protect her than the man who lies bound upon a plundered vessel's deck has power to protect his wife on board the pirate schooner disappearing in the horizon. She may be well treated, she may be outraged; it is in the powerlessness that the agony lies. There is, indeed, one thing more which we do know of this young woman: the Virginia newspapers state that she was tortured under the lash, after her husband's execution, to make her produce his papers: this is all.

What his private experiences and special privileges or wrongs may have been, it is therefore now impossible to say. Travis was declared to be "more humane and fatherly to his slaves than any man in the county;" but it is astonishing how often this phenomenon occurs in the contemporary annals of slave insurrections. The chairman of the county court also stated, in pronouncing sentence, that Nat Turner had spoken of his master as "only too indulgent;" but this, for some reason, does not appear in his printed Confession, which only says, "He was a kind master, and placed the greatest confidence in me." It is very possible that it may have been so, but the printed accounts of Nat Turner's person look suspicious: he is described in Gov. Floyd's proclamation as having a scar on one of his temples, also one on the back of his neck, and a large knot on one of the bones of his right arm, produced by a blow; and although these were explained away in Virginia newspapers as having been produced by fights with his companions, yet such affrays are entirely foreign to the admitted habits of the man. It must therefore remain an open question, whether the scars and the knot were produced by black hands or by white.

Whatever Nat Turner's experiences of slavery might have been, it is certain that his plans were not suddenly adopted, but that he had brooded over them for years. To this day there are traditions among the Virginia slaves of the keen devices of "Prophet Nat." If he was caught with lime and lampblack in hand, conning over a half-finished county-map on the barn-door, he was always "planning what to do if he were blind;" or, "studying how to get to Mr. Francis's house." When he had called a meeting of slaves, and some poor whites came eavesdropping, the poor whites at once became the subjects for discussion: he incidentally mentioned that the masters had been heard threatening to drive them away; one slave had been ordered to shoot Mr. Jones's pigs, another to tear down Mr. Johnson's fences. The poor whites, Johnson and Jones, ran home to see to their homesteads, and were better friends than ever to Prophet Nat. . . .

When he came, therefore, to the barbecue on the appointed Sunday, and found not these four only, but two others, his first question to the intruders was, how they came thither. To this Will answered manfully, that his life was worth no more than the others, and "his liberty was as dear to him." This admitted him to confidence; and as Jack was known to be entirely under Hark's influence, the strangers were no bar to their discussion. Eleven hours they remained there, in anxious consultation: one can imagine those dusky faces, beneath the funereal woods, and amid the flickering of pine-knot torches, preparing that stern revenge whose shuddering echoes should ring through the land so long. Two things were at last decided: to begin their work that night; and to begin it with a massacre so swift and irresistible as to create in a few days more terror than many battles, and so spare the need of future bloodshed. "It was agreed that we should commence at home on that night, and, until we had armed and equipped ourselves and gained sufficient force, neither age nor sex was to be spared: which was invariably adhered to."

John Brown invaded Virginia with nineteen men, and with the avowed resolution to take no life but in self-defence. Nat Turner attacked Virginia from within, with six men, and with the determination to spare no life until his power was established. John Brown intended to pass rapidly through Virginia, and then retreat to the mountains. Nat Turner intended to "conquer Southampton County as the white men did in the Revolution, and then retreat, if necessary, to the Dismal Swamp." Each plan was deliberately matured; each was in its way practicable; but each was defeated by a single false step, as will soon appear.

We must pass over the details of horror, as they occurred during the next twenty-four hours. Swift and stealthy as Indians, the black men passed from house to house,—not pausing, not hesitating, as their terrible work went on. In one thing they were humaner than Indians, or than white men fighting against Indians: there was no gratuitous outrage beyond the death-blow itself, no insult, no mutilation; but in every house they entered, that blow fell on man, woman, and child, —nothing that had a white skin was spared. From every house they took arms and ammunition, and from a few money. On every plantation they found recruits: those dusky slaves, so obsequious to their master the day before, so prompt to sing and dance before his Northern visitors, were all swift to transform themselves into fiends of retribution now; show them sword or musket, and they grasped it, though it were an heirloom from Washington himself. The troop increased from house to house,—first to fifteen, then to forty, then to sixty. Some were armed with muskets, some with axes, some with scythes, some came on their masters' horses. As the numbers increased, they could be divided, and the awful work was carried on more rapidly still. The plan then was for an advanced guard of horsemen to approach each house at a gallop, and surround it till the others came up. Meanwhile, what agonies of terror must have taken place within, shared alike by innocent and by guilty! what memories of wrongs inflicted on those dusky creatures, by some,—what innocent participation, by others, in the penance! The outbreak lasted for but forty-eight hours; but, during that period, fifty-five whites were slain, without the loss of a single slave. . . .

When the number of adherents had increased to fifty or sixty, Nat Turner judged it time to strike at the county-seat, Jerusalem. Thither a few white fugitives had already fled, and couriers might thence be despatched for aid to Richmond and Petersburg, unless promptly intercepted. Besides, he could there find arms, ammunition, and money; though they had already obtained, it is dubiously reported, from eight hundred to one thousand dollars. On the way it was necessary to pass the plantation of Mr. Parker, three miles from Jerusalem. Some of the men wished to stop here and enlist some of their friends. Nat Turner objected, as the delay might prove dangerous; he yielded at last, and it proved fatal.

He remained at the gate with six or eight men; thirty or forty went to the house, half a mile distant. They remained too long, and he went alone to hasten them. During his absence a party of eighteen white men came up suddenly, dispersing the small guard left at the gate; and when the main body of slaves emerged from the house, they encountered, for the first time, their armed masters. The blacks halted; the whites advanced cautiously within a hundred yards, and fired a volley; on its being returned, they broke into disorder, and hurriedly retreated, leaving some wounded on the ground. The retreating whites were pursued, and were saved only by falling in with another band of fresh men from Jerusalem, with whose aid they turned upon the slaves, who in their turn fell into confusion. Turner, Hark, and about twenty men on horseback retreated in some order; the rest were scattered. The leader still planned to reach Jerusalem by a private way, thus evading pursuit; but at last decided to stop for the night, in the hope of enlisting additional recruits.

During the night the number increased again to forty, and they encamped on Major Ridley's plantation. An alarm took place during the darkness,—whether real or imaginary, does not appear,—and the men became scattered again. Proceeding to make fresh enlistments with the daylight, they were resisted at Dr. Blunt's house, where his slaves, under his orders, fired upon them; and this, with a later attack from a party of white men near Capt. Harris's, so broke up the whole force that they never re-united. The few who remained together agreed to separate for a few hours to see if any thing could be done to revive the insurrection, and meet again that evening at their original rendezvous. But they never reached it.

Gloomily came Nat Turner at nightfall into those gloomy woods where forty-eight hours before he had revealed the details of his terrible plot to his companions. At the outset all his plans had succeeded;

every thing was as he predicted: the slaves had come readily at his call; the masters had proved perfectly defenceless. Had he not been persuaded to pause at Parker's plantation, he would have been master before now of the arms and ammunition at Jerusalem; and with these to aid, and the Dismal Swamp for a refuge, he might have sustained himself indefinitely against his pursuers.

Now the blood was shed, the risk was incurred, his friends were killed or captured, and all for what? Lasting memories of terror, to be sure, for his oppressors; but, on the other hand, hopeless failure for the insurrection, and certain death for him. What a watch he must have kept that night! To that excited imagination, which had always seen spirits in the sky and blood-drops on the corn and hieroglyphic marks on the dry leaves, how full the lonely forest must have been of signs and solemn warnings! Alone with the fox's bark, the rabbit's rustle, and the screech-owl's scream, the self-appointed prophet brooded over his despair. Once creeping to the edge of the wood, he saw men stealthily approach on horseback. He fancied them some of his companions; but before he dared to whisper their ominous names, "Hark" or "Dred,"—for the latter was the name, since famous, of one of his more recent recruits,—he saw them to be white men, and shrank back stealthily beneath his covert.

There he waited two days and two nights,—long enough to satisfy himself that no one would rejoin him, and that the insurrection had hopelessly failed. The determined, desperate spirits who had shared his plans were scattered forever, and longer delay would be destruction for him also. He found a spot which he judged safe, dug a hole under a pile of fence-rails in a field, and lay there for six weeks, only leaving it for a few moments at midnight to obtain water from a neighboring spring. Food he had previously provided, without discovery, from a house near by.

Meanwhile an unbounded variety of rumors went flying through the State. The express which first reached the governor announced that the militia were retreating before the slaves. An express to Petersburg further fixed the number of militia at three hundred, and of blacks at eight hundred, and invented a convenient shower of rain to explain the dampened ardor of the whites. Later reports described the slaves as making three desperate attempts to cross the bridge over the Nottoway between Cross Keys and Jerusalem, and stated that the leader had been shot in the attempt. Other accounts put the number of negroes at three hundred, all well mounted and armed, with two or three white men as leaders. Their intention was supposed to be to reach the Dismal Swamp, and they must be hemmed in from that side. . . .

Meanwhile the cause of all this terror was made the object of desperate search. On Sept. 17 the governor offered a reward of five hundred dollars for his capture; and there were other rewards, swelling the amount to eleven hundred dollars,—but in vain. No one could track or trap him. On Sept. 30 a minute account of his capture appeared in the newspapers, but it was wholly false. On Oct. 7 there was another, and on Oct. 18 another; yet all without foundation. Worn out by confinement in his little cave, Nat Turner grew more adventurous, and began to move about stealthily by night, afraid to speak to any human being, but hoping to obtain some information that might aid his escape. Returning regularly to his retreat before daybreak, he might possibly have continued this mode of life until pursuit had ceased, had not a dog succeeded where men had failed. The creature accidentally smelt out the provisions hid in the cave, and finally led thither his masters, two negroes, one of whom was named Nelson. On discovering the formidable fugitive, they fled precipitately, when he hastened to retreat in an opposite direction. This was on Oct. 15; and from this moment the neighborhood was all alive with excitement, and five or six hundred men undertook the pursuit.

It shows a more than Indian adroitness in Nat Turner to have escaped capture any longer. The cave, the arms, the provisions, were found; and, lying among them, the notched stick of this miserable Robinson Crusoe, marked with five weary weeks and six days. But the man was gone. For ten days more he concealed himself among the wheat-stacks on Mr. Francis's plantation, and during this time was reduced almost to despair. Once he decided to surrender himself, and walked by night within two miles of Jerusalem before his purpose failed him. Three times he tried to get out of that neighborhood, but in vain: travelling by day was of course out of the question, and by night he found it impossible to elude the patrol. Again and again, therefore, he returned to his hiding-place; and, during his whole two months' liberty, never went five miles from the Cross Keys. On the 25th of October, he was at last discovered by Mr. Francis as he was emerging from a stack. A load of buckshot was instantly discharged at him, twelve of which passed through his hat as he fell to the ground. He escaped even then; but his pursuers were rapidly concentrating upon him, and it is perfectly astonishing that he could have eluded them for five days more.

On Sunday, Oct 30, a man named Benjamin Phipps, going out for the first time on patrol duty, was passing at noon a clearing in the woods where a number of pine-trees had long since been felled. There was a motion among their boughs; he stopped to watch it; and through a gap in the branches he saw, emerging from a hole in the earth beneath, the face of Nat Turner. Aiming his gun instantly, Phipps called on him to surrender. The fugitive, exhausted with watching and privation, entangled in the branches, armed only with a sword, had nothing to do but to yield,—sagaciously reflecting, also, as he afterwards explained, that the woods were full of armed men, and that he had better trust fortune for some later chance of escape, instead of desperately attempting it then. He was correct in the first impression, since there were fifty armed scouts within a circuit of two miles. His insurrection ended where it began; for this spot was only a mile and a half from the house of Joseph Travis.

Torn, emaciated, ragged, "a mere scarecrow," still wearing the hat perforated with buckshot, with his arms bound to his sides, he was driven before the levelled gun to the nearest house, that of a Mr. Edwards. He was confined there that night; but the news had spread so rapidly that within an hour after his arrival a hundred persons had collected, and the excitement became so intense "that it was with difficulty he could be conveyed alive to Jerusalem." The enthusiasm spread instantly through Virginia: M. Trezvant, the Jerusalem postmaster, sent notices of it far and near; and Gov. Floyd himself wrote a letter to the Richmond *Enquirer* to give official announcement of the momentous capture.

When Nat Turner was asked by Mr. T. R. Gray, the counsel assigned him, whether, although defeated, he still believed in his own Providential mission, he answered, as simply as one who came thirty years after him, "Was not Christ crucified?" In the same spirit, when arraigned before the court, "he answered, 'Not guilty,' saying to his counsel that he did not feel so." But apparently no argument was made in his favor by his counsel, nor were any witnesses called,—he being convicted on the testimony of Levi Waller, and upon his own confession, which was put in by Mr. Gray, and acknowledged by the prisoner before the six justices composing the court, as being "full, free, and voluntary." He was therefore placed in the paradoxical position of conviction by his own confession, under a plea of "Not guilty." The arrest took place on the 30th of October, 1831, the confession on the 1st of November, the trial and conviction on the 5th, and the execution on the following Friday, the 11th of November, precisely at noon. He met his death with perfect composure, declined addressing the multitude assembled, and told the sheriff in a firm voice that he was ready. Another account says that he "betrayed no emotion, and even hurried the executioner in the performance of his duty." "Not a limb nor a muscle was observed to move. His body, after his death, was given over to the surgeons for dissection."

The confession of the captive was published under authority of Mr. Gray, in a pamphlet, at Baltimore. Fifty thousand copies of it are said to have been printed; and it was "embellished with an accurate likeness of the brigand, taken by Mr. John Crawley, portrait-painter, and lithographed by Endicott & Swett, at Baltimore." The newly established *Liberator* said of it, at the time, that it would "only serve to rouse up other leaders, and hasten other insurrections," and advised grand juries to indict Mr. Gray. I have never seen a copy of the original pamphlet; it is not easily to be found in any of our public libraries; and I have heard of but one as still existing, although the Confession itself has been repeatedly reprinted. Another small pamphlet, containing the main features of the outbreak, was published at New York during the same year, and this is in my possession. But the greater part of the facts which I have given were gleaned from the contemporary newspapers.

Who now shall go back thirty years, and read the heart of this extraordinary man, who, by the admission of his captors, "never was known to swear an oath, or drink a drop of spirits;" who, on the same authority, "for natural intelligence and quickness of apprehension was surpassed by few men," "with a mind capable of attaining any thing;" who knew no book but his Bible, and that by heart; who devoted himself soul and body to the cause of his race, without a trace of personal hope or fear; who laid his plans so shrewdly that they came at last with less warning than any earthquake on the doomed community around; and who, when that time arrived, took the life of man, woman, and child, without a throb of compunction, a word of exultation, or an act of superfluous outrage? Mrs. Stowe's "Dred" seems dim and melodramatic beside the actual Nat Turner, and De Quincey's "Avenger" is his only parallel in imaginative literature. Mr. Gray, his counsel, rises into a sort of bewildered enthusiasm with the prisoner before him. "I shall not attempt to describe the effect of his narrative, as told and commented on by himself, in the condemned hole of the prison. The calm, deliberate composure with which he spoke of his late deeds and intentions, the expression of his fiend-like face when excited by enthusiasm, still bearing the stains of the blood of helpless innocence about him, clothed with rags and covered with chains, yet daring to raise his manacled hands to heaven, with a spirit soaring above the attributes of man,—I looked on him, and the blood curdled in my veins." . . .

While these things were going on, the enthusiasm for the Polish Revolution was rising to its height. The nation was ringing with a peal of joy, on hearing that at Frankfort the Poles had killed fourteen thousand Russians. The *Southern Religious Telegraph* was publishing an impassioned address to Kosciuszko; standards were being consecrated for Poland in the larger cities; heroes like Skrzynecki, Czartoryski, Rozyski, Raminski, were choking the trump of Fame with their complicated patronymics. These are all forgotten now; and this poor negro, who did not even possess a name, beyond one abrupt monosyllable,—for even the name of Turner was the master's property,— still lives, a memory of terror, and a symbol of wild retribution.

16

The Civil War and
Slave Rebellion

*From the beginning of the Civil War there were those
in the northern states who insisted that the slaves should be
emancipated and armed by the government. Some, like the anonymous "Insurrectionist" who wrote an article in* The Liberator
*of April 26, 1861, urged the government to foment slave rebel-
lions as a means of quickly bringing the South to its knees. And
when, yielding to pressure from radicals and abolitionists, black
and white, Lincoln in September, 1862, issued his preliminary
emancipation proclamation, the Richmond* Enquirer *equated
abolition with slave insurrection, and denounced the president
as a "Fiend." In the next year, as blacks were mustered into the
Union Army, black leaders like Frederick Douglass traveled
throughout the North, urging free Negroes to enlist, and calling
on them to "Remember Denmark Vesey . . . remember Nathaniel Turner. . . ."*

RICHMOND *ENQUIRER,* OCTOBER 1, 1862

Lincoln and His Proclamation

Abraham Lincoln's Proclamation ordaining servile insurrection in
the Confederate States has not been for a moment misunderstood
either North or South. After undertaking to destroy four thousand
millions of our property at the dash of a pen, Lincoln proceeds to say:

"And the Executive government of the United States, including the
military and naval authority thereof, will *recognize and maintain* the
freedom of such persons, and *will do no act or acts to repress such
persons, or any of them, in any efforts they may make for their actual
freedom."*

This is as much as to bid the slaves to rise in insurrection, with the
assurance of the aid of the whole military and naval power of the
United States. . . . Deliberately, and with full purpose, our enemies
have entered upon this step.

Is there anyone who has not reflected upon the nature of the agency
which Lincoln now invokes? A servile war is necessarily one of extermination, and the peculiar character of the negro, adds to its inevitable horrors. Released from authority, he is at once a savage; and the
very ignorance which drives him to his own destruction, stimulates

him to the darkest excesses. How was it in Southampton in 1831, when
Nat Turner engaged in the work to which Lincoln now invites? Not
satisfied with murdering the few men who fell into their power, they
massacred even the babe in the cradle. They in this manner exterminated the family of Mr. Travis, Turner's kind and indulgent master.
Next, Mrs. Waller and her *ten* children were slain and piled in a
heap on the floor. Near by, a school of little girls was captured, and
all massacred except one who escaped. The family of Mrs. Vaughan
was next destroyed. In this manner between Sunday night and Monday noon, they had murdered fifty-five persons, nearly all of whom
were women and children.

This is the sort of work Lincoln desires to see. This is the agency
which Lincoln now invokes! . . . Butler has been called infamous—
by common consent he is known as the Beast. But Butler is a saint
compared to his master. In addition to all that Butler authorized,
Lincoln adds butchery—even the butchery of *babes!* Language is too
poor to furnish a name suitable for such a character. . . . What shall
we call him?—coward? assassin? savage?—the murderer of women and
babes, and the false destroyer of his own deluded allies?—Shall we
consider these as all embodied in the word "fiend!" and shall we call
him *that?*—Lincoln, the Fiend! let history take hold of him, and let
the civilized world fling its scorpion lash at him!

We have described Lincoln's *intentions* and *wishes* towards us. . . .
But, thank Heaven, we are not delivered over to his will! We are
abundantly able to maintain a salutary domestic authority at the same
time that our armies meet Lincoln's in the field. Lincoln would simply
drive our servants to their destruction. Cheerful and happy now, he
plots their death. An insurrection is their swift destruction. How was
it in the long-hatched Southampton case to which we have already
referred? Sunday night the insurrectionists began their work. Monday
at noon they were in full flight, and hiding in the swamps. It needs
scarcely to be asked how they fared.—They suffered a terrible retribution. They were hunted like wild beasts, as they were, and were at
first killed wherever found. Several of these murderers of women and
children were taken at the Cross Keys, and their heads cut off on the
spot; afterwards captives were tried and hung—among them Nat
Turner, the leader. Some innocent ones are believed to have perished
with the guilty.

So it will ever be with servile insurrections if attempted here. They
can gain no foodhold with proper vigilance. They will, at any rate,
be as quickly suppressed as a common riot, and terrible punishment
will fall on the guilty. But what does the Fiend care for that? He is
the common enemy of both white and black. . . .

17

A Pioneer Black Historian
and Nat Turner

In August, 1861, in the obscure abolitionist publication Pine and Palm, *there appeared an article on Nat Turner by the former slave and abolitionist leader, William Wells Brown. Based largely on the* Confessions, *Brown's essay was republished two years later in* The Black Man, *a collection of fifty-three sketches of black leaders. An abridged version of the essay appeared in 1867 in Brown's most important work,* The Negro in the American Rebellion. *To Brown, writing in 1861, Nat Turner was a "martyr to the freedom of his race." The account includes a number of incidents which probably reflect Brown's imagination rather than historical reality, such as Turner's speech to his followers at the inception of the rebellion.*

By 1880, when Brown published another interpretation of Turner, he was somewhat more restrained. Turner was now "an insane man—made so by slavery." Brown still felt that slave rebellions were proofs to the world of black humanity and courage, but he warned his people not to "live upon the past," but to emulate the "cultivated whites" and therefore prove the falsity of notions of racial inferiority. The difference between Brown's interpretations of 1861 and 1880 reflects perhaps a personal disillusionment at a time when the gains of the Civil War and Reconstruction seemed to be disappearing.

NAT TURNER [1]

Biography is individual history, as distinguished from that of communities, of nations, and of worlds. Eulogy is that deserved applause which springs from the virtues and attaches itself to the characters of men. This is not intended either as a biography or a eulogy, but simply a sketch of one whose history has hitherto been neglected, and to the memory of whom the American people are not prepared to do justice.

On one of the oldest and largest plantations in Southampton county, Virginia, owned by Benjamin Turner, Esq., Nat was born a slave, on the 2d of October, 1800. His parents were of unmixed African descent. Surrounded as he was by the superstition of the slave quarters, and

[1] From William Wells Brown, *The Black Man: His Antecedents, His Genius, and His Achievements* (Boston, 1863), pp. 59–75.

141

being taught by his mother that he was born for a prophet, a preacher, and a deliverer of his race, it was not strange that the child should have imbibed the principles which were afterwards developed in his career. Early impressed with the belief that he had seen visions, and received communications direct from God, he, like Napoleon, regarded himself as a being of destiny. In his childhood Nat was of an amiable disposition; but circumstances in which he was placed as a slave, brought out incidents that created a change in his disposition, and turned his kind and docile feeling into the most intense hatred to the white race.

Being absent one night from his master's plantation without a pass, he was caught by Whitlock and Mull, the two district patrolers, and severely flogged. This act of cruelty inflamed the young slave, and he resolved upon having revenge. Getting two of the boys of a neighboring plantation to join him, Nat obtained a long rope, went out at night on the road through which the officers had their beat, and stationing his companions, one on each side of the road, he stretched the rope across, fastening each end to a tree, and drawing it tight. His rope thus fixed, and his accomplices instructed how to act their part, Nat started off up the road. The night being dark, and the rope only six or eight inches from the ground, the slave felt sure that he would give his enemies a "high fall."

Nat hearing them, he called out in a disguised voice, "Is dat you, Jim?" To this Whitlock replied, "Yes, dis is me." Waiting until the white men were near him, Nat started off upon a run, followed by the officers. The boy had placed a sheet of white paper in the road, so that he might know at what point to jump the rope, so as not to be caught in his own trap. Arriving at the signal he sprung over the rope, and went down the road like an antelope. But not so with the white men, for both were caught by the legs and thrown so hard upon the ground that Mull had his shoulder put out of joint, and his face terribly lacerated by the fall; while Whitlock's left wrist was broken, and his head bruised in a shocking manner. Nat hastened home, while his companions did the same, not forgetting to take with them the clothes line which had been so serviceable in the conflict. The patrolers were left on the field of battle, crying, swearing, and calling for help.

Snow seldom falls as far south as the southern part of Virginia; but when it does, the boys usually have a good time snow-balling, and on such occasions the slaves, old and young women and men, are generally pelted without mercy, and with no right to retaliate. It was only a few months after his affair with the patrolers, that Nat was attacked by a gang of boys, who chased him some distance, snow-balling with all their power. The slave boy knew the lads, and determined upon revenge. Waiting till night, he filled his pockets with rocks, and went into the street. Very soon the same gang of boys were at his heels, and pelting him. Concealing his face so as not to be known, Nat discharged his rocks in every direction, until his enemies had all taken to their heels.

The ill treatment he experienced at the hands of the whites, and the visions he claimed to have seen, caused Nat to avoid, as far as he could, all intercourse with his fellow-slaves, and threw around him a gloom and melancholy that disappeared only with his life.

Both the young slave and his friends averred that a full knowledge of the alphabet came to him in a single night. Impressed with the belief that his mission was a religious one, and this impression strengthened by the advice of his grandmother, a pious but ignorant woman, Nat commenced preaching when about twenty-five of age, but never went beyond his own master's locality. In stature he was under the middle size, long armed, round-shouldered, and strongly marked with the African features. A gloomy fire burned in his looks, and he had a melancholy expression of countenance. He never tasted a drop of ardent spirits in his life, and was never known to smile. In the year 1828 new visions appeared to Nat, and he claimed to have direct communication with God. Unlike most of those born under the influence of slavery, he had no faith in conjuring, fortune-telling, or dreams, and always spoke with contempt of such things. Being hired out to cruel masters, he ran away, and remained in the woods thirty days, and could have easily escaped to the free states, as did his father some years before; but he received, as he says in his confession a communication from the spirit. . . .

The plan of an insurrection was now formed in his own mind, and the time had arrived for him to take others into the secret; and he at once communicated his ideas to four of his friends, in whom he had implicit confidence. Hark Travis, Nelson Williams, Sam Edwards, and Henry Porter were slaves like himself, and like him had taken their names from their masters. A meeting must be held with these, and it must take place in some secluded place, where the whites would not disturb them; and a meeting was appointed. The spot where they assembled was as wild and romantic as were the visions that had been impressed upon the mind of their leader.

Three miles from where Nat lived was a dark swamp filled with reptiles, in the middle of which was a dry spot, reached by a narrow, winding path, and upon which human feet seldom trod, on account of its having been the place where a slave had been tortured to death by a slow fire, for the crime of having flogged his cruel and inhuman master. The night for the meeting arrived, and they came together. Hark brought a pig; Sam, bread; Nelson, sweet potatoes; and Henry, brandy; and the gathering was turned into a feast. Others were taken in, and joined the conspiracy. All partook heartily of the food and drank freely, except Nat. He fasted and prayed. It was agreed that the

revolt should commence that night, and in their own master's house-
holds, and that each slave should give his oppressor the death blow.
Before they left the swamp Nat made a speech, in which he said,
"Friends and brothers: We are to commence a great work to-night.
Our race is to be delivered from slavery, and God has appointed us
as the men to do his bidding, and let us be worthy of our calling. I
am told to slay all the whites we encounter, without regard to age or
sex. We have no arms or ammunition, but we will find these in the
houses of our oppressors, and as we go on others can join us. Remember that we do not go forth for the sake of blood and carnage, but it
is necessary that in the commencement of this revolution all the whites
we meet should die, until we shall have an army strong enough to
carry on the war upon a Christian basis. Remember that our is not a
war for robbery and to satisfy our passions; it is a struggle for freedom.
Ours must be deeds, and not words. Then let's away to the scene of
action."

. . . After going through a mere form of trial, he was convicted
and executed at Jerusalem, the county seat for Southampton county,
Virginia. Not a limb trembled or a muscle was observed to move. Thus
died Nat Turner, at the early age of thirty-one years—a martyr to the
freedom of his race, and a victim to his own fanaticism. He meditated
upon the wrongs of his oppressed and injured people, till the idea of
their deliverance excluded all other ideas from his mind, and he devoted his life to its realization. Every thing appeared to him a vision,
and all favorable omens were signs from God. That he was sincere in
all that he professed, there is not the slightest doubt. After being defeated he might have escaped to the free states, but the hope of raising
a new band kept him from doing so.

He impressed his image upon the minds of those who once beheld
him. His looks, his sermons, his acts, and his heroism live in the hearts
of his race, on every cotton, sugar, and rice plantation at the south.
The present generation of slaves have a superstitious veneration for
his name, and believe that in another insurrection Nat Turner will
appear and take command. He foretold that at his death the sun would
refuse to shine, and that there would be signs of disapprobation given
from heaven. And it is true that the sun was darkened, a storm gathered, and more boisterous weather had never appeared in Southampton county than on the day of Nat's execution. The sheriff, warned by
the prisoner, refused to cut the cord that held the trap. No black man
would touch the rope. A poor old white man, long besotted by drink,
was brought forty miles to be the executioner. And even the planters,
with all their prejudice and hatred, believed him honest and sincere. . . .

From this insurrection, and other manifestations of insubordination
by the slave population, the southern people, if they are wise, should

learn a grave lesson; for the experience of the past might give them some clew to the future.

Thirty years' free discussion has materially changed public opinion in the non-slaveholding states, and a negro insurrection, in the present excited state of the nation, would not receive the condemnation that it did in 1831. The right of man to the enjoyment of freedom is a settled point; and where he is deprived of this, without any criminal act of his own, it is his duty to regain his liberty at every cost.

If the oppressor is struck down in the contest, his fall will be a just one, and all the world will applaud the act.

This is a new era, and we are in the midst of the most important crisis that our country has yet witnessed. And in the crisis the negro is an important item. Every eye is now turned towards the south, looking for another Nat Turner.

The great struggle for our elevation is now with ourselves.[2] We may talk of Hannibal, Euclid, Phyllis Wheatly, Benjamin Bannaker, and Toussaint L'Overture, but the world will ask us for our men and women of this day. We cannot live upon the past; we must stand the test, one that we have a legitimate right to. To do this, we must imitate the best examples set us by the cultivated whites, and by so doing we will teach them that they can claim no superiority on account of race.

The efforts made by oppressed nations or communities to throw off their chains, entitles them to, and gains for them the respect of mankind. This, the blacks never made, or what they did was so feeble as scarcely to call for comment. The planning of Denmark Vesey for an insurrection in South Carolina, was noble, and he deserved a better fate; but he was betrayed by the race that he was attempting to serve.

Nat Turner's strike for liberty was the outburst of feelings of an insane man—made so by slavery. True, the negro did good service at the battles of Wagner, Honey Hill, Port Hudson, Milliken's Bend, Poison Springs, Obistee and Petersburg. Yet it would have been far better if they had commenced earlier, or had been under leaders of their own color. The St. Domingo revolution brought forth men of courage. But the subsequent course of the people as a government, reflects little or no honor on the race. They have floated about like a ship without a rudder, ever since the expulsion of Rochambeau.

The fact is the world likes to see the exhibition of pluck on the part of an oppressed people, even though they fail in their object. It is these outbursts of love of liberty that gains respect and sympathy for the enslaved. Therefore, I bid God speed to the men and women of the South, in their effort to break the long spell of lethargy that hangs over the race.

[2] From William Wells Brown, *My Southern Home: or, the South and Its People* (np, 1880), pp. 243–44.

18

Nat Turner Remembered: The 1880s

Despite the frustrations of the post–Reconstruction era and the beginning of the ascendancy of Booker T. Washington and his policy of racial accommodation, interest in Nat Turner among blacks did not wane. A publisher in Petersburg, Virginia reprinted the Confessions *in 1881, and during this decade there appeared two mammoth contributions to black history, George Washington Williams's* History of the Negro Race in America, *and Rev. William J. Simmons's* Men of Mark, *both of which included sketches of Turner. For Williams, Turner was a "martyr to freedom," a "Black John Brown," who would never be forgotten by black Americans. Simmons' portrait was positive, but more restrained, reflecting his view that most slaves were patient under slavery and loyal even during the Civil War. In 1884, the young black editor, T. Thomas Fortune, published a eulogistic if somewhat pedestrian poem on Turner, and five years later two black newspapers engaged in a debate over whether it was more appropriate to build a statue to a white hero—John Brown, or a black one—Turner. The debate illustrated the tension between an older tradition of color-blind abolitionism, represented by Frederick Douglass, Jr. of the Washington, D.C.* National Leader, *and the racial consciousness of the New York* Age.

NAT TURNER [1]

By T. Thomas Fortune

> He stood erect, a man as proud
> As ever to a tyrant bowed
> Unwilling head or bent a knee,
> And longed, while bending, to be free:
> And o'er his ebon features came
> A shadow—'twas of manly shame—
> Aye, shame that he should wear a chain
> And feel his manhood writhed with pain,
> Doomed to a life of plodding toil,
> Shamefully rooted to the soil!

[1] From Cleveland *Gazette*, November 22, 1884.

He stood erect; his eyes flashed fire;
His robust form convulsed with ire;
"I will be free! I will be free!
Or, fighting, die a man!" cried he.

Virginia's hills were lit at night—
The slave had risen in his might.
And far and near Nat's wail went forth,
To South and East, and West and North,
And strong men trembled in their power,
And weak men felt 'twas now their hour.
"I will be free! I will be free!
Or, fighting, die a man!" cried he.
The tyrant's arm was all too strong,
Had swayed dominion all too long;
And so the hero met his end
As all who fall as Freedom's friend.

The blow he struck shook slavery's throne;
His cause was just, e'en skeptics own;
And round his lowly grave soon swarmed
Freedom's brave hosts for freedom arm'd.
That host was swollen by Nat's kin
To fight for Freedom, Freedom win,
Upon the soil that spurned his cry:
"I will be free, or I will die!"

Let tyrants quake, e'en in their power,
For sure will come the awful hour
When they must give an answer, why
Heroes in chains should basely die,
Instead of rushing to the field,
And counting battle ere they yield.

NEW YORK AGE, JANUARY 12, 1889

John Brown and Nat. Turner

The Washington National Leader, of which Mr. Frederick Douglass Jr., is associate editor, recently wanted to know if it was not almost time that the colored people were doing something to perpetuate the memory of John Brown.

We think not. We think John Brown's memory is strong enough to perpetuate itself, even if all the Negroes in the universe were suddenly to become extinct. His memory is a part of the history of the government. It is embalmed in a thousand songs and stories. Your own father, Mr. Douglass, has written a lecture on the life of John Brown, which will help along the perpetuation of that great and good man. A German scholar has just given a brochure to the world, which competent critics declare a most judicial and thorough study of the character of John Brown ever produced.

No; John Brown's memory stands no immediate prospect of vanishing into oblivion.

But there is another, a fore-runner of John Brown, if you please, who stands in more need of our copper pennies to be melted down into a monument to perpetuate his memory than John Brown. We refer of course to Nat. Turner, who was executed at Jerusalem, Southampton County, Virginia, for inciting and leading his fellow slaves to insurrection long before John Brown invaded Kansas and planned his unfortunate raid on Harpers Ferry.

Nat. Turner was a black hero. He preferred death to slavery. He ought to have a monument. White men care nothing for his memory. We should cherish it.

It is quite remarkable that whenever colored men move that somebody's memory be perpetuated, that somebody's memory is always a white man's.

Young Mr. Douglass should mend his ways in this matter. His great father will some day have a monument which he will have eminently deserved and it will have to be built by the pennies of colored people. White people build monuments to white people.

WASHINGTON *NATIONAL LEADER*, JANUARY 19, 1889

The editor of the New York Age draws the color line over our proposition to erect a monument to the memory of the life and character of John Brown and suggests that Nat. Turner stands more in need of one. We have no fault to find with his suggestion; but when he sluringly remarks "that whenever colored men move that somebody's memory be perpetuated, that somebody's memory is always a white man's," he helps to sustain the charge made against us by the whites of the South, "that it is the colored people who draw the color line." We have always been of the opinion that the character and good acts of a man were worthy of emulation and perpetuation, and not his color. But the young gentleman who edits the Age makes color the condition of action towards erecting a monument in honor of one who broke the chains from about his neck and made him free to act for himself. The suggestion made by the Leader has led the Age to discover no good traits in Nat. Turner's character that precedes his being black. "Nat. Turner was a black hero. He preferred death to slavery.

He ought to have a monument. White men care nothing for his memory. We should cherish it."

Nat. Turner has been dead many years, and the editor of the Age has never found time to suggest a monument for him until now, and he only suggests it now in opposition to one being erected in honor of John Brown, because he was so fortunate or unfortunate as to be born white. Prejudice among the white people of this country is dying out; but the editor of the Age would encourage it among the blacks. This is not wise nor just, but what does the Age care? We trust you will get straight on this matter. If you wish to slur at the proposer of a monument for John Brown, do so; but don't set up such a ridiculous strain of reasoning as an objection, based on color. You can do better we know, if you will only try.

NEW YORK *AGE*, JANUARY 26, 1889

Nat. Turner

Fred Douglass, Jr., in the National Leader, exhibits too much temper in replying to our editorial suggesting a monument to Nat. Turner instead of one to John Brown. It indicates that we touched the Achillesean weak spot in his armor.

"That Nat. Turner has been dead many years" is almost equally true of John Brown. John Brown lost his life in urging and leading an insurrection of slaves. Nat. Turner at an earlier date did the same. The conduct of the one was no more heroic than that of the other. The whites have embalmed the memory of John Brown in marble and vellum, and Fred Douglass, Jr., now wants colored people to embalm it in brass; while the memory of the black hero is preserved neither in marble, vellum nor brass.

What we protest against is Negro worship of white men and the memory of white men, to the utter exclusion of colored men equally patriotic and self-sacrificing. It is the absence of race pride and race unity which makes white men despise black men all the world over.

We do not draw the color line. Fred Douglass, Jr., knows that his insinuation in this regard is a baseless invention. We simply insist that in theory "do unto others as you would have them do unto you" is splendid, but that in practice the philosophy of conduct is "do unto others as they do unto you," the sooner to make them understand that a dagger of the right sort has two edges, the one as sharp of blade as the other.

We yield to none in admiration of the character and sacrifices of John Brown. The character and sacrifices of Nat. Turner are dearer to us because he was of us and exhibited in the most abject condition the heroism and race devotion which have illustrated in all times the sort of men who are worthy to be free.

NEW YORK *AGE*, DECEMBER 28, 1889

Nat Turner: A Senior Oration by a Student of the New York City College

Arthur W. Handy is a young man who graduated from Grammar School No. 81, of which Prof. Charles L. Reason is principal, some few years ago and entered the New York City College. He is at present a member of the graduating class and a candidate for the post of class orator next June. The following is his senior oration, entitled "A Hero," it being one of three essays, limited to 550 words each, required to decide who shall occupy the position so highly prized.

"In every age, in every clime, heroes have arisen. Men who have laid down family ties, honor, and even life itself for the maintenance of a principle. Men whose courage and devotion under the most trying circumstances have caused mankind to wonder in silent admiration. The world knows nothing of some of its greatest heroes, for there are forms of greatness which die and make no sign. There are martyrs that miss the palm, but not the stake. Heroes without the laurels and conquerors without the triumph. It has been said and said truly that the times make the man. Greece had her Leonidas, Rome her Horatius and England her Cromwell. Nathaniel Turner was a hero! Characterized from the rest of his down trodden brethren by natural aptitude, by dint of hard work in secret places Turner learned to read and write.

"Exercising his knowledge by reading such documents as the Right to Petition, Turner's eyes were opened. He saw that all men were created free and equal. Immediately like a flash of lightning his whole being was suffused with a noble idea. Like Joan of Arc, he saw his mission in the flash of meteors, he heard his summons in the roaring of the wind. Collecting about him those whom he could trust, he planned a formidable uprising stretching from the land of Dixie to the palmetto groves of South Carolina. Slowly but surely the movement progressed. The time at last arrived when the blow was to have been struck. When the slave with sword in hand was to strike one blow for liberty. Was it done? Your histories do not record it. Nathaniel Turner was betrayed and by one of his own number. And yet how history repeats itself. How many such causes have been lost through treachery. Yet he died like a hero. No murmur escaped his lips. No sigh of regret for the failure of his plans.

"With his death ceased all such attempts for freedom until the immortal John Brown took up the cause. And yet how different were the surroundings of these two men, and still both aimed at the same result.

Turner alone, friendless, with nothing but his ignorant companions to cheer him in the mighty struggle, worked with undaunted fortitude. Brown was watched and encouraged by a host of admiring friends. Thousands of dollars were appropriated for his scheme and some of the noblest spirits on this continent bade him God-speed. How strange it is that these two men, brought up under such different influences, should have been animated by the same desire. The crime for which Brown died at Harpers Ferry was identical with the one for which Turner died in South Carolina, the means by which it was to have been accomplished the same. And yet all the world unites in giving glory and honor to Brown while Turner is forgotten.

"Let those of us in whom the love of humanity responds to the spirit of the Bard Burns, who in his 'Honest Poverty' declares that 'a man's a man for a' that,' lift the veil of obscurity that shrouds the deeds of black men at the South. When the Nation's history shall be written in the days to come Nathan Hale and Crispus Attucks will be accorded places side by side. May we not hope that John Brown and Nathaniel Turner will be surrounded with an equal halo of glory? Then rest in peace, thou more than hero, in other ages, in distant climes, when truth shall get a hearing, thy name shall be mentioned with reverence and with honor."

that sat on him had a bow; and a crown was given unto him: and he went forth conquering and to conquer." Though Nat was a religious fanatic, yet he deemed any means justifiable for the accomplishment of his purpose and for making the impression that he was a prophet and servant of God. He wrote hieroglyphics and quotations on leaves and blades of fodder, and these found, according to his prediction, caused the slaves to believe him a miraculous being, endowed with supernatural powers. He spat blood at pleasure, but it proved to be the coloring matter of the log-wood, stolen from his master's dye pots. At his baptism crowds gathered, some from curiosity and others from a belief in his prophecy that a white dove would descend from heaven and alight upon his shoulder. This prophecy explains the reviling to which he refers in his confession, no doubt, with the intention of making the impression that the white people disapproved of religious toleration. That Nat was believed must not be taken as proof of the ignorance and exclusive superstition of the blacks. It is the custom to consider the whites as far advanced as they are at present, and the slaves as debased, ignorant, and superstitious creatures as in their native state. But the eclipse of the sun in February, and its peculiar appearance in August, 1831, had as grave an effect upon the former as upon the latter. The "green" or "blue" day is still remembered by some of our citizens, and at the time something terrible was hourly expected. Upon the scaffold Nat declared that after his execution it would grow dark and rain for the last time. It did actually rain, and there was for some time a dry spell. This alarmed many of the whites as well as the negroes. Conjuring was the Southern counterpart of the old Puritan belief in witchcraft. It is generally attributed to the negroes, some of whom professed to be "conjur doctors," but many a gouty master believed himself conjured. Nor are such signs of superstition and fear wanting at the present day. The negroes are still afraid to pass graveyards and places where murders have been committed, and see the wrath of God in every unusual occurrence.

Thus the insurrection "was not instigated by motives of revenge or sudden anger, but the result of long deliberation and a settled purpose of mind, the offspring of gloomy fanaticism acting upon materials but too well prepared for such impressions," and of love of self-importance, encouraged by the efforts of negro preachers, who were influenced by external affairs, and employed in circulating inflammatory and seditious periodicals. Those who have received most are the most jealous and ready to complain. Nat Turner, as the Southampton slaves in general, was like a spoiled child, who, having been allowed too many privileges in youth, soon thinks he ought to be master of all he surveys. The calling of a Constitutional Convention, to meet in October, 1829, inspired in the slaves of Matthews, Isle of Wight, and the neighboring counties hopes of emancipation, and in case of failure of such declaration a determination to rebel and massacre the whites. Doubtless Nat had heard the same subjects discussed, and, being conscious of the results of the convention, which not only failed to emancipate the slaves, but limited the right of suffrage to the whites, he considered it time to carry out his threats. He was undoubtedly inspired with the hope of freedom, and the mere discussion of emancipation by a convention may have led him to believe that many of the whites would sympathize with his schemes. He is said to have passed the home of some poor white people because he considered it useless to kill those who thought no better of themselves than they did of the negroes. He also said that after he had gained a firm foothold he intended to spare all the women and children and the men who offered no resistance. But the watchword of all was indiscriminate slaughter and plunder. . . .

The Southampton insurrection was a landmark in the history of slavery. Little was known of it on account of the suppression by the Southern States of all such reports as were likely to arouse an insurrectionary spirit and because of exaggerated accounts given in the North. It was the forerunner of the great slavery debates which resulted in the abolition of slavery in the United States, and was, indirectly, most instrumental in bringing about this result. Its importance is truly conceived by the old negroes of Southampton and vicinity, who reckon all time from "Nat's Fray," or "Old Nat's War." It is, in fact, the only plot by rebellious Southern negroes which deserves the name of insurrection. More negroes were connected with the Gabriel insurrection, but they were discovered, dispersed, and their leader executed without the loss of one white person. Both were influenced by the attempts of former insurgent slaves, but the Southampton rebellion was directly encouraged by the abolition movement in the United States, while Gabriel met with encouragement only from foreigners. The two insurrections also agree in that, in both, religious fanaticism and delusion played a very important role. The true character of the negro and the nature of the institution of slavery in the American colonies and States can best be learned from a thorough study of slave revolts. . . .

History records no instance in which two races equally free have lived together in harmony. The Anglo-Boer dispute in the Transvaal is a question of race supremacy, and Sir Alfred Milner, the British Commissioner in South Africa, says: "It seems a paradox, but it is true that the only effective way of protecting our subjects is to help them to cease to be our subjects." Mr. Jefferson said that the negro and white races, equally free, could not live under the same government. They cannot amalgamate and solve the question as did Greece and Rome. Consequently, either the negro must be colonized or occupy an inferior position. But that the negroes may occupy an inferior position in the United States, they must be equally distributed in all sections of the country. Otherwise in those sections farthest removed there will exist sympathy for the negro, and a misconception and misrepresentation of the relation of the two races. The whites of the North and West believe the negro is cheated and persecuted. In many sections it is actually believed that rejected lovers in the South black themselves and commit the outrages so frequently perpetrated by negroes. So far the two races have lived in the South as equals before the law, because the majority of the negroes remain conscious of the superiority of the white race. For this reason negro labor has been preferred to white. The negro gladly accepts gifts in the form of food, old clothes, etc., and performs menial services, as cook, coachman, and servant of every description. Custom and habit exclude the poor whites of the South from such offices. In this way the negroes are rapidly acquiring property which, together with the free schools, supported principally by the whites, free amusement, and cheap newspapers, enables them to give their children educations equal to that of the ordinary whites, while the poorer whites are unable to secure even common-school education. Consequently, the number of servants in the South is gradually decreasing, and the white people learning to perform for themselves the ordinary services. But this education of the negro, which fits him for the highest offices in the land, renders him a useless and discontented citizen. The whites cannot submit to negro rule and self-assertion. With the negroes equally distributed over the Union, this could be easily avoided. But so long as they remain with equal citizenship in the South they will continue a burden to themselves and to the white population. The South will remain the "Solid South" and prefer exclusion from national offices rather than allow the State offices to fall into the hands of negroes. . . .

In conclusion, the following considerations may be submitted:

First. The possibility and danger of negro insurrection are largely responsible for the suppression of the slave trade and the substitution of negro slavery for negro servitude. The negroes at first enjoyed the same rights and privileges as the white indented servants, with the exception of the possibility of social distinction and amalgamation with the white inhabitants. The Indians, English, French, and native whites of bad character took advantage of these facts to stir up discontent among the servants as well as the free negroes. Consequently, stringent legislation, which gradually led to the enslavement of the negro was necessary to put an end to such evils.

Second. The condition of slavery in Virginia was not such as to arouse insurrections among the slaves. An affection existed between master and slave which has been handed down to their descendants, which dispelled that physical aversion and incompatibility of character and temper of the superior race for the inferior, stopped internecine wars, and prevented the general tendency of civilization to gradually blot out the inferior race. By this means alone has the perpetuity of the negro race been assured. Not one insurrection was due to cruel treatment or inbred desire for freedom.

Third. Superstition, religious fanaticism, and love of plunder and pillage have played a part in every slave insurrection in Virginia. Delusion has always been active. The weak and cowardly have participated, while the brave and intelligent slaves, in general, remained loyal.

Fourth. French and English intrigues, especially the latter, have, from the earliest colonial period, exerted a powerful influence over the slaves of Virginia. Sierra Leone, on the west coast of Africa, was settled by negroes who fought on the British side in the War of Independence.

Fifth. The contiguity of three large bodies of free negroes—those of the West Indies, of South America, and of the Northern States and Canada—tended to incite the slaves of the South and to convince the people that the days of slavery were numbered.

Sixth. The Indian troubles not only incited the slaves to rebellion, but aroused in those sections more remote a sympathy for the negro which bore evil fruit.

Seventh. No slave insurrection would have occurred in Virginia but for the abolition movement in other sections. On the contrary, the emancipation sentiment in Virginia would ultimately have led to the freedom of the slave and his colonization in Liberia. This example would have been followed by other Southern States. What Virginia and the South feared was not emancipation, but fanaticism. Self-preservation, the first law of nature, was the basic principle in the origin as well as in the continuance of negro slavery in Virginia.

Eighth. The slave legislation of Virginia was efficient and mild. It rendered the success of slave insurrection impossible, and laid the foundation of a training which rendered the negro a good and worthy citizen.

Ninth. Servile insurrections delayed the emancipation of the slaves in the United States. The emancipation sentiment was strong in the South as well as in the North, but abolition without colonization beyond the limits of the United States was advocated by few. Abolition was a war measure rather than the result of unanimity of Northern sentiment therefor.

Tenth. The negro, conscious of his inferiority, and equally distributed over the country, will make a peaceful and useful citizen. But educated for the highest offices, which he can never fill, he will remain a source of disturbance and insurrection, and under such circumstances it will be best for both races that the negro be transported beyond the limits of the United States.

20

1931: The 100th Anniversary of the Turner Insurrection

> *The 100th anniversary of the Southampton insurrection, in 1931, passed without much fanfare in either the white or black press. The large black newspapers—the Baltimore* Afro–American, *Pittsburg* Courier, *New York* Age, *and Chicago* Defender *ignored the anniversary, although the* Defender *did mark the anniversary of John Brown's raid with a long article and a cartoon. Among the periodicals which did commemorate Turner were the* Crisis, *the organ of the N.A.A.C.P., edited by W. E. B. DuBois;* The Communist; The Liberator, *the publication of the League of Struggle for Negro Rights, an organization of black Communists; and the National Urban League's* Opportunity. *The articles in* The Liberator, *written by the West Indian-born Cyril Briggs, tried to relate Turner to black struggles of 1931, while in* Opportunity, *the black historian Rayford Logan was more historical in approach. Both called on blacks to honor the rebel's memory, and a few years later, Logan organized a committee which unsuccessfully attempted to raise funds for a monument to Turner.*

THE LIBERATOR, JUNE 6, 1931

The Scottsboro Case and The Nat Turner Centenary, by Cyril Briggs

This coming November 11, 1931, will mark the one hundredth anniversary of the murder by the State of Virginia of the heroic Negro revolutionary, Nat Turner.

Not many Negro workers know about Nat Turner and the scores of other brave leaders of the numerous slave insurrections which constantly challenged the brutal power of the slave-owners and kept them in fear and trembling.

Traitors Soft Peddle Revolutionary Traditions

The American bosses, with the support of the treacherous Negro petty bourgeois misleaders (preachers, landlords, business men, etc.) have nearly succeeded in wiping out of the consciousness of the Negro masses all memory of their glorious revolutionary traditions. For the bosses, whose oppression of the Negro masses is today as brutal as under chattel slavery, do not wish the exploited Negro masses to have any traditions of revolt and struggle against their oppressors. Such traditions would serve to stiffen their resistance to present-day share cropper slavery, lynching, etc., and would make it unpleasant for the bosses. In this, the bosses are ably seconded by the Negro Uncle Tom reformists who constantly try to stifle the protests of the Negro masses, as so clearly evidenced today in the Scottsboro case where reformist organizations and papers like N.A.A.C.P., the Chattanooga Ministers Alliance, the Pittsburgh Courier, etc., are trying their best to stop the nation-wide mass protest against the outrageous frame-up and planned legal murder of nine innocent Negro children.

Set Up Servile Example

In the effort to develop a slave psychology in the Negro masses, the American bosses and their Negro tools have done their best to kill the revolutionary traditions of the Negro masses. In place of such heroic figures as Nat Turner, Frederick Douglass, Denmark Vesey, etc., the white ruling class and their despicable agents within the Negro race have set up instead the servile figures of Booker T. Washington and the even more despicable Moton.

In support of this policy, the utmost care is taken by the prostitute bourgeois historians to consistently present the picture of the Negro as a slave, immemorially servile and subordinate, satisfied with his slave status and incapable of revolt. This boss policy is faithfully supported by the misleaders like Kelly Miller, the leadership of the N.A.A.C.P., the Urban League and other reformist organizations.

Misleaders Aid Murder of Boys

To these misleaders any thought of the frightfully oppressed Negro masses joining ranks with the revolutionary white workers in the fight against their common oppressors is unthinkable and horrible. That is why the leaders of the N.A.A.C.P., the Chattanooga Ministers Alliance and other Uncle Tom reformists are today opposing with every weapon at their command the united fight of white and Negro workers to save the nine innocent Scottsboro Negro children. To these shameful misleaders it is preferable that these innocent children are murdered than that the Negro masses should smash through the barriers of Jim Crow isolation and join the white workers in a fighting alliance against the capitalist starvation system with its murderous lynch terror against the Negro masses.

Must Revive Our Revolutionary Traditions

The centenary of the murder of Nat Turner must be made the
occasion for reviving the revolutionary traditions of the Negro masses,
and for smashing the treacherous influence of the Uncle Tom reformists. Nat Turner Centenary memorial meetings must be held throughout the country on November 11. Hundreds of thousands of Negro
and white workers must be made acquainted with the daring insurrection launched by Nat Turner against the Virginia slave power, and
with his heroism on the scaffold to which he was condemned by the
government of Virginia.

In order to make the Nat Turner Centenary a nation-wide event
and to draw in the largest possible masses, the League of Struggle for
Negro Rights should at once take up the question of organizing the
widest possible united front basis. For this purpose it is necessary that
the National Committee of the L.S.N.R. should at once get busy on
the task of drawing up a plan and sending out instructions to the
various groups and affiliated bodies of the L.S.N.R. The time is already
short if we are to mobilize a real mass celebration that will draw in
hundreds of organizations and wide masses of Negro and white workers
and poor farmers.

The Nat Turner Centenary meetings can be very effectively connected up with the Scottsboro campaign and made to serve as a further
mobilization base for the fight to stop the legal lynching of the nine
Alabama boys and to smash the system of boss oppression and lynching.

THE LIBERATOR, NOVEMBER 7, 1931

Nat Turner Marches On

Nat Turner—forgotten, ignored or distorted by the Negro up-
holders of the "white supremacy" system such as the N.A.A.C.P.—is
deeply entrenched in the hearts of revolutionary workers, both Negro
and white.

Notwithstanding all his religious phantasies, Nat Turner, in deeds,
was a revolutionary leader of the enslaved Negroes. With the utmost
courage and determination he led the slaves of Virginia with sword and
musket against the slaveowners. No idle dreams of freedom were his.
He fought for freedom, leading the slaves in battle. The revolt led by
him was one of the most powerful of the 30 slave revolts recorded in
this country. He lost—his remains were scattered among the white
land owners as souvenirs—but his revolt added new strength to the
revolutionary traditions of the Negro people. He added to that tradi-

tion, which took root in the first courageous resistance of the Negro tribes against the slave raiders on the African coasts, grew in the revolts on the horrible slave ships, progressed with the earliest slave revolts in this country, bloomed into temporary success in the Haitian Revolution and expanded with the revolutionary struggles in the West Indies.

Today, this revolutionary tradition of which Nat Turner was a bearer is alive and growing. It finds expression in the revolutionary movement directed at the slavery of today, which still holds the Negro people in subjection. This revolutionary tradition is maturing and fusing itself with the whole revolutionary tradition of the working class. Just as Nat Turner led his followers against chattel slavery in 1831, today, 100 years later, modern day revolutionists, the Communists, are leading both white and Negro masses against the system that breeds starvation and mass misery.

The Communist Party and the League of Struggle for Negro Rights is in the forefront of the struggle for the 9,000,000 Black Peons of the South, leading the struggle for the right of self-determination—the right of the Negro majority of the Black Belt to set up their own government, proclaim their own state unity and determine for themselves their relation with other governments, especially the U.S.

A new march is on the way. It is forming in all four corners of this country. It is a march representing the starving millions of white and Negro toilers. In its columns march white and Negro proletarians. They will reach Washington on December 7, when Congress convenes, and demand a lump sum of $150 for each unemployed worker for the winter, $50 for each dependent and unemployment insurance. They will sweep aside all jim-crow barriers in the onward march of the working class.

In the National Hunger March, the tradition of Nat Turner will go marching on. Starving Negro toilers of the cities and farms, march in solid ranks with the starving white workers!

Long live the Tradition of Nat Turner! Join the National Hunger March!

RAYFORD W. LOGAN: NAT TURNER: FIEND OR MARTYR? [1]

Down the River Dundy floated black, bloated corpses, rotting under the African sun. The village of a thousand huts along its banks was no longer filled with the prattle of children—vultures contended with beasts of prey for their tender carcasses. Here Yanee had once loved King Omloo, but a bullet had sent Yanee to Kanno Beyond the Grave and King Omloo was trudging in a slave coffle to the coast.

[1] From *Opportunity*, IX (November, 1931): pp. 337–39. Reprinted by permission of the National Urban League, Inc.

The White Man had brought his civilization to Africa.

The slaves "were tied to pole in rows, four feet apart; a loose wicker bandage around the neck of each, connected him to the pole, and the arms being pinioned by a bandage affixed behind above the elbows, they had sufficient room to feed, but not to loose themselves. . . . Often did they look back with tears in their eyes." Some went mad and laughed back at the hyenas. Some died under the leash. Others sought certain death through flight or mutiny. Still others refused to die before they had a chance to kill.

Death marched with the Black Ivory—but would it be always to the black man to whom it beckoned?

Death reaped another black harvest in the barracoons and during the embarkation. Some slaves preferred the shark's belly to the journey beyond the seas. Death revelled in the vile ship's hold amid the offal of those dying with dysentery and groaned with those going blind from ophthalmia. It led the slaves to promise not to throw themselves overboard if given a breath of air on deck. They promised—and threw themselves to the sharks.

A ship hails in sight. Is it rescuer or kidnaper? Their ship, every sail gasping for wind, runs away. The sea is becalmed; their pursuer closes. The captain manacles the slaves to the anchor chain on the far side of the ship. Just before the English officers come on board, he cuts the chain and six hundred men, women, and children go to Davey Jones' locker. The captain is not arrested, because there is no "evidence." He returns to Africa and a thousand more children are left orphans, a dozen more wenches are chosen to grace the sailors' bed, and a thousand more men die so that five hundred or four hundred or one hundred may till the fields of the Land of the Free.

> *The skipper on arriving in port closes*
> *". . . the Bible carefully, putting it down,*
> *As though his fingers loved it."*

For two centuries the gentle souls of the Western Hemisphere lolled at their ease on their plantations, their *habitations,* and their *haciendas* while fifty million corpses were rotting in Africa, the depths of the seas, and on the coasts of the western world. The fate of the living was sometimes worse: husband was torn from wife and mother from child. And yet they sang. They had to sing or die or kill.

On August 21, 1831 Nat Turner, a deeply religious, highly moral Negro slave belonging to one Travis of Southampton County, Virginia, stopped singing and praying and led an insurrection in which fifty-five white men, women, and children were killed. One white for each million of Africans. Nat was a long way from a reckoning either according to the Bible or the Constitution of the United States which rated five Negroes equal to three white men.

So long as Nat was at large, Virginia shuddered. A thousand troops could not find him. The imagination of the planters heard bare feet gliding on the roof when the autumn leaves fell. In the twilight it saw burly black forms assemble silently behind ghostlike trees. The sighing winds brought chants from Dismal Swamp where the murderers were whetting their axes. From North Carolina came rumors of "Walarums and excursions." The *Macon Messenger* barely got off the press because all the able-bodied men were on patrol. New Orleans trembled at the report that a black man had twelve hundred stand of arms in his cellar. "Pity us!" implored a correspondent from Kentucky. The South was scared—scared as it perhaps never was before or since. The least frightened denied Divine Retribution.

Such terror demanded relief. Since Nat could not be found, any "nigger" would do. One man admitted killing ten or fifteen. General Eppes, commanding the troops, officially denounced the "revolting, inhuman, acts of barbarity." The slaughter continued. At the same time Virginia was praying for further success to the Poles who were reported as having butchered 14,000 Russians.

The coincidences of history afford alluring speculation. November eleventh is now an occasion for rejoicing at the conclusion, stupefaction at the beginning, of the greatest holocaust of the modern age, and preparation for the next. To 12,000,000 black folk it should be a day of pride—for on that day one hundred years ago a black man kept his "Rendezvous with Death" rather than live a bondsman. His simple courage surpassed the comprehension of his executioners as did that of the Man of Galilee.

There are those who would have you believe that Nat Turner's Insurrection was a failure. It is true that his executioners divided his remains for souvenirs, thus setting perhaps a precedent for a later American outdoor sport. The punishment meted out to him and to his accomplices effectively discouraged any other insurrections of note. The board of education of a Virginia county recently denied a petition for a colored training school because of the execrable memory of Nat Turner. No monument commemorates his deed. And in 1930 a Negro college professor told a white audience that the Negro will probably be back in captivity in the next twenty-five years.

But did he die in vain? By a peculiar and unwitting coincidence the lock and key of the jail in which Nat was confined lie in a case in the Virginia State Library next to the call to arms issued in Lexington County, Virginia, at the outbreak of the Civil War. No one would be foolhardy enough to assert that Nat Turner's insurrection caused the Civil War. One may safely declare, however, that it did reveal the only

solution to America's Gordian knot—the sword. Slavery had rung
again as "an alarum bell in the night," and some already realized that
the "panacea of palaver" was as worthless as all other nostrums.

At first the South sought to repress any other attempts to gain freedom by force. Systematic conversions to the Christian Church taught
the proper submission. Dialecticians proved that converting a slave
did not make him free. The most rigorous and drastic regulations were
enacted to prevent any recurrence of insurrections.

The planters blamed Garrison and his *Liberator* for the insurrection.
This accusation is probably unfounded, but who will deny that Nat's
effort crystallized the fighting ideals of the Abolitionists? Let him who
would be free strike the first blow. Lovejoy and John Brown would
not have been ashamed to be called the spiritual descendants of this
black slave. Wendell Phillips in eulogizing Toussaint Louverture must
have seen in him a kindred spirit. Even the Quakers, who suffered
ostracism and imprisonment for their underground activities, must
have gained respect for a race that produced men who preferred death
to slavery.

And finally, the South erected a gigantic defense mechanism to
justify their "peculiar institution." Only savages, they shouted, would
revolt against such an idyllic state as slavery. The slave was better off
than he would have been in Africa. Had he not come to know the
Anglo-Saxon God, and, hence, gained a passport to Heaven? His fate
was better than that of white laborers in the North or in Europe, than
that of free Negroes. He was sure of his job, was he not? Black mam-
mies, although not allowed to keep their own children, had the privilege and honor of allowing the best blood of the South to suckle at
their breasts. Some white men held black wenches in such high esteem
that they used them to increase their human stock exactly as they used
studs to increase their stables. Though slaves, they were erecting a
Kingdom of Cotton that all of Europe would not dare attack. They
made possible as fine a breed of gentlemen as ever knew how to ride
to hounds, drink mint juleps, betray their wives, turn a "bon mot,"
dance the reel, carve a wild boar, and amass debts that they could not
pay. Had the Roman *latifundia* or the *haciendas* of New Spain created
anything finer? Why in the name of an Almighty and Just God should
these beasts want to kill fifty men, women, and children?

The dead tell no tales, not even fifty million of them.

No reputable historian doubts that the period from 1831 to 1861
was the most horrible era of slavery. As the abolitionists redoubled
their attacks, the South increased its drastic regulations and pious
preachments. Driven from post to post, the planters finally proclaimed
slavery such a fine thing that it could not, by the laws of man or the
will of God, be kept out of the newly acquired federal territory, out

of the Caribbean, out of the old Northwest Territory, out of the free states themselves. In 1860 a man practically unknown but destined to become the Greatest American, peculiarly ugly but performing perhaps the only true "beau geste" in American history, was elected on a platform that declared, among other things, the power of Congress to exclude slavery from federal territory. The South, proclaiming "Better out of the Union with slavery than in it without slavery," placed its trust in the arbitrament of war and the justice of God. The gallantry of the South fighting a lost cause is still the theme of poetry and history. Nat Turner, ignominiously hanged for seeking liberty, is mentioned only to be execrated as a bloodthirsty beast.

Every one is free to form his own opinion of Nat Turner. It is interesting to note, however, the sentiment of a man still shuddering from the shock. Samuel Warner, writing in 1831, declared:

"It seems almost incredible that there could be found an individual of the human species, who rather than to wear the goading yoke of bondage, would prefer becoming the voluntary subject of so great a share of want and misery (as that which Nat found in his hiding place)! —but, such indeed, is the love of liberty—the gift of God!—and while we shall ever feel it a duty which we owe to humanity to lend our aid if necessary in suppressing insurrections so fatal to the lives of our countrymen as the one of recent occurrence in the South when fifty-five innocent persons were in the space of a few hours most inhumanly butchered by a band of ill-advised wretches, who heeded not the entreaties of the aged and infirmed or the heart piercing screeches of the expiring infant! yet, we can not hold those entirely blameless who first brought them from their native plains—who robbed them of their domestic joys—who tore them from their weeping children and dearest connections, and doomed them in this 'Land of Liberty' to a state of cruel bondage!"

Thirty years later Thomas Wentworth Higginson was not afraid to write:

"Who now shall go back thirty years, and read the heart of this extraordinary man, who, by the admission of his captors, 'never was known to swear an oath, or drink a drop of spirits;' who, on the same authority, 'for natural intelligence and quickness of apprehension was surpassed by few men,' 'with a mind capable of attaining anything;' who knew no book but his Bible, and that by heart; who devoted himself soul and body to the cause of his race, without a trace of personal hope or fear; who laid his plans so shrewdly that they came at last with less warning than any earthquake on the doomed community around; and who, when that time arrived, took the life of man, woman, and child, without a throb of compunction, a word of exultation, or an act of superfluous outrage? Mrs. Stowe's 'Dred' seems dim and melodramatic beside the actual Nat Turner, and De Quincy's 'Avenger' is his only parallel in imaginative literature."

The South no longer shackles black bodies—that is, in general. It has, however, enslaved the minds of black folk just as surely as it once did their bodies. What a glorious task on this, the one-hundredth anniversary of Nat Turner's Insurrection, to dedicate ourselves to the emancipation of the minds of twelve million black folk. One may even hope for some little intelligence from the white master minds. If not, who will dare predict that there will never be another Nat Turner?

21

Nat Turner Remembered: The 1960s

Within the past decade, interest in Nat Turner has been stimulated by two developments. First, the growing militance of the black movement has led increasing numbers of black spokesmen to commemorate Turner as a revolutionary forebear. In 1968, Eldridge Cleaver wrote, "Nat Turner, Gabriel Prosser and Denmark Vesey . . . are the spiritual fathers of today's urban guerillas," and two years later, an advocate of "black guerilla warfare" praised "Nat Turner's philosophy of 'strike by night and spare none.' " Secondly, the appearance of William Styron's Pulitzer Prize-winning novel, The Confessions of Nat Turner *and the controversy which surrounded it made many whites aware for the first time of Turner's existence, and led blacks to articulate their own conception of Turner's character and aims. One of the most striking evocations of Turner was created by the black poet Robert Hayden, whose "Ballad of Nat Turner," based on a vision related in the* Confessions, *captured the religious mysticism central to Turner's life. And another black writer, Addison Gayle, in a short essay attempted to relate Turner to the contemporary philosophy of Black Power.*

THE BALLAD OF NAT TURNER [1]

Then fled, O brethren, the wicked juba
    and wandered wandered far
from curfew joys in the Dismal's night.
    Fool of St. Elmo's fire

In scary night I wandered, praying,
    Lord God my harshener,
speak to me now or let me die;
    speak, Lord, to this mourner.

And came at length to livid trees
    where Ibo warriors
hung shadowless, turning in wind
    that moaned like Africa,

[1] From Robert Hayden, *Selected Poems* (New York, 1966), pp. 72–74. Copyright © 1966 by Robert Hayden. Reprinted by permission of October House, Inc.

167

Their belltongue bodies dead, their eyes
   alive with the anger deep
in my own heart. Is this the sign,
   the sign forepromised me?

The spirits vanished. Afraid and lonely
   I wandered on in blackness.
Speak to me now or let me die.
   Die, whispered the blackness.

And wild things gasped and scuffled in
   the night; seething shapes
of evil frolicked upon the air.
   I reeled with fear, I prayed.

Sudden brightness clove the preying
   darkness, brightness that was
itself a golden darkness, brightness
   so bright that it was darkness.

And there were angels, their faces hidden
   from me, angels at war
with one another, angels in dazzling
   combat. And oh the splendor,

The fearful splendor of that warring.
   Hide me, I cried to rock and bramble.
Hide me, the rock, the bramble cried. . . .
   How tell you of that holy battle?

The shock of wing on wing and sword
   on sword was the tumult of
a taken city burning. I cannot
   say how long they strove,

For the wheel in a turning wheel which is time
   in eternity had ceased
its whirling, and owl and moccasin,
   panther and nameless beast

And I were held like creatures fixed
   in flaming, in fiery amber.
But I saw I saw oh many of
   those mighty beings waver,

Waver and fall, go streaking down
    into swamp water, and the water
hissed and steamed and bubbled and locked
    shuddering shuddering over

The fallen and soon was motionless.
    Then that massive light
began a-folding slowly in
    upon itself, and I

Beheld the conqueror faces and, lo,
    they were like mine, I saw
they were like mine and in joy and terror
    wept, praising praising Jehovah.

Oh praised my honer, harshener
    till a sleep came over me,
a sleep heavy as death. And when
    I awoke at last free

And purified, I rose and prayed
    and returned after a time
to the blazing fields, to the humbleness.
    And bided my time.

NAT TURNER AND THE BLACK NATIONALISTS [2]

. . . Turner engaged in a violent revolution against the institution of slavery; and yet it is not the violent revolution that is most important. Black people have engaged in violent revolution before and since. Turner is important because he attempted to destroy an oppressive system totally; he saw himself always as one of the oppressed, and his actions were undertaken in the spirit of liberty for all, with the intent of bringing freedom to all. Turner demanded destruction of the oppressive apparatus not coexistence with it, realizing, as today's moderate Negro leaders do not, that coexistence (integration) is only another way of enabling the many—though many more many—to oppress the few.

But most important, Turner was able to say that that moment in history for him and his people was the worst, therefore negating a moral and ethical scripture against violence. The laws, morals, and ethics constructed by a totalitarian society are, due to their very nature,

[2] From Addison Gayle, *The Black Situation* (New York, 1970), pp. 68–70. Copyright © 1970. Reprinted by permission of Horizon Press.

invalid. No victim has a moral responsibility to recognize the laws of the oppressor. And, in the same way, he owes no allegiance to a moral code which he did not help to construct, about which he was not consulted, and which operates continuously to keep him in his oppressed status.

In addition, Turner's actions negate the philosophy of the late Martin Luther King. Violence, argued King, binds the oppressor and the oppressed together, robbing the victim of that nobility inherent in suffering, pushing him further from his oppressor; and worst of all the victim is psychologically damaged in the process. Undoubtedly, there is psychological damage incurred by the victim who engages in violence, but this must be measured against the psychological damage incurred by the victim who does not.

Was it psychologically healthier, for example, for the family of Emmett Till to watch passively as men led their son away to certain death? Is it psychologically healthy for young people today to accept non-violently the excesses of a system which ravages their minds, bodies, and spirits, bringing a more lingering and painful death than that suffered by Emmett Till? Alongside the psychic damage inherent in acts of violence must be placed, especially for the victim, what Franz Fanon has called the purgative effect of violence. Which is the more damaging is a question for psychologists.

Turner was restricted by no such philosophy. From that moment when he realized that the conditions which he lived under were the worst, he became a revolutionary in the true sense of the word; he dedicated himself to the elimination of the oppressive social and political apparatus, not in the interests of a few but in the interest of all. He envisioned a revolution which would free every man in chains, enable every victim to breathe the air of freedom, and grant every man the right to choose his own destiny. Thus Turner accepted the formula which has now become the guiding ethic of the Black Power revolution: salvation for all or salvation for none.

No philosophy which does not demand change in the American power structure for the benefit of all the victims can be called revolutionary in any sense of the term. The Black Power proponent, like Nat Turner, realizes this fact, and for this reason he is the only true nihilist in twentieth-century America, believing with his heart, head, and soul that the conditions which exist at the moment are the worst.

In this way the Black Power philosophy differs from philosophies espoused by other black theoreticians, for its advocates envision a future—indeed the central meaning of the rebellion is predicated upon a future—in which the dignity of all men will have been restored. But the future is possible only after the complete and total destruction of the existing oppressive apparatus.

That the system is oppressive and has always operated to deny dignity to black people, to rob black people of any conception of themselves, of their worth, of their historical positions, and further, to deny them life, freedom of movement and choice is a point which all moderate Negro leaders readily concede. Such leaders differ only in the means to correct the abuses, to so transform the system that it will remedy all defects, make some restitution—if not to the victims, then to the sons and daughters of the victims.

Their plans are well known. One calls for an economic miracle, a Marshall plan; another for increased legal, legislative, and political action; still another for mass assaults upon the American conscience. And the majority of Afro-Americans accept one, sometimes all of these plans simultaneously, primarily because most still believe in the American Dream, remain wedded to the Christian myth, and see salvation and redemption in the rhetoric of leaders who promise a piece of this earth not for all but for a chosen few.

Few are capable of believing with Nat Turner that the conditions under which they live at this moment are the worst, for dedication to such a belief mandates revolution. Only the advocates of Black Power have arrived at this position, and thus Black Power is the only philosophy in America demanding revolution in the common interest of all black people.

The Black Power advocate seeks a higher meaning for man. He seeks a higher freedom. He seeks not only a more equal society, but a more just one; not a larger share of the fruits of production, but a more humane and precise definition of the human condition. As such, the advocates of Black Power are the champions of an ethic which goes far beyond existentialism, leading from property values to human ones, from degradation to dignity, from a preoccupation with some to a preoccupation with all. With Nat Turner, the Black Power proponent ignores the call of the Negro middle class and the Black Nationalists alike for a system which will only save some of the people, and demands instead a system in which no black men will wear chains and all black men will be free.

22
The Folk Memory of Nat Turner

Nat Turner was not forgotten by black people in America, either during slavery or after emancipation. In 1861, Thomas Wentworth Higginson observed, "to this day there are traditions among the Virginia slaves of the keen devices of 'Prophet Nat,'" and twenty years later, George W. Williams wrote, "southern black women have handed down the tradition to their children, and the 'Prophet Nat' is still marching on." When William Drewry did his research in the late 1890s for the first book-length study of Turner, he found many former slaves in Southampton county who had keen memories of the rebellion, and some who "reckon all time from 'Nat's Fray.'" But few historians since Drewry have tried to tap the folk memory of Turner, and many have doubted that it exists at all.

In 1969, Henry I. Tragle, a Massachusetts writer investigating the Southampton insurrection, interviewed a seventy-year-old black man, Percy Claud, to whom the story of Turner had been handed down by his parents and grandparents. Claud's remarks show that the folk memory of Turner is still alive in Southampton County, although somewhat intermingled with local superstitions. Claud's statement about how Turner learned to read, however, is clearly related to the Confessions, *in which Turner told of seeing "hieroglyphics" and "numbers" on leaves in the woods. And the classic declaration of millenarian religious faith with which Claud closes gives us a glimpse into the black culture of this backward, isolated rural area, where religious beliefs have not, apparently, changed much since Turner's day.[1]*

Tragle: You told me that you had heard about Nat Turner from your mother when you were a little boy. Would you tell me what it was that you had heard from her?

Claud: . . . My mother was telling me that Nat Turner was at the old Travis place. . . . She just told me he has a man that was God man, he was a man for war, and for legal rights, and for freedom. . . .

T.: You told me also, Mr. Claud, about something that they did to Nat, after they caught him. What was this?

C.: . . . They told me when I was a boy, after they caught him,

[1] From an interview with Mr. Percy Claud, of Boykins, Virginia, by Henry I. Tragle, April 24, 1969. Used by permission of Mr. Claud and Mr. Tragle. (Transcribed from a tape recording in the possession of Mr. Tragle.)

some say they drug him and whipped him to death. . . . I heard some say they didn't do that.

T.: How did you know about [Nat Turner's cave]?

C.: I knowed about it by, we worked the farm over there and my father carried us there and showed us the old cave round there. . . .

T.: Did he tell you that was Nat Turner's cave?

C.: Yes, sir.

T.: And what did he tell you about Nat Turner?

C.: He told me that that was his cave and that was where he left from his home up there, he left his mistress and master's home, and come to build him a cave there to hisself, and while he was up there to hisself, he begin to get in union with many of his friends. And said then they began to come over here and have my table, and began to discuss the problems, what they want to do. . . .

C.: Mr. Claud, what did the people tell you about what Nat Turner actually did, do you know what he did?

C.: They told me what he actually did. First, he killed his mistress and master.

T.: Mr. Travis and his wife.

C.: Yes, at Travis' place, yes, sir.

T.: But he had a whole group of people with him.

C.: That's right, sir. . . . After that, he went on out . . . down to Cross Keys. And that's why they begin to find, that, to get into his business, and find where he was located at. And after they found where he was located at, then they surround him. . . . They put him in jail in Jerusalem, and kept him in jail in Jerusalem for a certain period of time, then they took him out. And that's why, after they took him out, they whipped him and beat him. . . . My mother told me . . . they hung him. She didn't know, but that's what she was told.

T.: You told me, Mr. Claud, something about after he'd been hung, they saw some signs, or some writing on his feet?

C.: They say they found on his feet, after they has killed him, they say they hate they killed him, because he found on his feet were blue letters, said war and rumors of war, written in the skins of his feet. That's what my mother told me when I was a little boy.

T.: . . . Do you think, yourself, Mr. Claud, that Nat thought that God had given him a mission to perform?

C.: Yes, sir.

T.: And is this why people followed him, and were willing to die, to do what he said do?

C.: Yes, because he said his feet said wars and rumors of war were coming up today. . . .

T.: How old a man was he when he received this mission, when he carried out this act, do you know?

C.: No, sir, I remember they told me . . . that God beguiled him, to come to teach him by fig leaves and holly leaves and apple bits.

T.: You mean that he found letters on the leaves, and that's the way he learned to read?

C.: That's they way he learned to read, and his mother didn't begin to come to teach him until then. He begin to come in by the leaves into his mother, showing the leaves to his mother, . . . they tell me his mother was read, and so she began to teach him. . . . They tell me that's where he first started from.

T.: Did you hear this from your mother?

C.: Yes, sir.

T.: Did your mother tell you who told her?

C.: . . . Her mother. . . .

T.: [Asks whether things will be better for Claud's children and grandchildren than today.]

C.: . . . God's going to destroy this here wicked race and he goin' to raise up a nation, a race that's goin' to be here, just like he did in Noah's day. . . . He's goin' to raise a nation, obey him, and do as his command, and love one another.

Afterword

The treatment of Nat Turner's rebellion by historians can be summed up in one word—neglect. Most accounts of the Jacksonian era ignore or barely mention this pivotal occurrence, and only a handful of historians have written detailed accounts of the insurrection. Only within the last few years, partly because of the controversy over William Styron's fictional treatment of Turner, and partly as a result of the black movement's search for a "usable past," has there been sustained interest in Turner and in what his revolt tells us about the institution of slavery.

The means by which blacks resisted slavery varied greatly. On the simplest and most widespread level, slaves engaged in what historians have termed "day-to-day resistance"—feigning illness, leaving plantations for a few days, and destroying or neglecting property. More serious, as far as the masters were concerned, were the crimes committed by slaves, including running away, arson, poisoning, and assaults on masters and overseers. Finally, there were slave conspiracies and rebellions. Although far less frequent than sporadic, individualistic, and unorganized resistance, and by no means as extensive as the rebellions in Brazil and the West Indies, slave revolts in the United States date back as far as 1663. In the eighteenth century, there were major conspiracies in New York in 1712, when two dozen slaves set fire to a group of buildings and killed the first nine whites to arrive on the scene, and in South Carolina in 1739, when a band of armed slaves attempted to fight their way to Spanish Florida.

The three greatest slave conspiracies—Gabriel Prosser's in 1800, Denmark Vesey's in 1822, and Turner's—took place in the nineteenth century. A comparison of the three is instructive in understanding the nature of slave rebellion. All three of these conspiracies developed outside the area of plantation slavery, where the system was most oppressive. Prosser's involved slaves in and around Richmond; Vesey's took place in Charleston; and Turner's in the isolated farming county of Southampton. In all three the slave church—a center of the alternative culture which slaves strove to create—played a crucial role. Prosser's brother Martin was a preacher, and the two often related to other slaves the story of "the days of old when the Israelites were in service to King Pharaoh" and how Moses led them to freedom. Vesey, another slave testified, "studied the Bible a great deal and tried to prove from it that slavery and bondage is against the Bible." Most of the Vesey plotters were members of Charleston's African Church, and one of the leaders, Gullah Jack, was an Angolese witch doctor who many slaves believed had the power to make them invulnerable.

Turner, of course, was a slave preacher and seems closely akin to the religious mystics who led the bloody medieval millenarian peasant outbreaks. Millenarian leaders tended to be members of the lower clergy, often obsessed for years with apocalyptic fantasies and visions, who believed themselves chosen by God to bring about a purging of the world's sins and a new era of divine rule on earth. The language of Turner's *Confessions* certainly seems to fit such a pattern. "It was plain to me," the rebel told Gray, after describing his visions, "that the Savior was about to lay down the yoke he had borne for the sins of men, and the great day of judgement was at hand." And when Gray asked Turner, after the suppression of the revolt, whether he did not believe himself mistaken, the imprisoned, manacled rebel replied, "Was not Christ crucified?" The Vesey and Gabriel conspiracies drew on political and humanitarian sources as well as slave religion for their ideological inspiration, while Turner seems to have been motivated exclusively by his mystical visions. But all three conspiracies show that while masters hoped that Christian training was an effective means of social control, the slaves could use Christianity for their own purposes. Moreover, illegal religious meetings, which whites allowed virtually without complaint, served as centers of rebel plotting. The ease with which slaves in Richmond, Charleston, and Southampton were able to gather together may help explain why conspiracies were easier to organize there than in the plantation areas of the deep South, where policing seems to have been far more strict.

Gabriel Prosser, Denmark Vesey, and Nat Turner were, by definition, unique individuals. All were located in positions in the slave system that gave them far greater access to information, skills, and the outside world than the average slave, and which enabled them to escape the system's most severe psychological impact. Prosser was a literate blacksmith, and many of his associates were skilled artisans of Richmond and the vicinity. Vesey was free, literate, and well-traveled; his associates were skilled urban slaves—carpenters, sawyers, mechanics, and blacksmiths of Charleston. Turner was a literate preacher. All seem to have been well-treated and afforded privileges by their masters. "Not only were the leaders of good character, and very much indulged by their owners," the Official Report of the Vesey conspiracy noted with a certain puzzlement, "but this was very generally the case with all who were convicted,—many of them possessing the highest confidence of their owners, and not one of bad character." The skilled, privileged slave in the antebellum South was in a far better position than either the field hand or house servant to develop the self-esteem, secular knowledge, and organizational skill essential to revolutionary leadership. By the same token, however, this class of slaves also had the most to lose from rebellion, and both Prosser and Vesey were betrayed by privileged slaves who did not wish to see their privileges jeopardized. As Turner himself recognized, a rebellion that involved little or no long-term planning stood less chance of being betrayed by virtue of its very spontaneity.

Of the lives of the mass of the slaves, we still know far too little. But the conduct of the slaves of Southampton in the face of Turner's revolt, and especially the sixty or so who joined the rebels, may give us some clues. Most slaves, while by no means content with their lot, would not openly confront the system but would seize opportunities to escape it when they arose. Thus one slave declared, when he heard of Turner's uprising, "if the negroes came that way he would join them and kill all the whites." If Turner's men did not come by, he would presumably continue to be content with sporadic day-to-day resistance, although when the Union army appeared during the Civil War, he might well have joined the thousands of slaves who took the opportunity to flee plantations and farms, and head for the Union lines. And in later years he might well have been one of those blacks for whom the memory of Nat Turner became part of folk culture and a source of inspiration in the struggle for their rights after 1831.

Bibliographical Note

The most important contemporary source for Nat Turner and the Southampton insurrection is *The Confessions of Nat Turner, The Leader of the Late Insurrection in Southampton, Va. As Fully and voluntarily made to Thomas R. Gray* . . . (Baltimore, 1831). The records of the trial of Turner and other rebels is in Southampton County, Virginia *Minute Book,* 1830–35, a microfilm copy of which is in the Virginia State Library. Also in this library are the *Executive Papers* of Governor John Floyd and Legislative Petitions, which shed considerable light on the reaction to the rebellion. Some petitions are printed in J. H. Johnston, coll., "Antislavery Petitions Presented to the Virginia Legislature by Citizens of Various Counties," *Journal of Negro History,* XII (October, 1927), 670–91. In the Library of Congress there is relevant material in the John Floyd Papers, William C. Rives Papers, and Nicholas Trist Papers; and in the North Carolina Department of Archives and History, that state's reactions are reflected in the Mordecai Family Papers, Nicholls Papers, and Governor Montfort Stokes *Letterbook.* For the abolitionist response, see the William Lloyd Garrison Papers, Boston Public Library.

The most important contemporary newspaper reports may be found in the Richmond *Enquirer,* Richmond *Whig,* Norfolk *American Beacon,* Washington, D.C., *National Intelligencer,* and *Niles' National Register.* For contemporary newspaper reactions, see the excerpts from northern and southern papers reprinted in *The Liberator*; and the New York *Daily Sentinel,* Albany *Evening Journal,* Albany *Argus, Ohio State Journal,* New York *Morning Courier and Enquirer,* New York *Commercial Advertiser,* and Boston *Courier.* There are also contemporary accounts in Samuel Warner, *Authentic and Impartial Narrative of the Tragical Scene which was witnessed in Southampton County* . . . (New York, 1831); Fitzhugh Lee, *General Lee* (New York, 1904); J. G. de Roulhac Hamilton, ed., *The Papers of Thomas Ruffin,* 4 vols. (Raleigh, 1918–20); Charles Ambler, *The Life and Diary of John Floyd* (Richmond, 1918), and Ira Berlin, ed., "After Nat Turner, a Letter from 1831," *Journal of Negro History,* LV (April, 1970), 144–51. Henry I. Tragle, *The Southampton Slave Revolt* (Amherst, Mass.: 1971), is a collection of the most important contemporary documents and accounts. In addition to the fugitive slave narratives cited in the text, there are accounts of the rebellion by slaves in Henry C. Bruce, *The New Man: Twenty-nine Years a Slave* (York, Pa.: 1895);

and Jamie Parker, *The Fugitive: Related to Mrs. Emily Pierson* (Hartford, 1851).

Among the many historical treatments of Nat Turner are: Robert R. Howison, *A History of Virginia, From its Discovery and Settlement to the Present Time*, 2 vols. (Richmond, 1848); Henry Bibb, *Slave Insurrection in Southampton Co. Va, . . .* (New York, 1850); William C. Nell, *Colored Patriots of the American Revolution* (Boston, 1855); Joshua Coffin, *An Account of Some of the Principal Slave Insurrections* (New York, 1860); Thomas Wentworth Higginson, "Nat Turner's Insurrection," *Atlantic Monthly*, VIII (August, 1861), 173–87 (also reprinted in James McPherson, ed., *Black Rebellion* [New York: 1969]); William Wells Brown, *The Black Man: His Antecedents, His Genius, and His Achievements* (Boston, 1863), and the abridged version of the same essay, in Brown, *The Negro in the American Rebellion* (Boston, 1867); Stephen B. Weeks, "The Slave Insurrection in Virginia, 1831," *Magazine of American History*, XXV (1891), 448–58; Jeremiah B. Jeter, *Recollections of a Long Life* (Richmond, 1891); William H. Parker, "The Nat Turner Insurrection," *Ole Virginny Yarns*, I (1893), 14–29; "Rodka," "A Page of History. One of the Tragedies of the Old Slavery Days," *Godey's Magazine*, CXXXVI (March, 1898), 288–92; and William S. Drewry, *The Southampton Insurrection* (Washington, 1900).

More recent historical accounts include: John W. Cromwell, "The Aftermath of Nat Turner's Insurrection," *Journal of Negro History*, V (April, 1920), 208–34; James H. Johnston, "The Participation of White Men in Virginia Negro Insurrections," *Journal of Negro History*, XVI (April, 1931), 158–67; Miles M. Fisher, "Nat Turner, A Hundred Years Afterwards," *Crisis*, XXXVIII (September, 1931), 385; Rayford Logan, "Nat Turner: Fiend or Martyr?" *Opportunity*, IX (November, 1931), 337–39; Harvey Wish, "American Slave Insurrections Before 1861," *Journal of Negro History*, XXII (July, 1937), 299–320; Joseph C. Carroll, *Slave Insurrections in the United States 1800–1865* (Boston, 1939); Herbert Aptheker, *American Negro Slave Revolts* (New York, 1943); Russell B. Nye, *A Baker's Dozen, Thirteen Unusual Americans* (East Lansing, 1956); Robert N. Elliott, "The Nat Turner Insurrection as Reported in the North Carolina Press," *North Carolina Historical Review*, XXXVIII (January, 1961), 1–18; William Styron, "This Quiet Dust," *Harper's* (April, 1965), 135–46; Nicholas Halasz, *The Rattling Chains* (New York, 1966); Herbert Aptheker, *Nat Turner's Slave Rebellion* (New York, 1966); F. Roy Johnson, *The Nat Turner Slave Insurrection* (Murfreesboro, N. C., 1966); Lerone Bennett, *Pioneers in Protest* (New York, 1968); and F. Roy Johnson, *The Nat Turner Story* (Murfreesboro, 1970).

On the Virginia background of Turner's rebellion, the following works are most useful: Charles Ambler, *Sectionalism in Virginia from 1776 to 1861* (Chicago, 1910); James C. Ballagh, *A History of Slavery in Virginia* (Baltimore, 1902); Joseph B. Earnest, *The Religious Development of the Negro in Virginia* (Charlottesville, 1914); Jane P. Guild, *Black Laws of Virginia* (Richmond, 1936); Luther P. Jackson, *Free Negro Labor and Property in Virginia 1830–1860* (Washington, D. C., 1942); James H. Johnston, *Race Relations in Virginia and Miscegenation in the South 1776–1860* (Amherst, 1970); Herbert Klein, *Slavery in the Americas* (Chicago, 1967); and Works Projects Administration, Writers' Program, Virginia, *The Negro in Virginia* (New York, 1940). For the Virginia Debate on Slavery and its aftermath, see William S. Jenkins, *Pro-Slavery Thought in the Old South* (Chapel Hill, 1935); Joseph C. Robert, *The Road From Monticello* (Durham, 1941); Theodore M. Whitfield, *Slavery Agitation in Virginia 1829–1832* (Baltimore, 1930); Clement Eaton, *The Freedom-of-thought Struggle in the Old South* (New York, 1964); the reports of the legislative speeches, printed in the Richmond *Enquirer* and *Whig* (January–April, 1832); *The Letter of Appomattox to the People of Virginia* . . . (Richmond, 1832); and Thomas R. Dew, *Review of the Debates* . . . (Richmond, 1832).

Abolitionist responses to Turner and their changing attitudes toward violence are discussed in: Robert B. Abzug, "The Influence of Garrisonian Abolitionists' Fears of Slave Violence on the Antislavery Argument 1829–1840," *Journal of Negro History*, LV (January, 1970), 15–28; Herbert Aptheker, *To Be Free* (New York, 1948); Howard H. Bell, "Expressions of Negro Militancy in the North, 1840–1860," *Journal of Negro History*, XLV (January, 1960), 11–21; John Demos, "The Antislavery Movement and the Problem of Violent 'Means,'" *New England Quarterly*, XXXVII (December, 1964), 501–26; Aileen S. Kraditor, *Means and Ends in American Abolitionism* (New York, 1969); and John L. Thomas, *The Liberator* (Boston, 1963).

Among fictional treatments of Nat Turner are Harriet Beecher Stowe, *Dred* (1856); G. P. R. James, *The Old Dominion* (1858); Mary Johnston, *Prisoners of Hope* (1899); Pauline C. Bouve, *Their Shadows Before* (1899); Randolph Edmonds, *Six Plays for a Negro Theater* (Boston, 1934); Daniel Panger, *Ol' Prophet Nat* (1967); and William Styron, *The Confessions of Nat Turner* (1968). In conjunction with the last book, see also John Henrik Clarke, ed., *William Styron's "Nat Turner," Ten Black Writers Respond* (Boston, 1968); Henry I. Tragle, "Styron and His Sources," *Massachusetts Review*, XI (Winter, 1970), 134–53; Melvin J. Friedman and Irving Malin, eds., *William Styron's "The Confessions of Nat Turner," A Critical Handbook* (Belmont, Cal., 1970); and John B. Duff and Peter M. Mitchell, eds., *The Nat Turner Rebellion: The Historical Event and the Modern Controversy* (New York, 1971).

Index

More general works on slavery which have important insights on the nature of slave resistance include: Winthrop D. Jordan, *White Over Black* (Chapel Hill, 1969); Kenneth Stampp, *The Peculiar Institution* (New York, 1956); Robert Starobin, *Industrial Slavery in the Old South* (New York, 1970); Richard Wade, *Slavery in the Cities* (New York, 1964); Stanley Elkins, *Slavery* (Chicago, 1959); Charles H. Nichols, *Many Thousand Gone* (Leiden, 1963); Stanley Feldstein, *Once a Slave* (New York, 1971); Gilbert Osofsky, *Puttin' On Ole Massa* (New York, 1969); Sterling Stuckey, "Through the Prism of Folklore: The Black Ethos in Slavery," *Massachusetts Review*, IX (Summer, 1968), 417–37; George M. Fredrickson and Christopher Lasch, "Resistance to Slavery," *Civil War History*, XIII (December, 1967), 315–29; and Eugene D. Genovese, "Rebelliousness and Docility in the Negro Slave: A Critique of the Elkins Thesis," *Civil War History*, XIII (December, 1967), 293–314.

Among the best recent more general works on slave rebellion are William F. Cheek, ed., *Black Resistance Before the Civil War* (Beverly Hills, 1970); Eugene D. Genovese, "The Legacy of Slavery and the Roots of Black Nationalism," *Studies on the Left*, VI (1966), 3–26; and the comments in the same issue by Herbert Aptheker, Frank Kofsky, and C. Vann Woodward; Vincent Harding, "Religion and Resistance Among Antebellum Negroes, 1800–1860," in August Meier and Elliot M. Rudwick, eds., *The Making of Black America*, 2 vols. (New York, 1969), I, 179–97; Marion D. Kilson, "Towards Freedom: An Analysis of Slave Revolts in the United States," *Phylon*, XXV (1964), 175–87; and George Rawick, "The Historical Roots of Black Liberation," *Radical America*, II (July–August, 1968), 1–12.